DATE DUE

BRODART, CO.   Cat. No. 23-221-003

Texas In Poetry 2

Edited by Billy Bob Hill

TEXAS
In Poetry 2

EDITED BY BILLY BOB HILL

TCU PRESS ★ FORT WORTH ★ TEXAS

Library of Congress Cataloging-in-Publication Data

Texas In Poetry 2 / edited by Billy Bob Hill.
        p. cm.
Includes index.
        ISBN 0-87565-267-0 (alk. paper) -- ISBN 0-87565-268-9 (pbk. : alk. paper)
  1. American poetry --Texas.   2. Texas--Poetry.   I. Hill, Billy Bob.
  PS558.T4 T354 2002
  811.008 ' 09764--dc21

                                                                    2002005057

Texas In Poetry is supported in part by a grant from the Writers' League of Texas and the Texas Commission on the Arts.

Jacket Illustrations/Kip Lott
Book Design/Margie Adkins Graphic Design

For Julia Giddens Hill (1917 – 2000):
reciter of poetry, public school music teacher,
frequent traveler, and friend.

Contents

1 I'LL TAKE TEXAS

2 FACES OF BLOOD KINDRED

3 Texas: A World in Itself

7 Tales of Old-Time Texas

_8_ Things about to Disappear

9 I'M GOING TO LEAVE OLD TEXAS NOW

11 No Quittin' Sense

Foreword

The present revised edition of *Texas in Poetry* updates and expands Billy Bob Hill's 1994 edition, which received excellent reviews and was sold out within two years of publication. In that volume Hill made it clear that the anthology was not a collection of the best that has been written in this state or about this state. His purpose then was to present a full and representative selection of the poetry just a few years after the sesquicentennial of Texas independence; in fact, the full title of the first edition is *Texas in Poetry: A 150-Year Anthology*. This edition, now eight years after the first edition, has the same goals—to give the reader a sampling of Texas poetry from the earliest times to the present. In this second edition, he could have eliminated many of the older works in favor of modern Texas verse that compare favorably with anything being written in the country today. But that would have gone against his standard for the first edition, for to give a full picture of Texas in poetry it is necessary to keep those poems that are by today's standards mawkish, amateurish, and oftentimes embarrassing to lovers of poetry. But they do represent the thoughts and language of a time when the state was in its infancy. And even before. Back to the years when the state was warring for independence. Back to the nascent republic hoping for admission to the Union.

But since so much that is first-rate is included, most of the poems in this large and definitive collection are works that will stand comparison with the best writing in the mainstream of American poetry. In fact, both editions are filled with excellent poems by writers recognized across the country as accomplished craftsmen. Writers like Vassar Miller, Walter McDonald, R. S. Gwynn, Betsy Feagan Colquitt, Betty Adcock, Pattiann Rogers, William Barney, Lorenzo Thomas, Cynthia Macdonald, Edward Hirsch, William Virgil Davis, Jack Myers, Robert Phillips, Ray González, Rosemary Catacalos, Harryette Mullen, Thomas Whitbread, James Hoggard, Jerry Bradley, Naomi Shihab Nye, Del Marie Rogers, and Sandra Cisneros are all writers well known in contemporary American poetry. And there are many other poets included here who are making names for themselves as this edition goes to press. I have in mind talented writers like Mary Loving Blanchard, Isabel Nathaniel, Jas. Mardis, Palmer Hall, Robert Fink, Carmen Tafolla, Teresa Palomo Acosta, Carol Coffee Reposa, Jerry Craven, Sherry Craven, Tim Seibels, Cynthia Harper, Njoki McElroy, Chip Dameron, and Carol Cullar. Needless to say, I have not named all the fine Texas poets, and I am sure my omissions will haunt me even before the book goes to press. But they are here in this volume and all add immeasurably to the picture of Texas poetry as it stands at the beginning of a new millennium.

Nor has Hill forgotten those Texas poets whose works have caused critics from around the nation take notice, poets who founded the Texas Poetry Society and nurtured Texas verse during the 1920s, '30s, and '40s when Texas poetry was almost always derided as doggerel about bluebonnets and cattle. But those serious poets of the poetry society paved the way for writers as sophisticated as those writing in Texas today. In those early hard days, Karle Wilson Baker, Whitney Montgomery, W. E. Bard, Lexie Dean Robertson, Grace Noll Crowell, Berta Hart Nance, Faye M Yauger, Gene Shuford, Vaida Stewart Montgomery, Arthur M. Sampley, Hilton Ross Greer, and Stanley E. Babb kept Texas poetry alive and smoothed a path for today's best writers.

In order to give a sense of the scope of verse in Texas, Hill has wisely included works by such barely recognized poets as Mirabeau B. Lamar, the second president of the Republic; Bonnie Parker, the notorious bank robber whose contribution is a long bit of frippery about the killers Bonnie and Clyde; and W. Lee O'Daniel, whose Lightcrust Doughboys were hillbilly radio stars in the 1930s (O'Daniel wrote "Beautiful Texas" before going on to be governor and a U. S. Senator—though he was undistinguished in all his pursuits). There is even Sam Houston's "A Texian's Call to Arms" from 1836. And certainly Hill has not neglected to include one of the "great bad" poems of all time, "Lasca"—remember the line "Scratches don't count in Texas/Down by the Rio Grande"? Not to mention Berta Hart Nance's now-unfashionable poem "Cattle" with its memorable (?) lines "Other states were carved or born/ Texas grew from hide and horn."

One of the interesting things about *Texas in Poetry* is that editor Hill has divided the poems into recognizable themes about life in the Lone Star State. And he has chosen for his subtitles the names of some celebrated works about Texas. His first chapter is called "I'll Take Texas," a title borrowed from Mary Lasswell's memoir about her return to the state from New York. His final chapter is borrowed from the Reverend C. C. White's wonderful dictated auto-biography, "No Quittin' Sense." Some of the other title divisions come from A. C. Greene's *A Personal Country*, William A. Owens' *This Stubborn Soil*, and George Sessions Perry's *Texas: A World in Itself*. There are eleven sections, and one of the ways to read the book is to start at the beginning and read all the poems in each section before moving on. But it is also instructive to read here and there in the book as one does in any general anthology. I have done it both ways. When the first edition was published, I was director of the Center for Texas Studies at the University of North Texas and was, in a way, the book's publisher. But since I didn't edit it or proofread it, I read it piecemeal. This time around, as an editor and proofreader at TCU Press, I read the entire manuscript from start to finish and saw, for the first time, how intelligent and interesting Hill's divisions are. I recommend reading the book from cover to cover the way one should attack Byron's *Don Juan* or any novel. For classroom use, such an approach will never sell, and the piecemeal approach will repay the reader almost equally well. I find that I am more impressed with the second edition than the first because of the way I read it this time around—and also because Hill has discovered many new poems and new poets.

Hill admits in an earlier preface that he did not include all the poems that he could have, and that is even truer now than it was in 1994. Now, an anthologist could produce a volume of Texas poetry that would include none of the poems from a time past when poetry in this state was still derivative and untutored and simplistic to human eye and ear. But, admirable though such a volume would be, it would not serve the purpose that Hill had in mind when he put together the first edition. I have no doubt that Billy Bob Hill, probably the most comprehensive and knowledgeable observer of Texas poetry we have, could—and may—produce such a volume. But it will not supersede his outstanding *Texas in Poetry.*

James Ward Lee
Fort Worth, Texas

Acknowledgments

I would like to thank my late seventh-grade social studies teacher, Margarette McDade and my graduate school professor A.C. Greene. I was lucky enough to have studied under only the best. The following living Texans directly contributed to this book: Theresa Palomo Acosta, and Don Graham, Mike Hennech, A.C. Greene, Marshall Terry, Terry Dalrymple, Thomas Edward Brawner, James Ward Lee, Jim Cody, Kent Biffle, James Gilbert Clarke, Robert Flynn, Guida Jackson, J. Paul Holcomb, Bryan Woolley, Dave Oliphant, Paul Kenneth Oswalt, Cheryl Chapman, James Mardis, F. E. Abernethy, Jill Paterson, John Graves, Paul Foreman, Judyth Rigler, Robert Compton, Anne Dingus, Laurie Champion, Mark Busby, Paul Ruffin, Barbara Miles, Clay Reynolds, Charles Daniel, Tom Pilkington, Robert Nelson, Jerry Craven, Mary Albright, Tom Dodge, Ann McVay, Fritz Lanham, L. D. and Laverne Harrell Clark, Joyce Gibson Roach, Margie West, Judy Alter, Judith Kroll, Thea Temple, Rick Sale, Lou Rodenberger, Kip Lott, and Betty Wiesepape. In addition, my deepest thanks go to: Becky Waskom, Grant Sisk, Chuck Taylor, Ron Tyler, George B. Ward, Fran Vick, F.E. Abernethy, and Susan R. Petty.

Introduction

Poetry seems to me to be a basic mode of human expression, like singing, dancing, or kissing. The rhythms, the rhymings, seem attached to the drumbeat of the heart, no matter in what language. Poetry is something that doesn't have to be taught or learned: listen to children skipping rope or playing hopscotch to homemade rhymes. And even for grownups, there is no more satisfactory way of counting off than

> Wire-briar limberlock
> Three geese in a flock.
> One flew east, one flew west,
> One flew over the cuckoo's nest. . . .

What is wire-briar, what is limberlock ...who knows or who cares; they are the poetry of intense decision-making.

Poetry seems to occur to us naturally in moments of deeply felt emotion, spurring us to put down words which express great love, great fear, great sorrow, or great celebration—we who might never before have thought of voicing our ideas in poetry. Take this anonymous, pencil-written poem found in a sixty-five-year-old Texas scrapbook:

You dont know how Ive suffered of late
You dont know how my heart does eake
But now I know Its to late, Yes Its all
　　　In vain
I've tried to Be Just as Calm as a lamb
But now I a all Broke down
Never more can I come home
And find my Mother dear at home
Its hard tho must be no human tong
can tell How It greaves me
I long to see her on that Beautiful Shore
Where greafe and pain Shall be no more.

　　Although President Mirabeau Lamar and a few other Republic of Texas figures wrote poetry, and some of the plains Indians developed chants which were quite poetic, probably the first true Texas poets were the black workers and the cowboys; both celebrated the events of their daily lives, the generally small happenings of their work, and did it in song: the boll weevil comes to Texas "lookin' for uh home"; Little Joe the wrangler falls beneath his horse during a stampede. Death, the vagaries of love, and a resignation toward life's disasters floats among and above most rural worker ballads.

　　Texans have always liked to celebrate their uniqueness in poetry, some of it very bad—the Alamo has been lamented far too often—but the power of Texas events challenged the old poetic world of the nineteenth century: even Walt Whitman mourned the Goliad massacre. But some *is* good, and even old standards deserve re-reading for the atmosphere they retain: "Lasca," probably the most famous of the old Texas verses, was written by an Englishman who had spent less than three years in Texas, but Frank Deprez caught a certain regional spirit, just as Larry Chittenden, "The Cowboy Poet" (from New Jersey and Maine), did in the 1890s when he wrote "The Cowboys' Christmas Ball" and his other rollicking West Texas verse.

Facing literary reality—charming they may be, but in early Texas (as Leonidas W. Payne observed in 1928), "there was, nevertheless, a vast amount of mediocre poetry produced." Should we forgive the rhymesters? Frank Dobie couldn't. He left the poetry out of his influential *Life and Literature of the Southwest.* Dobie was torn between two worlds. He wanted to be acknowledged as an intellectual, and no intellectual in his time could even use the phrase "Texas poetry" without shuddering or making faces. On the other hand, Dobie, who prided himself on being a man of the soil and of its people, couldn't but admit the songs of those earthen folks were as valid an expression of their lives as the folk tales of lost mines, buried treasures, and oral mythology.

So, there was a lot of bad poetry written in Texas, and continues to be written, be warned. But there has been enough good verse, sometimes hidden in small anthologies, sometimes a diamond glowing among its rhinestone companionship. The Poetry Society of Texas has been both elevated and condemned for its role in Texas poetry for the last seven or so decades, but when its work is summed up, the Poetry Society has more positives than negatives. And publications like the old *Southwest Review* contributed Texas verse of a recognizable high quality. Much of that lost-era verse deserves to be resurrected—and read again. Vaida and Whitney Montgomery, Fay M. Yauger, even Berta Hart Nance ("Other states were carved or born; / Texas grew from hide and horn") deserve being looked at once more, compared only with what they are saying.

Today Texas has a proud line of what could be called new poets. Their quality is unquestioned, their poetic thoughts powerful, moving, instructive. Not everyone who calls himself "poet" is one, or is a good one, but poetry has moved into a new phase all over the world, which (believe it or not) includes Texas. Poetry has become politicized, but the best such work is gentle and insistent without slamming the reader over the head with its message. Poetry has become personal, internal, thoughts that come bubbling up in no order but with passionate conviction. The one form of poetry that seems missing today is that oldest of passionate verse, the love song. Poets are afraid to write love songs because, I suppose, the world of poetic peers might laugh. And today's poet has to be careful, also, that anything celebrating a public event must be coolly phrased, detached, with slightly elevated eyebrows.

But Texas still arouses the poetic instinct in its citizens. Some of today's poets, like Walter McDonald, write almost exclusively of how and what the land means, what it does to the people who live on it, successfully and unsuccessfully. Others, like Pat LittleDog, find the incongruities of Texas life to be a useful means of locating one's self. Naomi Nye discerns Texans in narrow but loving detail, looking at them—approvingly and, hinting, disapprovingly, but always forgiving them—through the small end of the poetic telescope. Jack Myers taught and retaught how to be both human and earthling. I must stop, for it is not fair to point out only a few Texas poets today. The Lone Star State is full of discernible writing as in few other periods.

Therefore, take up this collection with an open mind, a reader's mind, not a critic's. These poems are not presented as the ultimate or even the best possible collection. In fact, one or two very good poems were denied the collection because the writer felt they were not worth the salvation of an anthology. Too bad. The writer never knows what of his will become a guide to safety, a deliverance from evil, or a reproof for selfish greed. Poetry can do all that, even mediocre poetry. Even Texas poetry.

A. C. Greene
Salado, Texas

1

I'll Take Texas

When I got out of the cab in front of the hotel, I thought I heard someone calling my name. I turned my head to see that it was only a truckload of lonesome, bawling, white-faced calves. But it was music to me: as Texas a welcome as anyone could wish.

Mary Lasswell

1

MARY VANEK
Homing Instinct

I drove all night from the red light
of dusk that stained the last of the Rockies true
to their given name—Sangre de Cristos.
I made the Valley of the Volcanoes south
of Raton by first dark. No moon that December
evening, perfectly cold, the air clear enough
to smell the irrigated fields of northwest Texas.
I was nearly home. All I wanted
after a month in Wyoming with two New Yorkers
and a crazy California woman
was the sound of my own vowels
in someone else's mouth. Until then,
I drank beer cold as the air
outside my rolled-down window
and sang along with Patsy Cline.

With my luck close to midnight,
I made the left-hand turn onto the Farm-to-Market
1719, Hazardous Cargo Route, and the road
that runs to the front door of my parents' house.
Stopped in the pure dark of the front pasture,
the music full and tinny, the car lights out,
I waited. It did not take long.
One yip, a yowl, then full-bodied howls
filled my head and aching sinuses
with the actual anthem of home.

—1994

✷ ✷ ✷ ✷ ✷ ✷ ✷ ✷ ✷ ✷ ✷ ✷ ✷

We Go Away at Home

Oklahoma lies on top of us like a sod quilt
thickened with manure. Once a year it turns over
and the black escapes. So we dream we drive all night
into the mouth of boredom, smelling sex,
betting that the long explosions of the stars
have stopped. By dawn the flags of radiation are flying
deep inside New Mexico and I wake you so you can sleep
against me as the ultra-colors pass through rock.

In the dusty sunlight I read the land out loud
while you explore the invisible ruins I describe
as silence. The Mexican gorge blasts up its hacking
yellow cough and you focus on a long-legged bird
pecking its way between the rocks. It takes off
as the curtain of heat thickens to a lens.

In Louisiana men in bogs are running from tree to tree.
They fall down peacefully and dissolve, then flash out
as green shoots in another life. We are sinking into ourselves
with the inward smile of vegetables as it gets dark.
The night air breathes the black trees in like smoke.
Lying here, disappearing, we remember why we stayed at home.

—1979

W. Lee O'Daniel
Beautiful Texas

You have all read the beautiful story
Of countries far over the sea,
From whence came our ancestors
To establish this home of the free,
There are some folks who still like to travel
To see what they have over there
But when they go look, it's not like the book
And they find there is none to compare.

To beautiful, beautiful Texas,
Where the beautiful bluebonnets grow,
We are proud of our forefathers
Who fought at the Alamo.
You can live on the plain or the mountains,
Or down where the sea breezes blow
And you are still in beautiful Texas
The most beautiful place that I know.

—1939

William D. Barney
Long Gone to Texas

Some of those pioneers who came
out of dead hopes, unevened scores,
wrote three stark letters on their doors,
shook disappointment off, and shame,
and headed here to kindle a new star.

At twelve I had no lasting hurt,
no stricken heart, no dream's debris.
Transplanted like an up-plucked tree,

my roots caught into splendid dirt,
and soon reset the running calendar.

Whoever cultivates this patch
earth color will stick to his hand.
Gladly I gather from this land
whatever harvest I can scratch.
The field, like the star, is large and singular.

Add one more letter to the three.
I'll carve the legend on my bark,
a culminating brand to mark
more than a half of century—
Long Gone to Texas. Here my horizons are.

    —1986

★ ★ ★ ★ ★ ★ ★ ★ ★ ★ ★ ★

WILLIAM ALLEN WARD
Texas

Texas,
Child of the West,
Who talks in the soft voice
Of the South, but packs a gun
On his hip.

Texas,
A two-gun killer
Who looks the gambling cheat
Straight in the eye—a pistol bark . . .
Then death!

Texas,
A rowdy boy,
With the wind for a pal

And the sunset to paint his cheeks
With health.

Texas,
A little girl,
Who plucks a wild flower
On the hill of June, to put in
Her hair.

—1934

* * * * * * * * * * * * * * * *

CALEY O'DWYER
Texas

The nosebleed
of the cottonwood. Land of God.

The land of aluminum siding and food.
I'm from the creek and the deep bayou,

the summer flower and the mockingbird.
Land of endless neighborhood.

Land of good. I'm from the green
grasshopper, the hornet and the dirt-dauber.

The millipede, the centipede, the spider.
The electric bug-snapper.

I'm from Texas. That's Southwest
of Northeast. And a bit to your left.

I'm from the land of the oil pump
and the trash dump.

The CB radio
and the tornado.

I'm from the land of "get up and let's go!"
Land of the Superbowl

and jello. I'm from the land of 52
types of cereal.

Odessa, Kermit and Louisville.
Land of the fall at Wichita

and the dunes below Penwell. The sea shell
of Galveston.

Land of the pecan tree,
and the oak,

where the locust
burns in the mulberry

and sings in the scarecrow's eye
and sings in the hull of the lakeboat

and the speedboat
and the gin.

Land of the yellow rose
and the Sunday sermon.

Land of the holy water
at Houston.

Land of the cow-chip, the corncob and the cornerback.
Land of the clogged artery heart attack.

Land of the blitz, the stomp and the sack.
Land of the crockpot

and the astronaut.
Land of the Black-eyed Susan.

And the black eye of the North.
Land of the beer can,

the barbecue, the brave
and the Dairy Queen milk shake.

Land of the warring sexes.
I'm from Texas.

Land of the loan shark.
Land of the handshake.

   —*2000*

 ✶ ✶ ✶ ✶ ✶ ✶ ✶ ✶ ✶ ✶ ✶

LEXIE DEAN ROBERTSON
Texas Memoranda

Lemon trees
Warm under a Texas sun,
Fragrant with the memories of old Spain
And yellow with the golden apples of Hesperides.

Bluebonnets
A bit of cobalt sky let down to earth
An unexpected turquoise lake
Spilled down a hillside.

Coastline
A curve of cool brown sand
Embracing the dim sapphire reaches of the sea

And a wild gull flying.

Galveston Beach
A sweep of sea and sand
With the unending loveliness of changing water
Weaving frothy lace against the shore.

Pecos River
A silver ribbon
Wending through dark sage-grass prairies
Reflecting always the ancient glory
Of the western sun.

—1940

DEL MARIE ROGERS
Some Nights I Love Everybody in Texas

287 Cafe, Dumas, Texas.
Dark plains around a truck-stop, flat as a plate.
(You see me with a great big smile)
Brainless neon shining, waitresses,
cheerful dog in the door, cowboys, chicken-fried steak.
Burl Ives sings "It's Just My Funny Way of Laughin'."
Outside, across the flatland, a black wind is blowing,
strong enough to make my sons old,
my daughters pinch-faced,
in a cold instant,
all but this island.

—1979

Berta Hart Nance
State Song

The singers filled the tiny schoolhouse stage
With youth and vigor in a studied pose,
I watched them from the peak of middle age, —
There was a chord; the sturdy voices rose:
    "God bless you, Texas,
      And keep you brave and strong."

And while they sang I thought, and pitied us,
Who had been young without that song to sing—
A bugle for a patriot, —and thus,
It made me glad to hear the voices ring.

Outside was Texas, sparkling to the door,
With rounded hill and prairie-mist of green,
Bluebonnets on the scented valley floor,
And mocking-birds that rhymed away unseen.

And here in Texas, in the simple hall,
The manly students with the chiming throats,
Their task the building of our country's wall, —
And with a sob I whispered to the notes:
    "Good bless you, Texas,
      And keep you brave and strong."

—1935

✦ ✦ ✦ ✦ ✦ ✦ ✦ ✦ ✦ ✦ ✦

Peggy Zuleika Lynch
A True Texan

A true Texan wears the Lone Star in his heart
    as well as over it.
A true Texan matches his valor
    against anyone's at the drop of a hat.

A true Texan clings to his land
     not as landed gentry
     but as gentle to the land.

     It's his domain.
     It's his kingdom.

Out of the sand, the brush, the cacti, the mesquite,
     the plush metropolitan cities
wherever the Lone Star flies,
     the people who are truly Texan vie and defy
the rugged tornadoes, the demolishing floods
     the burning droughts, the inexplicable crime.
They take what comes
     and stretch the mind
to weather fortune's decree:
     true men of grit.

(Chorus)

We are Texas rugged individualists.
     We can live in a hovel
       or live in a palace.
It makes no great difference
     and we have no malice.
We're game to whatever destiny deals us
     YES, WE ARE TEXANS;
     the nation loves us?
We are fundamentally antagonists
     to whatever "out does" us!
     We just go on and buck up!
YES, WE ARE TEXAS RUGGED INDIVIDUALISTS.
     WE'RE TEXANS!
     The nation loves us?

—1980

Richard Sale
Stilts and Other Vehicles

The old masters posed themselves at a window,
Forearm along the sill to form a base.
From that vantage they could view the world.
I learned to walk in Sweetwater, Tex.
In Athens, next, I got good enough on them
To climb the high steps of the First Baptist Church.
Then on to Palestine, to fence balancing,
To Corpus Christi, to surfboards, filled glasses
On a bent arm. Classical names, classical poses.

Now I have walked on my Western stilts
In London, Paris, Seville, standing on one foot
In awe and a self-conscious perversity of pride.
I may progress to some exotic Polynesian posture before
       it's over.
The High Plains and Piney Woods and the low
Dunes of the coastal flats are far behind.
But a jingling spur: What you thought you outgrew
Shaped whatever gait you've grown into.

—1978

2

Faces of Blood Kindred

. . . *A*nswered any speechless question, atoned for blind failing, the outrage and the pain on the face of his blood kindred?

William Goyen

Ai
Family

The old man sent for Papa,
but he wouldn't go.
That's what they tell me.
I don't know.
He had land to give him.
He was on his death bed,
but Papa wouldn't go.
Papa said, "Die like a dog, Old Man."
He said it in the shed
where he kept the horse tack.
He said it when he fed the horses.
He said it in bed like a prayer,
then he kissed the only picture
he had of his mother, fell asleep
and woke up another day
and they sent word again.
The Old Man was calling out for him,
but Papa said, "I got a hen's neck to wring.
We're having baked chicken for dinner,"
and he went in the barn
and came out with eggs still warm from laying
and he took them in the kitchen
washed off the shit, put them in a basket
and went to sit on the front porch.
He rocked back and forth in his glider
and Mama brought him a glass of hot apple cider.
"Where's that chicken, John?"
"Nevermind, I'll do it myself," she said.
"The way he treated my mother," said Papa.
He remembered riding to Texas in a wagon
from Oklahoma when he was five
with his Choctaw mother
and his white father.

An older brother left behind
because he resembled Choctaws more than Papa did.
"That," he went on, "was a time."
The Old Man on a bay horse,
just staring at him,
until Papa waved,
then turning and riding off.
His father, Charles' silence at dinner,
biscuits and a basket of fried chicken
sent from the ranch house
and a teddy bear with all its fur nearly gone.
"That was mine," said his father.
"Now it's yours."
Papa nodded and picked up a chicken leg.
He ate ranch beans, potato salad
and washed it down with buttermilk.
Then his mother put him to bed.
Her long black braid had come undone
and he touched her hair
and it made a sound like silk rustling
in his dreams anyway.
The next day, his father took him to see cattle grazing
as far as the eye could see and farther.
He saw a pond for fishing, horses, and a bunk house,
a dog house, an outhouse his father once used
and he met a lot of people—cowboys, two cooks,
a man who took him up in the saddle of his horse.
That was his uncle, but he didn't know it then.
He died in the Great War.
He didn't see his grandfather.
His father took him in the kitchen of the ranch house.
"You be quiet as a little mouse," he told him.
The cook gave him hot chocolate and a book about the ABC's.
When his father came back, he just said, "Let's go, son."
He didn't return to that house,
until he was twenty,

after his father got killed when a steer trampled him
and ran clear to Abilene,
before anybody could catch it,
at least that's what they say.
Papa didn't know what would happen,
so he started packing.
Then a message came from The Old Man,
whose name was never uttered in their house.
John went that time.
He didn't know what he expected to find.
I'll tell you what he didn't, The Old Man.
The foreman had a letter for him.
It said, "I need a good drover."
He talked it over with his mother,
but she was ready to go back to her people,
so he took her home to Oklahoma,
where he met his brother
and Mama and went back to Texas
with his new bride, a job
and a life this side of respectable.
And so they lived that way for fifteen years.
Grandson and grandfather,
who couldn't put asunder the divisions of race.
Papa gets up. He walks to the gate,
opens it and just waits
for God knows what,
then he steps back and shuts it.
He remembers again the Christmas presents
sent from the ranch house,
always one for him, nothing for his mother
and smothers the urge to kick in the door
of the ranch house
pour gasoline on The Old Man, light it
and watch him burn to a cinder
with a smile on his face.
The same kind The Old Man wore

the day they first came face to face
and The Old Man rode off.
It had no love in it, it had no hate,
but it had kinship.

—2002

* * * * * * * * * *

CARMEN TAFOLLA
This River Here

This river here
is full of me and mine.
This river here
is full of you and yours.

Right here
(or maybe a little farther down)
My great-grandmother washed the dirt
out of her family's clothes,
soaking them, scrubbing them,
bringing them up
clean.

Right here
(or maybe a little farther down)
My grampa washed the sins
out of his congregation's souls,
baptizing them, scrubbing them,
bringing them up
clean.

Right here
(or maybe a little farther down)
My great-great grandma froze with fear
as she glimpsed
between the lean, dark trees

a lean, dark Indian peering at her.
She ran home screaming, "Ay, los indios!
A'i vienen los i-i-indios!!"
as he threw pebbles at her.
Till one day she got mad
and stayed
and threw pebbles
right back at him!

After they got married,
they built their house right here
(or maybe a little farther down.)

Right here,
my father gathered
mesquite beans and wild berries
working with a passion
during the depression.
His eager sweat poured off
and mixed so easily
with the water of this river here.

Right here,
my mother cried in silence,
so far from her home,
sitting with her one brown suitcase,
a traveled trunk packed full with blessings,
and rolling tears of loneliness and longing
which mixed (again so easily)
with the currents of this river here.

Right here we'd pour out picnics,
and childhood's blood from
dirty scrapes on dirty knees,
and every generation's first-hand stories
of the weeping lady La Llorona,

haunting the river every night,
crying "Ayyy, mis hi-i-i-ijos!"
(It happened right here!)
The fear dripped off our skin
and the blood dripped off our scrapes
and they mixed with the river water,
Right here.

Right here,
the stories and the stillness
of those gone before us
haunt us still,
now grown, our scrapes in different places,
the voices of those now dead
quieter,
but not too far away…

Right here we were married,
you and I,
and the music filled the air,
danced in,
dipped in,
mixed in
with the river water.

    …dirt and sins,
    fear and anger,
    sweat and tears,
    love and music,
    Blood.
    And memories…

It was right here!

And right here we stand,
washing clean our memories,

baptizing our hearts,
gathering past and present,
dancing to the flow
we find
right here
or maybe—
a little farther
down.

—2000

* * * * * * * * * * * * *

Mary Loving Blanchard
Bloodlines

Borders
stretch my slender vision
to reveal grand old missions

wilting in the fierce East Texas sun;
here the ghosts languish:
in damp alcoves, behind secret doors

in the marrow of women
who recount their mothers' history
with circumscribed tongue
to recall the mingling of blood—

A rebel Spaniard and a runaway slave, outsiders
who sought a life in these piney woods
where nothing foreign can live

did cheat this infertile place
and bear a daughter, remarkable in their sight.
Beyond my slender vision
I see Dolóres slamming her doors

in disbelief, I watch
as her rejection of his vow
to christen the bastard
at her exalted altar
is carried by the silty dirt
that coats the floors of this old town

to the ears of mothers
who looked into their daughters' faces
and being moved
to brush breath across the bronze cheeks

of girls
mangled by blood
would keep quiet no longer: Stood clamoring
before her walls
casting their complaints
at Dolóres' deaf ears. Beyond my slender vision

I hear their screams
as they relate the story, I taste the tears
that spill onto their bosoms
into the waiting mouths
of women
who carry history in their veins
who move through these piney woods
like quiet shadows

and keep watch
for the rebel's return.

—2001

  ✦   ✦   ✦   ✦   ✦   ✦   ✦   ✦   ✦   ✦   ✦   ✦

Violette Newton
Going Back to Ireland

When we saw Grandma come running out
of the bedroom, crying, we knew
it had happened, the thing
they were waiting for, the old man's
death. They hadn't let us in the room,
had shooed us away from the door
when they caught us looking.
But we wanted to see Grandpa lying there,
frail and white-haired, in the high old bed,
with swaths of mosquito netting pulled up
so it looked like a cloud over him.

We had come on the train from Texas to be
there, had seen our mother and aunts
take turns fanning him
with palmetto fans,
calling him "Papa" as they whispered
together. We wondered about the map
of Ireland on his wall. It looked
like a little green leaf on the brown sea …
the sea was brown because the map
was so old. We knew he had sailed
a winter ocean to get here
in another century
and had lived long enough
to see an airplane take off
and fly. He had said this.

The daughters followed their mother
out of the room, and soon the house
was filled with people coming to hug,
to bring gumbo and layer cake, people
saying it was a blessing. After all,

he was ninety-one. But Grandma,
so much younger, was inconsolable.

They ran us out to the back yard
where chickens were taking
dust baths under the fig trees,
and suddenly I looked up
to the white-hot morning sky
and saw angels, a bevy of them
swishing over the roof, taking
his soul with them, angels with wings
and white raiment, the soul surrounded
so I couldn't see it, but I knew
it was there, leaving us, going
back, I hoped, to Ireland
where he always said
his heart was.

 —1993

   ✴ ✴ ✴ ✴ ✴ ✴ ✴ ✴ ✴ ✴ ✴ ✴

ROSEMARY CATACALOS
Katakalos

The Old Man, we always called him.
We said it with respect.
Even when he embarrassed us
by wearing his plaid flannel work shirt
to church under the fine blue suit
one of his up-and-coming sons,
the three prides of his life,
had brought him.
Even when he spent hours
straightening used nails when
we could afford to buy him new ones
so he could build the hundreds
of crooked little plant stands

that still wobble in the corners
of our houses.

He had come off a hard island birthplace,
a rock long ago deserted by the gods
but still sopping with the blood
of its passing from hand to hand,
Greek to Turk, Turk to Greek
and back again,
as if everything had not always
belonged to the sea, he said,
and to the relentless light
that hurt the eyes
of statues and children alike.
He was brought up on routine whippings
every Sunday, before-the-fact punishment
to fit any crime. His father, the miller,
followed the wisdom that parents
can't be everywhere at once
and in seven days any boy is bound
to do something deserving a beating.
Besides, by his own admission
he was not such a good shepherd,
always getting sidetracked caring
for some sick bird or dog or donkey
that followed him everywhere ever after
and got mixed up with the goats and sheep.

A draft dodger from the Turkish Army,
he braved the maze of Ellis Island
alone at sixteen,
escaping with his last name intact
and his first name changed to Sam.
New York fed him dog food
those first few months
when he couldn't read the labels

and only knew from the pictures
that the cans were meat and cheap.
He used to laugh about that.
Said it was just as good as some of
that Spam and stuff they sell nowadays.
Anyway, Sam was
the darling of immigrant flophouses,
giving away counsel and sometimes money,
always finding someone who was
a little worse off than he was.

He hoboed all the way to Seattle
where he pretended to be a high-flying carpenter
and was saved by *Hagia Sophia* from a fall that
would otherwise have meant certain death.
Then he came to where they were
burning Greeks out of Oklahoma
and anyone who could kept moving
and opened a hamburger stand
a little farther south.
In San Antonio he rigged up
a brightly painted horse-drawn
popcorn and ice cream wagon
and made the rounds of the West Side,
never quite making more than a living
since he always told poor kids
to pay him whenever they got the money.
The hamburger stands came next.
The cafe on Produce Row that some
old market hands still remember.
The Ideal Spot on South Presa,
where every hobo and derelict
from here to either coast
knew he could collect a free meal.
Good Old Sam.
But his wife was always angry.

She wanted a house of her own,
something more than glass beads.
She hated the way he was always
attracting winos and gypsies
and cousins from everywhere
who camped on her red velvet cushions
while he was out working hard
to give it all away.
She was from Lagos, Jalisco,
and when they'd met
it hadn't been so much about love
as it had been simply time to get married.
That's what she always said.
Sam never said much about it
one way or the other,
except to smile and tell us
she'd had a hard life.

Still, they must have had a
little something special going.
Seeing how back then
he spoke only Greek,
a little broken English,
and she spoke only Spanish.
They were married through an interpreter.
Sam wore an ill-fitting suit
and carried a brown paper bag
full of sandwiches he had made
so as not to let the few guests go hungry.

Years later when they were old
she had never learned English
and he had never bought her a house.
He'd spend years in his by-now-perfect
Spanish trying to get her to see
how there was always some poor devil

who needed just a little help.
When she complained the loudest
he just listened patiently
and went about setting out his
sugar water in bottle caps
to feed the ants.
A smiling survivor.
A fat soft heart.
The Old Man.
We still say it with respect.

—1981

* * * * * * * * * * * * * *

CHARLES BEHLEN
My Grandfather's Hammer

A hard head.
A straight back.
When I tossed it down
it kicked the dirt
curtly,
slept at attention
like a Prussian.
Its voice was the
cry of a nail
clawed from a plank,
the gripe of a coin
pried from an acre
of Texas cotton
from 1918
to 1957.

—1985

* * * * * * * * * * * * * *

JIM LINEBARGER
Oppa

You lived in hardy commonness: the feel
of gritty linoleum, the smell of snuff,
the cornbread and beans and onions you preferred
for diet, a faulty hearing aid, a ball
of string, assorted buttons, an embossed
red-letter Bible, dearly paid for with dimes
and pennies from a knotted handkerchief.

But miracles attended you as well.
My father laughs and swears he sweated dust
in the creaking wagon that you drove across
the Llano Estacado, but raised his eyes
to marvel at peaks topped with a white glaze
of winter. From your swept yard, behind a piece
of smoked glass, I saw an invisible moon
black out the sun. A patchwork quilt became,
under the light of kerosene lamps, a rose
window as we giggled and hid from the tame
and moral beasts of your imagination.
Closer to death, when your laboring tears
would gather to tell us of a new sensation,
your face was like a baby's taking love.

The ways of living are as various
as those of dying, but I fear them all.
Teach me your secret way for the dark times,
something to live by, perhaps a single word,
some kind of myth for your inheritors
who have no understanding with the sun.

—1969

NJOKI McELROY
Present Moments

I started the day with a jog/fast walk
Into crisp fresh air. Breath exhausting
Past present future terrors. Cooling down
With rhythms of Tai Chi
I know this won't be always.

AFTERNOON

Creamed the butter and brown sugar by hand
Saved some of the crumbly mix to top the batter
Two well beaten eggs and buttermilk with dissolved
Baking powder turns the crumbly mix to rich brown batter
Cinnamon, nutmeg, ginger, vanilla go in last
In the oven the spicy aroma seeps out and into my pores
Light like cake and spicy Perfecto
It is my Xmas gift to Cousin Twoshoe.

At her house she savors
The warm morsels and says:
Oh how did you know I've had a taste for Gingerbread?
She's my grandmother's first cousin
And at 103 (she says she's 111) is my
Last contact to my maternal ancestor's memories.

I'm not bragging, Cousin Twoshoe confides
But God has led me on a wonderful journey
And when He comes for me, I'm ready.
Granny Marinda (Let's see, she's your great great great)
Was 110 when He came for her.

I was a little tot when she came to live with us
But I never forgot my little dark brown
Granny dressed in a long dress, starched apron, bonnet

High button shoes, smoking a pipe, sightless eyes searching
A distant past, talking about slavery

Dear Granny was sold several times.
She was a troublesome Runagate, always running
Running to find her freedom
Climbing trees to escape her captors.

Evening

Green apples in Mom's red glass bowl, evergreen
Wreaths, Kwanza candles, spicy scents fill the room
My main squeeze pedicures my tired feet with patience
And happy-to-pleaseness. He pats my legs and says:
O.K. Cleopatra?
I smile and run my fingers through his soft beard
My feet are smooth
My soul is rejuvenated I'm ready to dance all night
I know this won't be always

Night

At the party John Nickels and the Five Pennies
Play Blues, Country, Xmas
I don't want to make the gods jealous
But in my long flared red form fitting dress
I flaunt my good fortune
When the party ends, a stranger says:
Such a handsome couple—The two of you dance so beautifully.
I've lived this day of Present Moments well
If only this could be always.

—2002

BERTA HART NANCE
Frontier Mystery

My uncle was a ranger
In old Fort Griffin days.
And there he saw a woman
He could not help but praise.

Her dress was dark and splendid,
Her hands were fair and long,
Her eyes were soft and shining,
Her voice was full of song.

You would not think to find her
In any gambling den,
But every night at poker
She played with all the men.

And no man dared insult her,
And no one knew her name;
When she had won a fortune,
She vanished like a flame.

Leaving in shoddy fabric,
A thread of gold and blue,—
The only touch of glamour
My uncle ever knew.

—1935

✦　✦　✦　✦　✦　✦　✦　✦　✦　✦　✦　✦　✦

BENJAMIN ALIRE SÁENZ
Benjamín
In Memory of my Uncles:
Guillermo Sáenz, Benjamín Sáenz,
Ricardo Alire, and Bernardo Alire

31

                On the day of his birth
He took a breath, opened his eyes, then
Closed them tight forever. There was
Something in the Texas air he could never
Be at peace with—too much blood in the dust,
Too much fire in the sun, too much wind,
Too much wind. There would never be enough
Rain. He was born too thirsty. Knowing this
Though he was born perfect and good,
He died.
                Many years passed before his
Surviving older brother (under instructions
From a mother who refused to forget)
Passed down his name to his son.

                This is how I
Came to be possessed of his name, which
In turn, made me fall in love with dead
Uncles who lie still and perfect. Perfect
And good in the ground.

        —1995

  *   *   *   *   *   *   *   *   *   *   *   *

SUSAN WOOD
Four Roses
C.W.M. 1910-1985

Outside my door four roses
languish in the late spring sun. They don't
smell of failure yet, though he did, who hid
Four Roses in a cardboard suitcase. In memory
they call my uncle "Rabbit" because he runs
like that. Red-faced, he crouches
in the infield, short, and makes the dive
and throws to first. One out. I'm six

and sitting in the bleachers the summer
Eisenhower thought to save the world again, proud
to be his niece. The Fort Worth Cats are all the sport
there is. My father says I have it wrong.
By 1952 the whiskey stopped him, he hadn't played
in years, just coached, and not that much.
But I'd rather believe him home
and safe than think of the day my father,
out with his boss, saw a bum weaving
down a city street, a bottle of Four Roses
in his hand. Something in his walk gave him away.
My father turned back to the road, drove on
and on. The last time I saw my uncle he stooped
and shuffled when he walked, left a pile
of crumbs around his plate. It's an old story.
Next week I'll be forty and he'll be dead
five months who raised Four Roses to his lips
and drank. And what is memory
if not the glare of a sun-drenched field
where an almost Texas Leaguer pops up
and up and Rabbit opens his glove
to catch it, one hand, and end the game?

—1991

LEXIE DEAN ROBERTSON
Aunt Gilly

Aunt Gilly was a Texas belle
When she was fair and twenty,
The cowboys for a hundred miles
Came courting her a-plenty.

> Her father said he couldn't stir,
> For leather boot and silver spur.

At Texas dances long ago
Folk thought her conduct shocking,
When she swirled ruffled petticoats
And showed a silken stocking.

> But Gilly swirled again with laughter,
> And kicked a toe at the dusty rafter.

Her father was a sober man,
Her mother was a prude,
They barred their hearts when she left home
And married some strange dude.

> But he owned a smile and a red guitar,
> And the road he offered led sweet and far.

Aunt Gilly lost her smiling man
In a gambling house affray,
When he was second at the draw
In a San Antone cafe.

> A screech owl warned of the news before
> They laid him dead at her kitchen door.

She'll need a tidy sum, they said,
To keep her from the cold,
So they passed around a gallon hat
And filled it full of gold.

> In thanking them her lips were brave,
> Gold could not pay for that new grave.

She bought herself a cattle ranch,
Just off the Chisholm Trail,
And settled down to raising steers
As well as any male.

> She rode the range in skirts, of course,
> But she was a demon on a horse.

My great-aunt Gilly lived alone
For threescore years and seven,
The preacher at her funeral
Said she went to heaven.

                          But my Aunt Gilly rides a star
                            With a mustached dude and a new guitar.

—1928

*   *   *   *   *   *   *   *   *   *   *   *   *

ROBERT A. FINK
Aunt May

She, too, had been taken in, her husband's
father and mother and grandmother
making room for her on the farm
just up the road from her daddy's place
where she had learned to work the fields
but not how to care for a husband—the youngest son,
the one destined to bring in each season's crops—
and three old people. She was sixteen and shy,
undressing each night with the light out
in the only room she and my uncle were allowed
to learn about each other, no lock on the door.

The only water had to be drawn from the well,
the only bathing room the side porch, its galvanized wash tub.
Each night, she stood naked in the tub and lifted water
in her cupped palms, let it trickle down her body.
Later she allowed her husband to draw clean water
from the well, carry it balanced in a dish pan
to the porch and, standing at her back as she squatted
in the tub, pour the rinse water over her head,
her shoulders—a kind of anointing.

The outhouse was not a place to walk to in the night,
no place to be sitting in the dark. She learned
to slide the slop jar out from under their bed,
pee as quietly as a metal pot permitted.

She shared the kitchen with her mother-in-law.
She learned how biscuits were to be made,
how thick to slice bacon from the slab
hanging in the smokehouse. She already knew
how to catch a chicken, wring its neck.

She was used to being married by the time I came along.
Tending me, she learned to laugh at the ways of a boy—
wading barefoot up a bar ditch; riding a sycamore limb
to the ground then pushing off to rise and fall indifferent
to the blades of disc plows underneath the tree;
running just because; choosing, then throwing, a stick;
climbing, all of a sudden, onto his aunt's wide lap.

—2001

* * * * * * * * * * * *

ROGER JONES
Uncle Fenster's Grave

When Uncle Fenster died,
Aunt Mabel had no money left,
so she had to bury him
among the vagrants and slaves
in a high-weeded plot
of the old county graveyard
miles from town, long since
neglected by even its grim keeper.
One cousin had fashioned
a pine box for him;
had shellacked an attractive

wooden cross for a headstone,
complete with names, dates and epitaph.
It was all probably no more or less
than Uncle Fenster would have wanted.
But Aunt Mabel's nagging love,
like the barb of a goathead thorn
broken off in the quick
flesh off the heel, came down,
having lasted out the years
of dry rows and grasshoppers,
beyond the cancerous end
when Uncle Fenster insisted on spending
his money on coon dogs
rather than have any doctor around
to check the swelling knot
of deadly water in his head.
So the cold north Texas winds
swept for years the hill
where Uncle Fenster dozed
beneath the grass, while Aunt Mabel
sold the cow, moved to a better shack,
and took up jobs quilting,
cooking, sewing, and feeding
kids from town until she had
the money to have Uncle Fenster's box
moved to the cold dust and honorable
company of the municipal cemetery.
Only then would she confess
the weariness of years
spent with Uncle Fenster
by lying down to sleep
beside him for good.

—1993

Carmen Tafolla
Mi Tía Sofía

Mi Tía Sofía
sang the blues
at "A" Record Shop
on the west side of downtown,
across from Solo-Serve's
Thursday coupon specials
she never missed
>—"Cuatro yardas de floral print cottons por solo eighty-nine
>cents—fíjate nomàs, Sara, you'll never get it at that price
>anywhere else!" she says to her younger sister.

And "A" Record Shop
grows up the walls around her like vines
like the flowers and weeds and everything in her
green-thumb garden
But here—
instead of cilantro and rosas
and Príncipe Dormido—
it's a hundred odd and only 45's
10 years too late
that'll never be sold
even after she dies
and a dozen hit albums that crawl up the wall,
smiling cool pachuco-young Sonny and the Sunglo's,
The Latin Breed, Flaco Jimenez, Toby Torres,
and the Royal Jesters.
Also: Little Stevie Wonder.
And The Supremes.
She sings to pass the time
"Ah foun' mah thr*ee*-uhl
own Blueberry H*ee*-uhl."
She also likes "Lavender Blue."
It seems to be her color,
but *bright*—in a big-flowered cotton print
(from Solo-Serve).

Tía Sofía speaks Tex-Mex
with Black English
and all the latest slang.
Not like the other aunts—
Tía Ester, always at home,
> haciendo caldo
> haciendo guiso,
> haciendo tortillas,
> she never left the house
> except to go to church,
> braided her hair on top of her head
> and always said
> "Todos los gringos se parecen."
> (All Anglos look alike.)
or Tía Anita—always teaching,
smart, proper, decent,
Tía Sara, Tía Eloisa, Tía Febe—
all in church, always in church.
Sofía said, "Well, I play
Tennessee Ernie Ford and Mahalia Jackson
on Sunday mornings."
And she *did*,
and sang along,
never learning that only singing in church
"counted."
> She never made it through school either.
> Instead of Polish jokes,
> the family told Sofía jokes:
> "Remember that time at the lake, con Sofía?
> —Sophie! Come out of the water! It's raining!
> —No, me mojo! (I'll get wet!)"
>> Always a little embarrassed by her lack of wisdom,
>> lack of piety.
After she died, they didn't know what to say.
Didn't feel quite right saying
"She's always been a good Christian."
So they praised the way

"Siempre se arreglaba la cara,"
"se cuidaba,"
and the way she never "fooled around"
even though she could've
after Uncle Raymond died,
When she was still young.
(Only 71).

Funeral comes every 2 years in the family now
—just like the births did
60 to 80 years ago.
I remember a picture of a young flapper
with large eyes—Tía Sofía.
Between the tears
we bump into the coffin by accident,
and get scared
and start laughing.
It seems appropriate.
I also feel like singing
in a Black Tex-Mex
"Blueberry H*ee*-uhl."

> —1983

* * * * * * * * * * * * * *

PAUL RUFFIN
Female Cousins at Thanksgiving

The old Thanksgiving game
    has brought them to the country
    to Grandma's house
    the full table
    and ageless talk of ageless aunts
    and uncles and things
    that used to be.

Boys ring the wood
       with man sound, their
       long shadows knifing the fields
       for rabbits and birds, their
       guns rolling the hills
with rhythms of the hunt,
the dance of young gods.

From the smoky, too-hot house
the girls slip
to loiter in the sun
at the edge of the back porch;
a radio tinkles between them,
the fields lie before them,
and then the woods and hills,
       the smoky distant shapes of boys.

Talk goes round in the thick room,
       the television shows a ballgame,
       bellies and memories are full;
But lean boys slip
       through the woods, intent
       on grey ghosts
While the girls huddle outside,
       whisper and giggle
       and wait for a glimpse of the gods.

—1976

*   *   *   *   *   *   *   *   *   *   *

SARAH CORTEZ
Reunion

There is a new family at our reunion,
descended from a girl who died bloody
giving birth. Her parents lying,

saying no baby survived,
throwing my grandfather off the land.

This new family is from The Valley.
Parched land, endless highways
graying into brown dust. The dream of water
shimmering silver below noon-high sun.
My new relatives. Three sons, one daughter
from that baby left by my grandfather, hurrying
out of Mexico into the States at sixteen.

Carlos. Javier. José. Martha. Three sons,
one daughter. José. The unmarried one
with pointed, snake cowboy boots, black
felt hat parked low on back of head.
A bandit mustache, silken and full,
hiding white teeth glistening strong
into easy smiles.

José. In a family
of men and women who love to dance
you dance every dance. Whirling
older aunts or teen nieces with grace.
Even your brother's toddler dances
with upraised, bent baby arms
holding your hands, circling
your palm legs and black boots.
Small-baby, blunt, white leather shoes
dancing to your steps.

I speak to you at the picnic on Saturday,
looking into wide pools
of tinted sunglass covering half your face.
Your grin broadens, full blooms. I see
a black star high in the soft pink gum
of your mouth. None of the children

are yours. You work on cars.

Mi primo, I come to you full
of the city's rush and starts,
where I sit encased in glass
behind a metal desk. I seek
the earth's warm, brown curve
in your hug. Between your blackened fingernails
stubbing out Camels, I search. Beyond
the rusty barbed wire prongs
curling through the mounds of sand, along
the thin ridge of backbone curving into mattress, I
search. Smelling the dusty soil in your sweat,
embraced by the Naval tattoos
spliced across your muscles.

I want to enjoy you slowly
in The Valley's afternoon,
in a darkened bedroom, water-cooler angled
in the doorway, pink bedspread crumpled
on the floor. Before a rainstorm's heavy,
dust-laden drops hurl into parched earth.

Unfamiliar terrain. Where
passion becomes mother. Nourishment
from a man. You are
naked to the waist. Darkened chest,
scarred ribs, gaunt belly, hairless,
hairless. Black, laughing eyes.
Flat, sticker nipples
Warm *tortillas*
fresh to eat
in a linoleum kitchen.

Stripped to belt buckle,
barefoot by the stove,

attending white dough rounds
of *masa* cooking, you laugh.

I wouldn't fit in here.
Where dark-haired, handsome men
come home for lunch every day,
babies crawling underfoot and precious.
Where womens' shoulders are rounded,
soft and brown, for a man's fingers.

Mi primo, I look into my mirror,
I see you.

—*2000*

* * * * * * * * * * * * *

Naomi Shihab Nye
The Little Brother Poem

I keep seeing your car in the streets
but it never turns at our corner. I keep finding
little pieces of junk you saved, a packing box, a white rag,
and stashed in the shed for future uses. Today I am cleaning
the house. I take your old camping jug, poke my finger
through the rusted hole in the bottom, stack it on the trash
wondering if you'd yell at me, if you had other plans for it.

Little brother, when you were born I was glad. Believe this.
There is much you never forgave me for but I tell you now,
I wanted you.
It's true there are things I would change. Your face bleeding
the day you followed me and I pushed you in front of a bicycle.
For weeks your eyes hard on me under the bandages. For years
you quoted me back to myself, mean things I'd said that I didn't
remember. Last summer you disappeared into the streets of Dallas
at midnight on foot crying and I realized you'd been serious,

some strange bruise you still carried under the skin.
You're not little anymore. You passed me up and kept reminding me
I'd stopped growing. We're different, always have been,
you're Wall Street and I'm the local fruit market,
you're Pierre Cardin and I'm a used bandanna.
That's fine, I'll take differences over things that match.

If you were here today we wouldn't say this.
You'd be outside cranking up the lawnmower.
I'd be in here answering mail.
You'd pass through the house and say "You're a big help"
and I'd say "Don't mention it" and the door would close.

I think of the rest of our lives. You're on the edge of yours today.
Long-distance I said "Are you happy?" and your voice wasn't sure.
It sounded small, younger, it sounded like the little brother
I don't have anymore, the one who ran miniature trucks up my arms
telling me I was a highway, the one who believed me
when I told him monkeys arrived in the night to kidnap boys
with brown hair. I'm sorry for everything I did that hurt.
It's a large order I know, dumping out a whole drawer at once,
fingering receipts and stubs, trying to put them back
in some kind of shape so you'll be able to find everything later,
when you need it, and you don't have so much time.

—*1980*

* * * * * * * * * *

FAY M. YAUGER
I Remember

My father rode a horse
    And carried a gun;
He swapped for a living
    And fought for his fun—
I remember his spurs
    A-gleam in the sun.

My father was always
    Going somewhere—
To rodeo, market,
    Or cattleman's fair—
I remember my mother,
    Her hand in the air.

—1935

*　*　*　*　*　*　*　*　*　*　*

JOSEPH COLIN MURPHEY
Texas Boomer

My father
was a graduate
of the second grade
a man who made
every strike
from Spindletop
to Eldorado
a jazz-hopping
rig-topping
bum!

You may gather
my dreams do not
equate my old spade
with grade A
bourbon-straight
He was diluted
a proud-booted
brassy sot
loud as a bass
drum!
In love he was
no man to be proud

of. His best deed
was the day his need
sowed me in a cloud
of blondness
Contrary to his wont
she was a woman
whose only evil omen
was he

Love to him was
a rabbit fit—
animal whose tail
is a white sail
over the hill! Split
his ears ever were
by a train whistle
thistle prick
of a cheap song
calling

His second-
best deed
was his going
*Christ pity his
lover's eyes.*

      —1977

* * * * * * * * * * * * *

JAMES HOGGARD
Dove Hunting Each Labor Day

Clay kept the river we had to cross red
though hunch-backed gangs of carp
stirred it white when gar
swarm in among them,

their crowds of teeth hard thorns,
and the barnacles down their heads
and backs: horned flint

It's nerves, my father said,
nerves drive the world, he'd say,
taking me to a cottonwood's shade
The sun's too high, he's say,
for the dove to fly, let's wait,
he'd say, till the sun slips down
and the dove flare up against the sky

But I like taking aim, I'd say,
and I like loud noise,
I can nail a can at ninety yards,
But Dad said, No, not just yet—
keep yourself in full control—
we have to—if any more shoot up
this lease we'll all burn down,
but he didn't really care
that acres of brush caught fire each year

He likes to talk more than shoot,
he wasn't worried about safety and crops
He was trying to mouth the world to death
All this, he said, his face turning red
as he swept his arm across the field
around our mott—all this, he said,
all this is what M. Pascal meant
when he had in mind stars,
the frightening spaces between them,
the eternal damn silence

But we never have that, I said
I know, he said: we're blessed with wind,
and laughing, I had to agree

The hot south wind, he'd say:
the shock of God's own breath

Each year he said we'd come back here
when the weather cooled down
and the trees went bare
We'll try for quail, he'd say,
but we rarely did:
he seldom got free after Labor Day

Nerves, he kept saying, nerves
drive the world, and guns, he'd add,
and dove and fish and deer, but by then
I was stretched out thinking
clay was river's blood
hunch-backed gangs of carp stirred white
when gar swam in among them
with thorn-crowded snouts,
the entire world before and within them—
my father was right—
a miracle of nerves, and appetite

    —1999

*   *   *   *   *   *   *   *   *   *   *   *

HARRYETTE MULLEN
Father

My mother told me that after he left us
and we moved back to Texas,
for weeks whenever she'd take me out
I'd run and grab the pantleg
of any man I saw
(no matter if he was black or white)
shouting, "Daddy, Daddy!"

She said the white men
backed away redfaced and stiff.
The black men only laughed.

—1980

* * * * * * * * * * * *

Betsy Feagan Colquitt
Honor Card

Five by seven, aged brown
it confers in fine penmanship
privileges on Miss Eddie Young
for her good scholarship,
Spring 1902, McElhaney's Academy,
the academy a note now
in someone's history
of Major Erath's county.

She was bright and had good bones,
now gone to earth, and heavy hair
that lasted almost long enough,
and in 1902, too poor to stay,
left the academy
with contempt for her father
who couldn't pay
couldn't manage hen and chickens,
squandered the little he made
on books, the only things he owned
or wanted to, and read
driving a borrowed plow
on a rented farm.

And from the womb was angry
with her mother, passive ninety years,
a cow birthing in season,

who widowed dragged
her stairstep progeny pillar-
to-post to bed in unwelcoming houses,
and spent her last twenty years
in spare rooms waiting death
to come like a dark bridegroom
and he did and found her sleeping.
And fifteen, their firstborn,
she my mother left
whichever rundown farm
where cotton never made
  furrows what they were
  and weevils rampant
to work for money
selling in a general store
and buying there almost her wages
  the gold bracelet delicately chased;
  apricot mull for dress so lovely
  it stayed sixty years unfading
   in her mind; and tortoise comb
   to become the lavish hair.

This of course is long ago
and finding honor card
of her abandoned school
in her death-abandoned house,
I conjure by this relic
this once girl
most recent to me old woman
who, wheelchaired, counted hour by hour
"one two three ten," beginning again
a hundred times, knowing such numbers
get no honor cards
nor starting the alphabet with *k*;
who screamed at thoughts
meandering like a buried river

through terrain of dying brain;
and cried at her one good hand
gauzed like a boxer's against her jerking
from her flesh
unwanted intensive cares.
Contemptuous of her pooring
     rich beside her father's
and of passiveness
     mighty beside her mother's
and angrier at herself
than she ever was at anyone,
she tried again and again
to escape her paralyzed world,
restore brain to order, body to use,
but numbers were random
letters lost
and motion only dearest fiction.

And frustrated
she raged at this old woman
unable to please the ghost
of Mr. McElhaney or God
and certainly not herself.

—1977

*   *   *   *   *   *   *   *   *   *   *   *   *

TERESA PALOMO ACOSTA
Fragile soy

Fragile.
A seven letter word.
Not one to hiss over.
It seems to be a mantra.
I hear it repeated in natural food stores
Where egos are re-financed each day

In cartons of eggless mayo
Thrown into the grocery cart
Next to the vanilla ice cream bars
Covered with bitter chocolate.

But in español
Frágil has only six letters
Usually mispronounced
Like my name is
In the roughest of Texas accents that fall hard
in restaurants hawking
"Tex-Mex" unfragilely.

I asked my mamá what Tex-Mex meant.
She shrugged her shoulders, saying only that
She was Mejicana and lived in Tejas
And didn't favor migas.

Ay, tan frágil estoy hoy,
Standing
With my bruised ego
Alongside everyone else
Purchasing eggless mayo wonders
To my memory of espanol's pronunciation of my name.

Softly and quietly as frágil can be
In an imperfectly lovely place Texas will be
If it ever toughens up enough to speak Español.

—1994

Momma Sayings

Momma had words for us:
We were "crumb crushers,"
"eating machines,"
"bottomless pits."
Still, she made us charter members
of the bonepickers' club,
saying, "just don't let your eyes
get bigger than your stomachs."
Saying, "Take all you want,
But eat all you take."
Saying, "I'm not made of money, you know,
and the man at the Safeway
don't give away groceries for free."
She trained us not to leave lights on
"all over the house,"
because "electricity costs money—
so please turn the light off when you leave a room
and take the white man's hand out of my pocket."

When we were small
she called our feet "ant mashers,"
but when we'd outgrow our shoes,
our feet became "platforms."
She told us we must be growing big feet
          to support some big heavyset woman
(like our grandma Tiddly).

When she had to buy us new underwear
to replace the old ones full of holes,
she'd swear we were growing razor blades in our behinds,
"you tear these drawers up so fast."

Momma had words for us, all right:
She called us "the wrecking crew."
"She said our untidy bedroom
looked like "a cyclone struck it."

Our dirty fingernails she called "victory gardens."
And when we'd come in from playing outside
she'd tell us, "You smell like iron rust."
She'd say, "Go take a bath
and get some of the funk off of you."
But when the water ran too long in the tub
she'd yell, "That's enough water to wash an elephant."
And after the bath she'd say
"Be sure and grease those ashy legs."
She'd lemon-cream our elbows
and pull the hot comb
through "those tough kinks on your head."

Momma had lots of words for us,
her never quite perfect daughters,
the two brown pennies
she wanted to polish
so we'd shine like dimes.

    —1981

  ✶   ✶   ✶   ✶   ✶   ✶   ✶   ✶   ✶   ✶   ✶   ✶

3
Texas: A World in Itself

It is manifest that nobody is going to write all about Texas in any one book, or in any one reasonably long shelf of books. The subject is myriad, multifarious, and endless.

George Sessions Perry

MARGARET BELL HOUSTON
The Old Oak Speaks

"For five hundred years, Treaty Oak, said to be the widest spreading tree in North America, has stood near the banks of the Colorado River in Austin. It has played a romantic part in the lives of the Indians and in the history of Texas. Beneath it Stephen Austin signed the compact that fixed the boundary line between the land of the Red Men and the town of Austin. The historic tree may soon be destroyed." —*The Poets' Scroll*, 1926

My roots are buried deep in Texas ground.
I grip the harder when the great winds blow.
I lift my face to drink the Texas rain.
I bow beneath her gifts of gentle snow.

I know the near white faces of her stars.
The prairie moon has bathed me centuries long.
From out my heart a million mocking birds
Have flown to fill the prairie world with song.

Comanche, Tejas, in my shadow stand
To pray the great All Father, and to sign
The treaty with young Austin, vowing peace.
Leaving me guardian of the boundary line.

For I am Texas' oldest pioneer,
Have weathered all her changes to this hour.
Have watched her travail and her victory,
Her urgent growth from poverty to power.

She built a city round about my tent
Whose growing towers, how shining fair they seem!
I brood unchanged, yet in my heart I keep
Memory on memory, dream on dream.

And have I known the last sweet Texas Spring?
No more the green beneath, the blue above?
Oh children, for whose hour I watched in hope,
Let me cling longer to the soil I love!

—1926

* * * * * * * * * * * *

PAUL FOREMAN
Pecans

We walk down a red clay road in Texas
toward the pecan bottom, totin' a towsack,
two gallon buckets, and a cane pole.
Gonna frail some pirate pecans.
We come to a halt and listen
to squirrels barkin' up the creek, and crows
cawin' further along the orchard;
I wonder, who owns these pecans.
Is it the man in town selling insurance,
with paper deeds locked in a steel vault?
Or do they belong to Earth, herself,
who keeps punching up pecan sap
through the veins that root the tree,
then lets the ripe nuts fall to her chest,
or fill the craws of coons and possums.
Certain these two hobos
whose four worn-out shoes
are sticking to the clay dirt
don't own those pecans. No sir,
I make no bones about it, but I'm sure
they'll fill their pockets and towsack
and hull a few on the spot
before they mosey on.

CAW!   CAW!   CAW!
Go on you old crows!

Swipe all these pecans
and leave old Insurance
to curse the sky when he comes
to gather his crop.
Here's clay mud in your eye,
old Insurance, and sweet native
Texas pecans in this old varmint's gut.

—*1973*

* * * * * * * * * * * * * * *

MAUDE E. COLE
Prairie Friend

I needed some familiar thing to ease
My heart of loneliness, but all was strange,
Or so I thought, until with taller trees
I found you, dear old symbol of the range.
Your pinnate leaves were waving in the wind,
Strong leaves and silvery green like prairie grass;
My spirit quickened, I had found a friend,
A rugged westerner I could not pass.

To others you were but a gnarled mesquite;
To me you were the prairie's haunting space;
Windmills and cattle, fields of corn and wheat,
A friendly handshake and a smiling face.
Two aliens in the city, you and I,
In need of open land and sunny sky.

—*1948*

* * * * * * * * * * * * * * *

ROBERT A. FINK
Mesquite

(A mesquite tree is like an iceberg. Those roots go a long, long way down.)

A.F. Henderson
West Texas Rancher

Each one the shape of its soul—
knotted like an old squaw
or pliant as young girls naked by a stream.
Tejas Indians, politely accepting the Catholic
word of God, already knew the word for *tree of life*:
Shade Whose Tap Root Drinks The Desert.
Female. Fat with many children.

For horseless tribes, mesquite beans
served more ways than buffalo.
A good woman ground forty kilograms
of flour a day. Each July, she and her sisters
gathered the beans in baskets woven tight
as that which rescued Moses.
Even during drought years, bean pods fell like manna,
husks curled like Manitou's smile.
The word for *bean* was the same as that for *rain*.

Dissolved, mesquite beans cured sore throats;
swallowed, they purged the system.
Medicine men, spitting on their palms,
worked the flour into a paste
some say healed the blind.
Pressed against the cheek and pricked with cactus needles,
the leaves left a blue tattoo—Thumbprint Of God—
protection from all evils.

Around 1850, the mesquite spread to grasslands:
Cowboys and trail herds. Soldiers.
Their horses ate the beans,

germinated the seeds and passed them on—
war and cattle trails remembered with mesquite.

Today, ranchers call them Scrub To Burn.
Tares In Wheat. In town,
home owners wear down chainsaws against the trunks
and, being long accustomed to sprinkler systems and
store-bought bread, curse the beans
nothing seems to stop from falling.

—1987

* * * * * * * * * * * *

CYD ADAMS
Azaleas and Dogwoods

Strange, almost, how azaleas and dogwoods bloom together.
Sensitive to identical weather,
they celebrate the unsure sun of Lent; and their quick beauty
is quickly spent, fading almost with Easter.

Not even neighbors, these, though both are trees liking shade,
And much of their blooming is always made by those who
make much of such things. And the contrast their comparison
brings . . . .
Strange . . . the dark borne bright,
polarities lapped like lovers—the blood on the white.

But that's the way of it all, isn't it, the blood on the white.
How else may night wrap the silly face of day in dignity?
How else to be made the rite of all ripening,
The furrow ripped open, fertility, and the ever-circular
sowing of the seed?

The blood on the white, for the scream which serves delight,
to give the maid the toothmark and the bridal sheet the stain;
to feed the falcon with the skylark, to sing the rose's pain,

so the earth can drink its tribute and each April again
incite the sodden gray of the still-wintry day to Spring's
ironic light—
to the blood on the white.

—1980

* * * * * * * * * * * *

KARLE WILSON BAKER
Texas Cowboy

From garden-beds I tend, it is not far
To those great ranges where he used to ride;
Time's shadowy Door still stands a rift ajar,
And Fancy, glancing backward and aside,

May glimpse him whirling in a storm of dust,
A flashing bronze against a burning sky,
Before a sea of tossing horns up-thrust,
A peril thousand-pronged, to breast or die;

Or lying with locked hands beneath his head,
Watching the stars beside a lonely fire,
About him dim immensity outspread,
Within, dim gulfs of question and desire.

He is a Thought; he is not flesh-and-bone;
He is immortal Youth astride a Dream:
The hungry flame that eats to ash and stone
The gorgeous fruitage of the things that seem;

And I (who sank, with pang and toil enough,
My roots at last down to the nether springs,
Yet born to coax the shapely from the rough,
Have shunned the red and jagged edge of things),
A woman with a bird, a book, a flower,

Who, sifting life, has kept the quiet part,
Whose days like pearls are sorted, hour by hour—
Why is it that he gallops through my heart?

     —1929

* * * * * * * * * * * * *

MARGIE B. BOSWELL
Girls of the Rodeo

Here come the dashing riders,
Girls who are Texas born,
Who know the rhythm of riding
Over prairie sage and thorn.

Watch how they cut and circle,
Canter and gallop and pace,
Each girl and horse united
In a flowing pulse of grace.

Surely such easy motion,
Free from strain and fear,
Comes only to those who are quickened
By the blood of the pioneer.

     —1949

* * * * * * * * * * * * *

JOSEPH COLIN MURPHEY
Re-stringing 100 Year Old Wire

The fence posts I set today
will stand watch, a true memorial
to my sense of life, the strife I keep
before me lest I fail

Dead hands stretched the original wire
I now stretch again. It is antique
and speaks of the early days of brutality
which cattle learn to avoid

The barbs are cruel and wait for horses
and men who never learn. The man
who strung this stretch hanged himself
in the basement when the barn burned

the final victim of a bad crop year
Things men do that endure, the fences
they made, the houses they caused to be
make more sense to me than tombstones

Somewhere else this fellow lies
who built these fallen gates, who set
the fossil rocks in the walk
whose trees still shade the porch

I've never seen his grave nor the carved
stone it bears, but he is more alive here
than he is anywhere else in this earth
The good he did lives after him

> I hope all the bad
> is interred with his bones

—1986

* * * * * * * * * * * *

LAWRENCE CHITTENDEN
The Cowboys' Christmas Ball
To the Ranchmen of Texas

'Way out in Western Texas, where the Clear Fork's waters flow,
Where the cattle are "a-browzin'," an' the Spanish ponies grow;

Where the Northers "come a-whistlin'" from beyond the Neutral strip;
And the prairie dogs are sneezin' as if they had "the Grip";
Where the cayotes come a-howlin' 'round the ranches after dark,
And the mocking-birds are singin' to the lovely "medder lark";
Where the 'possum and the badger, and rattle-snakes abound,

And the monstrous stars are winkin' o'er a wilderness profound;
Where lonesome, tawny prairies melt into airy streams,
While the Double Mountains slumber, in heavenly kinds of dreams;
Where the antelope is grazin' and the lonely plovers call—
It was there that I attended "The Cowboys' Christmas Ball."

The town was Anson City, old Jones's county seat,
Where they raised Polled Angus cattle, and waving whiskered wheat;
Where the air is soft and "bammy," an' dry an' full of health,
And the prairies is explodin' with agricultural wealth;
Where they print the Texas Western, that Hec. McCann supplies,
With news and yarns and stories, uv most amazin' size;
Where Frank Smith "pulls the badger," on knowin' tenderfeet,
And Democracy's triumphant, and mighty hard to beat;
Where lives that good old hunter, John Milsap from Lamar,
Who "used to be the Sheriff, back East, in Paris, sah!"
'T was there, I say, at Anson, with the lively "Widder Wall,"
That I went to that reception, "The Cowboys' Christmas Ball."

The boys had left the ranches and come to town in piles;
The ladies—"kinder scatterin'"—had gathered in for miles.
And yet the place was crowded, as I remember well,
'T was got up for the occasion, at "The Morning Star Hotel."
The music was a fiddle an' a lively tambourine,
And a "viol come imported," by the stage from Abilene.
The room was togged out gorgeous—with mistletoe and shawls,
And candles flickered frescoes, around the airy walls.
The "wimmin folks" looked lovely—the boys looked kinder treed,
Till their leader commenced yellin', "Whoa! fellers, let's stampede,"

And the music started sighin', an' awailin' through the hall,
As a kind of introduction to "The Cowboys' Christmas Ball."

The leader was a feller that came from Swenson's Ranch,
They called him "Windy Billy," from "little Deadman's Branch."
His rig was "kinder keerless," big spurs and high-heeled boots;
He had the reputation that comes when "fellers shoots."
His voice was like a bugle upon the mountain's height;
His feet were animated, an' a mighty, movin' sight,
When he commenced to holler, "Neow fellers, stake yer pen!"
"Lock horns ter all them heifers, an'rustle 'em like men."
"Saloot yer lovely critters; neow swing an' let 'em go,"
"Climb the grape vine' round 'em—all hands do-se-do!"
"You Mavericks, jine the round-up—Jest skip her waterfall,"
Huh! hit wuz gettin' happy, "The Cowboy's Christmas Ball!"

The boys were tolerable skittish, the ladies powerful neat,
That old bass viol's music just got there with both feet!
That wailin', frisky fiddle, I never shall forget;
And Windy kept a singin'—I think I hear him yet—
"O Xes, chase your squirrels, an' cut 'em to one side,"
"Spur Treadwell to the centre, with Cross P Charley's bride,"
"Doc. Hollis down the middle, an' twine the ladies'chain,"
"Varn Andrews pen the fillies in big T Diamond's train."
"All pull yer freight tergether, neow swallow fork an' change,"
"'Big Boston' lead the trail herd, through little Pitchfork's range."
"Purr 'round yer gentle pussies, neow rope 'em! Balance all!"
Huh! hit wuz gettin' active—"The Cowboys' Christmas Ball!"
The dust riz fast an' furious, we all just galloped 'round,
Till the scenery got so giddy, that Z Bar Dick was downed.
We buckled to our partners, an' told 'em to hold on,
Then shook our hoofs like lightning, until the early dawn.
Don't tell me 'bout cotillions, or germans. No sir 'ee!
That whirl at Anson City just takes the cake with me.
I'm sick of lazy shufflin's, of them I've had my fill,

Give me a frontier break-down, backed up by Windy Bill.
McAllister ain't nowhar! when Windy leads the show,
I've seen 'em both in harness, and so I sorter know—
Oh, Bill, I sha'n't forget yer, and I'll oftentimes recall,
That lively gaited sworray—"The Cowboys' Christmas Ball."

—1893

* * * * * * * * * * * * *

WHITNEY MONTGOMERY
Death Rode a Pinto Pony

Death rode a pinto pony
Along the Rio Grande,
Beside the trail his shadow
Was riding on the sand.

The look upon his youthful face
Was sinister and dark,
And the pistol in his scabbard
Had never missed its mark.

The moonlight on the river
Was bright as molten ore,
The ripples broke in whispers
Along the sandy shore.

The breath of prairie flowers
Had made the night-wind sweet,
And a mocking bird made merry
In a lacy-leafed mesquite.

Death looked toward the river,
He looked toward the land,
He took his broad sombrero off
And held it in his hand,

And Death felt something touch him
He could not understand.

The lights at Madden's ranch-house
Were brighter than the moon,
The girls came tripping in like deer,
The fiddles were in tune,

And Death saw through the window
That man he came to kill,
And he that did not hesitate
Sat hesitating still.

A cloud came over the moon,
The moon came out and smiled,
A coyote howled upon the hill,
The mocking bird went wild.

Death drew his hand across his brow,
As if to move a stain,
Then slowly turned his pinto horse
And rode away again.

—1934

CLYDE WALTON HILL
The Little Towns of Texas

The little towns of Texas
That nestle on her plains
And gather close the inland roads,
The homing trails and lanes;
The little towns of Texas
That sleep the whole night long
Cooled by a scented southern breeze,
Lulled by its drowsy song!

The little towns of Texas
Will ever seem to me
Like stars that deck a prairie sky
Or isles that dot the sea:
Like beads that sparkle here and there
On Texas' flowered gown;
Like figures on its rich brocade
Of purple, green and brown.

The little towns of Texas
Seen through the prairie haze,
How fair and fresh and free they lie
Beneath the golden days!
Not crowded in deep valleys,
Not buried in tall trees,
But open to the sun, the rain,
The starlight, and the breeze!

The little towns of Texas,
What pretty names they bear!
There's Echo, Garland, Crystal Springs,
Arcadia, Dawn, and Dare;
There's Ingleside, and Prairie Home,
And Bells, and Rising Star.
God keep them childlike, restful, clean,
Pure as the prairies are!

—1924

★ ★ ★ ★ ★ ★ ★ ★ ★ ★ ★ ★ ★

RICHARD SALE
Farm-to-Market #4

Giles likes it flat.
He says those wide-spaced skies
turn the flat into hills

once you stop and look
and pace the territory on foot.
The dun limestone outcrops
tell of folded, crimped millenniums
if you have the patience to look.

I distrust the Giles in me
turning plains into plain-song.
Ecstasy must pay its own admission.
Giles distrusts the grammarian in me.

We're talking about little towns like Ponder,
little towns that lie so flat you wonder
how Ponderites ever got a wrinkle in their
brain.

Giles' eye is sharp, is sharp,
and his heart is clean as Amanda.
Why should I dare distrust the Giles in me
and feel, instead, the heartiest despair?

     —1990

*   *   *   *   *   *   *   *   *   *   *   *

NAOMI SHIHAB NYE
The Endurance of Poth, Texas

It's hard to know how well a town is when you only swing
through it on suspended Sunday evenings maybe twice a year.
Deserted streets. The dusty faces of stores: elderly aunts with
clamped mouths. I like to think Monday morning still buzzes
and whirls—rounded black autos roll in from farms, women
measure yard goods, boys haul empty bottles to the grocery,
jingling their coins. Nothing dries up. I want towns like Poth
and Panna Maria and Skidmore to continue forever in the flush,
red-cheeked, in love with all the small comings and goings of

cotton trucks, haylifts, peaches, squash, the cheerleader's
sleek ankles, the young farmer's nicked ear. Because if they
don't, what about us in the cities, those gray silhouettes off on
the horizon? We're doomed.

—1991

* * * * * * * * * * * *

BETSY FEAGAN COLQUITT
Poetry and Post, Texas

out of a high school writing contest
what miracle is wrought
except a poet? whose land
is jackrabbits big as coyotes,
mesquites with china roots,
and dust bowling over dust
through sun lanterns
and stars lacquer the wide sky.

he's never seen a daffodil
nor does Pecos flow like Avon,
yet this marvelous boy manned of language
visions his landscape whole:
jackrabbits graced as unicorns
roam these lines
where mesquites laurel their prickly legend,
and dust, sun, stars metaphor his universe
full of bad typing, worse spelling.
and overcome by poetry.

sick of paltered lines
on paltry passions, i find
these lifting craft to heaven's gate
and ringing by his sight.

it's not enough to judge he's won:
he's by God a poet, and Post
and all the West of Texas
can never be proclaimed again
the same.

     —1982

ROBERT A. FINK
The Atmosphere for Poetry in Abilene

It's no worse than say Odessa or Post or Snyder.
Any given inspiration passes through pillars of fire
cowboys and roughnecks say is only sun or B-1 bombers,
not Jehovah's wrathful eye preachers proclaim
from street corners, brandishing burlap sacks of rattlesnakes.
Nothing mysterious about clouds of dirt
boiling up from Lubbock, a close reminder of rain
the old prophet from View knows always returns
at West Texas Fair time if the first diamondback
he shoots in September is draped from his barbed
wire fence like his daddy and his daddy before him
did to draw down gully washers on unbelievers—
now mostly Dallas or Houstonites hawking civic art
to the Chamber of Commerce who bought
the twelve-foot flamingo
complete with Art Deco sun glasses,
the jigsaw cut-out aluminum Holsteins
cemented in upright positions,
and the Texas-size longhorn's plaster-cast skull
bleaching beside the Culture Center. They gambled
such would draw folk in from as far as Potosi
to gawk and spend and return home changed,
witnessing to friends of wonders they won't believe.

We who lost our way here from the East
know this is our breakdown point
where sins we lugged along in the belly of the Greyhound
were driven out of town while we cupped our hands
beneath the faucet in the terminal rest room
and splashed our faces, cleansed of ambition,
direction, knowing Abilene was our waiting room
where angels and tornadoes are foretold
from all directions; and the ticket agent
who knocked on the rest room door to say
we should come out now, offered the census book
for us to sign whatever name we chose,
like the Wood boys—Cord and Fire,
and we laughed, for the first time not
looking over our shoulder. We breathed in
the language of stock tanks, not pools
that could be bottomless, of quarter-horses
promising three-fourths remained to be invented,
and pick-up trucks no threat, meaning only
we'd never be passed by, the carbine in the gun rack
straight-shootin' as the open palm of handshakes.

So we fell in line at the Taylor County Coliseum
for elephants and high-wire acts, bull riders,
monster trucks and tractor pulls, country and western
yodelers, passing evangelists, but we kept in training
just in case—running ten miles a day, twenty on Saturday,
pacing the loop around the city, staying within hailing distance
of the Interstate. Then, as they say, that day dawned
when halfway through the local marathon, we reached
the stone ranch house turnaround point and saw
an old woman on the porch, waving her hand for help.
We slowed, then stopped, and entered the house
where, after phoning an ambulance and the woman's son,
we stood sweaty and aching as she sat on the edge
of the bed, doing all she knew to do—rubbing her husband's hand

and saying over and over like a mother to her child,
like a supplicant invoking safe passage for the dead,
"There, there. There, there." When we heard the ambulance,
we walked outside to wave the driver in and noticed
what we would swear was a rain cloud building on the horizon.
And it wasn't even September. And we laughed out loud,
believing somehow we were all forgiven.

—2002

VIOLETTE NEWTON
Texas Poetry

Up East, they do not think much
of Texas poetry. They think Texans
have no soul for aesthetics, that all
they do is pound their own chests,
talk loud and make money.
But every time I'm nearing Austin,
I look up at a painted sign
high on the side of the highway
that says, "Bert's Dirts"
and to pyramids of many-colored soils
sold by Bert, and I swell with pride
at that rhyming sign, I puff up
and point to that terse little title
and wish we could stop
so I could go in
and purchase
a spondee of sand
to make a gesture of my support
for poetry in Texas.

—1981

JACK MYERS
The Experts

When the man in the window seat
flying next to me
asks who I am
and I tell him I'm a poet,
he turns embarrassed toward the sun.
The woman on the other side of me
pipes up she's four-foot-ten and is going to sue
whoever made these seats.

And so it is I'm reminded how I wish I were
one of the aesthetes
floating down double-lit canals
of quiet listening, the ones
who come to know something as
mysterious and useless
as when a tree had decided to sleep.

You would think for them
pain lights up the edges of everything,
burns right through the center of every leaf,
but I've seen them strolling around,
their faces glistening with the sort of peace
only sleep can polish babies with.

And so when a waitress in San Antonio
asks me what I do, and I think
how the one small thing I've learned
seems more complex the more I think of it,
how the joys of it have overpowered me
long after I don't understand,

I tell her "Corned beef on rye, a side of salad,
hold the pickle, I'm a poet," and she stops to talk

about her little son who, she says, can hurt himself
even when he's sitting still. I tell her
there's a poem in that, and she repeats
"Hold the pickle, I'm a poet,"
then looks at me and says, "I know."

—1993

* * * * * * * * * * * * *

FREDERICK TURNER
The Poet Gets Drowsy on the Road

He pulls off into the picnic area,
rolls down the seat, and goes to sleep.
An unkempt fifty-six-old transient
with a strong body, aching joints,
the sleep-narcosis of incontinence:
a possible problem for the Highway Patrol.
Over his dreaming head
pass the immense skies of Texas,
the roar and rush and whine of the interstate
and the remembered images of a life.

—2000

* * * * * * * * * * * * *

DEL MARIE ROGERS
Customs of the Country

1.   Greeting

You don't have to know a person. Out this far
most any sign of life is welcome.
It's important to raise one or two fingers
from the steering wheel, when you meet someone
on the road to Pecos.

They'll respond, or make the first gesture.
Be careful: if you raise
four fingers from the wheel
or—God forbid—your whole hand, to wave it,
they'll think you're effusive.

2.   Religion

Of course you know the "new" people
are the ones who came since World War II.
Even the "old" people fight at times
over who got to Ft. Davis first.
But it's wonderful, still, to be accepted.

Though people at Marfa church
make Mama welcome, I understand this:
for Sunday service, she wants most to walk
to the remotest drop-off
and stand in high weeds for comfort.

3.   Rare

One rancher, having his fun
with a batch of Audubon bird-loving ladies
told them of weaver finches
at his place, gave directions.
They were off in a hurry, trailing binoculars.

Man knew he'd given them
another name for the small birds,
sparrows, as much a part of this country
as golden grass in the winter,
or stubborn cows, or ranchers.

—1994

ROBERT PHILLIPS
Drive Friendly
(Texas interstate road sign)

How to accomplish this latest admonition
from the Texas Department of Public Safety:
Will I become a better driver if I take one
or both hands off the wheel and wave gaily
at approaching automobiles? Or blink my lights?

Or toot the horn in amicable fashion
when passing through sleeping neighborhoods?
To operate a motor vehicle deep in this part
of Texas, do I need a ten-gallon hat
to tip at every woman driver?

I don't observe my fellow Texans driving
especially friendly, especially that S.O.B.
in the black Porsche convertible,
cutting me off in the middle lane.
OR THAT PICKUP WHO TOOK AWAY MY RIGHT OF WAY.

The Jeep behind me never dims its high beams.
The recreational vehicle up ahead zigs
and zags between lanes like a water beetle.
What gives them the license to drive
so unfriendly? Can't they read?

Native Texans know "Drive Friendly"
is merely the flip side of a warning:
In inclement weather it reads,
"Watch for Ice on Bridge" —
a sign giving Friendly the cold shoulder.

I envision a day when everyone will
Drive Friendly. Drivers will fling flowers

from open windows, blossoms sailing
from car to car in convivial exchange.
Highways will be strewn like on Palm Sunday.

Or perhaps they fling confetti,
toilet paper fluttering down gently—
even a trip to the Stop 'n Shop
will become a ticker-tape parade,
every citizen a returning astronaut.

Balloons will hang like rubber clouds,
over the beltways. Banners will festoon
traffic signals. Every driver will blow
kisses from car to car like Miss America,
and it will be friendly, friendly, friendly.

—2002

* * * * * * * * * * * * *

DAVID C. YATES
Sunset Along U.S. Highway 90
Between Langtry and Sanderson

Imagine a long brown poem—
As brown and as long as you can
Stretch it beneath a blazing sun
That melts your meters and leaves them

Broken and cracked upon the sand.
Omit all imagery and leave
Nothing to stretch for tension, nothing
To glue any adjectives to,

Nothing but an ocean of dull
Brown lines and an unbroken rhyme
That rhymes the same line after line
Far, far into the horizon.

Now, draw a line down the middle
Of your poem for a highway
And wait, just wait for that blazing
Sun to fall and hug the horizon.

—1979

* * * * * * * * * * * * *

GRACE NOLL CROWELL
Texas Autumn

Now autumn beats like music at my breast,
The color down the land is like a cry,
The winding roadways will not let me rest,
And distance is a call against the sky.
The haze runs shouting out across the hills,
Where autumn follows with its smoke and flame,
Upon a day like this the landscape spills
A glory that has never had a name.

Who has not seen a Texas field grown old
With clinging cotton—waiting some dark hand—
Who has not seen long miles of Texas gold
Where the flowers of a late sun light the land—
Or seen blurred fields—where purple thistles glow—
Has missed too much of beauty—this I know.

—1934

* * * * * * * * * * * * *

BOBBY BYRD
The Good Life
(—*after playing basketball on Tuesday night*)

Down at the Pine Knot Junior
on Yandell Street
the Mexican lady says,

You got pretty eyes.
I believe anything she says.
Muchas Gracias. Yo te amo.
She laughs and blushes.
Me too.
She sells me and my friends
Big Boys of Beer
—16 oz. of Busch or Old Milwaukee
in a mason jar for 80 cents each.
Plus tax.
On the TV the Braves play the Astros.
Jose Cruz is an old man.
So is Nolan Ryan.
So am I.
So are most of my friends.
It's almost October, and nobody cares.
The Astros were done for last month.
We sit outside instead.
The sun goes down over the mountain.
Saturn is hung right next to the moon
between two pink clouds and the twilight blue sky.
Yeah, that's right.
Eternity.
Texas is like this sometimes.
Not all the time.
But sometimes.
And that is usually enough.

—1992

JAMES HOGGARD
November

for John Graves

Shimmering spreads of golden fire,
oak leaves fan Comanche Bluff
where the Brazos de Dios turns deep
against a cliff, high limestone wall,
current speeding up at the curve
hard toward a white water roar:
shouts of giants trapped in rock,

and a russet granite boulder,
monolithic in the river's wide rush,
organizes the water slapping at it:
whirlpools drilling into sinkholes,
and down them cold November purls
when fierce blue northern winds
come beating the brilliance off limbs.

—1991

* * * * * * * * * * * *

VIOLETTE NEWTON
A Mythology of Snow

Here in the warm counties
in cold months, we practice
a mythology of snow. Long before
Texas plays A&M and fall coats
and boots are everywhere, shop windows
quiver in icicles, and gawky girl
models step like giraffes through
glittered cotton on their way
to a winter never coming.

As leaves fall and grass burns brown
from frost, the myth builds. We spray
foam on cross-batted windows, and
snowmen in mufflers come out
of closets to stand around,
pretending carols.
But when snow really comes,
we never know what to do with it.
Our heating systems quit, our tires
won't grip, our vegetation falls
in a heap. But we go on kidding
ourselves that this is the season
of snow, and as long as we
believe it, we can run around
in our sunclothes, shivering
ourselves into Currier and Ives
impossibilities, knowing
in the hard core of our minds,
no matter what scientists and
weathermen say, snow is pure
imagination anyway, it doesn't
last, it is only icing on the plain
cake of winter, which, in our case,
is only make-believe most of the time.

It takes more than snow, imitation
or otherwise, to make Christmas,
which can happen anywhere, even
in the warm rooms of the heart.

—1981

Sandra Cisneros
Bienvenido Poem for Sophie

This morning that would've meant
a field of crumpled snow if we
were in Vermont, brought only
a crumpled sky to Texas,

And you and Alba for breakfast
tacos at Torres Taco Haven
where you admired my table
next to the jukebox and
said, Good place to write.

You promised we could come back
and have tacos together and sit
here with coffee and our writer's
notebooks whenever we want.
And nobody would have to talk
if we didn't want to. Next time

you come by my house, I want
to take you up to the roof.
At sunset the grackles
make a wonderful racket.
You can come whenever you want.
And nobody will have to talk
if we don't want to.

—1994

BRYCE MILLIGAN
trusting steel

Here in the flux of flood and drought
that is south Texas, my Decembers
are wheelbarrows of freshly split oak.

Here where I have the luxury of abhorring
the evening splitting rasp and growl
of the chainsaw, I allow myself
to trust a simpler tool.

It is best when the streets have gone silent
and the heavy stroke of steel on oak resounds
house to house,
here, deep in this city.

The chunk and thud assumes
a natural meter
and again I hear Frost
rasping out memories of all his
maple and birch woods,
and here is Hall
tucking up the leaves
against the house at Eagle Pond,
banking the cold fragile flames
that await the deeper insulation
of the silencing snow.
With each fall of my red axe their lines
rear up like the faces
of forgotten friends
and I hear a cautious halting pace
in frozen woods
I shall never call
my own.

A thousand miles to the west, Ortiz
cuts piñon, loosing a wilder smell,
preparing a different spell,
but aching
with the same ritual.

Here I cut the green oak into lengths
then let it lie a single summer.
A San Antonio August will almost
split it for you
so it leaps apart at the touch
of December's blade.

  —1993

* * * * * * * * * * * *

CHARLES BEHLEN
Two Ice Storms

Between contractions,
my mother dreamed
of black water,
a lake by a road
I fell in and fell in.
She'd reach shoulder-deep,
feel my small hand slipping
down and away, and
startle awake to the
hospital radiator
crackling its spine,
the crazed wind
glazing everything.

So I was born wet and cold,
my cradle tipped
by an iced howl
I never forgot.

On the edge of the Caprock,
where the prairie drops
its glacial face to a
warm, rolling south,
I wrapped frozen pipes
while a deer carcass creaked
from the wellhouse rafter,
creaked and swung its
bloodied shoulders
against my breath.

The sights of my 12-guage
held miles of prairie;
held the alert, empty
eye-thoughts of rabbits;

held the buried light
of Cherokee flint;
held the fast hearts
of wintered sparrows.
And the sky's mouth
held my life,
thawless and grinding
an edge of the Caprock.

When the Great Storm of '62
closed the school early,
I tramped the miles home
through ice-stubbled acreage
and cut ice from the
door with a hoe.

Inside, the rooms
were chilled brittle,
waiting.

I huddled with a pot
of bitter coffee,
braced, pushed, and
dropped out of childhood.

  —1988

CHRIS WILLERTON
Winter at the Intersection

At Guthrie, Texas, snow-rimed afterthought
to the Four-Six Ranch, the square Texaco station
squats like a low, hollow tooth
in the gray mouth of winter.
The highway brings brief people
in both directions, a few at a time,
agreeing to give Guthrie a pulse a few hours
while sleet turns the guard-light on the telephone pole
to ectoplasm. The old frame courthouse
across the road hunkers down like a settler
to wait it out, collects the snow
slat by slat. Next door the brick office building
fades its red against the hooting blizzard,
crusting with stucco of snow.
Tumbleweeds out back are wadded white steel wool
becoming hummocks as snow clogs them over.
Under the yellow lights the bony boy
pumps gas, one hand in his jacket.
The pump nozzle gives no fumes.
On the black and white TV inside,
there is snow. When the jowly rancher
climbs into the cab, he flicks away
a just-lit cigarette. It sticks,
red tip up, a stick of incense
in the smutted slush.

Snow sops the white paper grey
and bears the leaves back to earth.

—*1986*

* * * * * * * * * * * * *

WILLLIAM VIRGIL DAVIS
Overnight Winter: Texas

Such a surprise to find icicles
inched along limbs outside the windows,
the glass frosted, the old dog

asleep beside the fire, content
to stay in. No one will be out
on the icy roads, in grocery stores.

We will sit together in one room,
with the fire and many candles,
and talk long into the dark

about days like this, other years;
of other places we have been.
Such times are wonderfully rare.

—*1992*

* * * * * * * * * * * * *

LAWRENCE CHITTENDEN
Ennui

At a lonely ranch 'neath a lonely sky
     On the tawny Texas prairie,
Where the owls hoo, and the plovers cry,
And the cayotes howl, and the Northers sigh,
     To-night I am sad and weary.

The fire dreams on in its chimney-bed,
　　　While the rain on the roof is sobbing
A requiem sad for a year that's dead,
For the shadowy faces flown and fled,
For the days misspent, and the words unsaid,
And the dreams that Time is robbing.

Without, in the wind and rain and gloom,
　　　The night is steeped in sorrow,
While spectral fancies haunt my room
With ghostly thoughts from Memory's tomb,
　　　And the cares of a dull To-morrow.
Ah, Life is at best a lonely lane
　　　O'ergrown with the rue and roses,
Though the flowers must wither, the thorns remain,
For each heart knoweth some secret pain;
Some fond regret, and some hope in vain,
　　　In each secret reposes.

Hast thou not sighed for some ideal shore
　　　'Midst groves and forests vernal—
Where pain and trials and griefs were o'er,
Where the world was fair as dreams of yore,
Where hearts were true and life was more,
　　　And love was a thing Eternal?
Ah, yes! and to-night 'neath a lonely sky,
　　　On the tawny Texas prairie,
Where the owls hoo and the Northers sigh,
Where the cayotes wail, and the plovers cry,
　　　To-night I am sad and weary.

December 31st.
—1893

GENE SHUFORD
Celebration

one fourth second after the earth had rolled
to that precise point opposite the sun
when we see the stars best, blow paper horns,
and all the bells in heaven and earth ring in
a new year, when Texans eat black-eyed peas,
and wine, hard liquor and champagne flow for the asking
merely because we are all still here, waiting for the light,
because we can slip out of the darkness again,
see the red ball in the east catch fire
one more time and not have to depend
on its memory and dream of it underground, lying
in some final and definitive darkness
                                        I say
at that precise chipped fragment of time
on a January first way back in the forties
Mrs. V. E. Tanner of Houston gave birth
to a son, the first Texan born that year

but later a woman bore her sixth child
a few hours after rescuing her five others
from her blazing farm home out near Lubbock
in a six-inch snow and eighteen-degree weather

AP editors seeking the woman of the year
overlooked this demonstration of female courage,
pioneer femininity, and heaven-sent motherhood,
and chose Princess Elizabeth of England—all
because of her Royal love story: in July
the King announced her engagement to Philip Mountbatten
and in November she married him, the new Duke of Edinburg,
in Westminster Abbey ceremonies broadcast
round the world for those who still believed in romance

that was the year necklines plunged as low
as the law allowed in after-five fashions
skirts dropped two inches (twelve above the floor)
but rebel Dallas women, defying Paris,
organized The Little Below the Knee Club

and don't forget:
Mitzi Soloman's modern sculpture "The Lovers"
was barred from the annual show
of the National Association of Women Artists

Seeking a definition of love, I keep thinking
of Mrs. Tanner and, more significantly, of the woman
who saved her five children from a fiery death
and two hours later gave birth to a sixth baby

had I been there I would have stood in the snow outside her window
and celebrated her divine mortality with music,
with poetry that floated across the white fields
and up toward the crystal stars.

    —1985

ROBERT BURLINGAME
Late Winter in West Texas

You never know the sky
in the beginning. This one
began quietly with sun.
We drove north along
       the river and saw
       a dark raft of ducks.

We got out. The land was brown,
pale yellow. But not unhappy. It
was quietly alive like the low
water held by the sand. Later
       in a shop, we bought
       wind chimes made of
       thin shells. I've hung
       them in our stripped
       mulberry

over the empty nest of the humming-
bird. A last year's nest slight and
pale brown, it rides on a small
branch the wind can never break.
For years it will look emptily
       into the sky near music.

    —1987

✳   ✳   ✳   ✳   ✳   ✳   ✳   ✳   ✳   ✳   ✳   ✳   ✳

FREDERICK TURNER
Early Warning

Spring comes in Dallas like a gunshot, like
A big transformer fuse, a missile strike.
Ninety degrees. Over the northern grid
Dances a disembodied pyramid.
Foam and dark water dries up in a flash
On the white-hot forecourt of the car-wash.
Air has the lilac tremor of cocaine,
Matter's dissolved to flakes of cellophane.
All along Hillcrest and Arapaho
Rises, pinkwhite, a radioactive glow
Of blanched pearblossom, apple, plum and quince,
Black redbud cankered with flushed innocence.
Don't drive there with the window open; you'll

Fall sick with the flower fumes. It's april fool,
It's mayday, mayday. Photochemical,
The carolina jasmine's cadmium fireball
Batters the sidewalk with a yellow shock
Releasing a sweet gas of poppycock.
The crocuses poke up their noses. "Urk!"
They gasp, and open with a purple jerk.
Don't know if that's blue sky or a fresh storm
The sun shines into, giddy, white and warm.
Yes, it's a cloud. The weathermap has grown
A newborn thunderworld all of its own,
Mushrooming up, neon and shadowhazy.
Out of it hail will tumble soon like crazy.
It smells of black disk brake powder, of guns,
Of pyramids and glass and pentagons.
Better take shelter in an underpass.
City of all desires, city of glass.

—2000

★ ★ ★ ★ ★ ★ ★ ★ ★ ★ ★ ★

JERRY CRAVEN
Spring in Palo Duro Canyon

Dancing between the darkness of dawn and twilight,
I, caught in burning April,
praise early the stations of the spring:
a land crowned with thorns, a desert stream,
buffalo grass, cottonwood, and careless weed
blessing brown soil with chlorophyll;
that canyon rim, aflame and vermillion
with sacred intercession from an exploding sun;
and all else that new-made Time creates
with tumbling light blazing winter earth
into this greening genesis of summer—
this air, a sacred confusion of bee, bird, and pollen,

this water, spawning shadows, alive with light,
this earth, holy with thistles and sage.

—*1988*

* * * * * * * * * * * * * *

MARY VANEK
Summer Begins Outside Dalhart, Texas

Clouds chinked together vertebrae fashion,
sunspots gilding the last of the winter wheat
make this May day the first true burst of summer.
School's out, littering the yard with children
tumbling over combines pulled out for repairs.
Mothers mutter "lockjaw" and wade in,
scattering kids, denying them the forbidden
sweet of rust in first blood ripped free
on a wingnut ragged with wear and winter rain.
Tonight, the aloe vera plants will be torn
and squeezed to relieve the first sunburns
of the season. And in their cool beds,
the children dream of dinosaur angels
in the sky, those bumpy, lumpy clouds
clear evidence of their belief
in a past alive and pressing as the present.

—*1989*

* * * * * * * * * * * * * *

GRACE NOLL CROWELL
Summer Nights in Texas

Days must be hot to make the cotton white,
And have their own peculiar yellow glare,
But when the Gulf wind booms its way at night,
There is no lovelier darkness anywhere.
I lift my face—I turn toward the South,

My hair blows loose—the wind along my path
Is like a drink to any thirsty mouth;
Is like a plunge in some soft-water bath.
I drink the wind! I bathe in it! I dive,
With outstretched arms, a swimmer in my glee!
The wind has made me gloriously alive,
Its waves roll in, and they sweep over me!
No day can be too hot, too long and bright,
If it be followed by a Texas night.

—1936

✦　✦　✦　✦　✦　✦　✦　✦　✦　✦　✦　✦

PAUL CHRISTENSEN
Summer Nights

Where the tracks sidewind through
tall grass, among the tumbledown shacks
of the Brazos bottoms, the boys
stand around keeping the moon company,
bottle in hand, swapping tall tales
and curses until the girls go dancing.

And the stark white houses rot in silence
with their lonely beds, and the heat
thick in the parlors, the old men
sleeping in their Lazy Boy loungers
before the muttering tv, the farm wives
playing bingo in the gymnasium

while the lights hum in the dance hall
and the small of sugar and sweat
mix in the breath, as an arm
goes tense with the feel of skin
in its bony hand, and a softness

wild as the sea gives in to love.

—1994

SUSAN BRIGHT
Riding the Currents

I want to ride the currents,
find light in the shallows
of the emerald water,
cool under an August sun
that heats Texas to a sizzle.

I want to ride the currents,
move my legs back and forth,
kick exactly these red flippers
that push me through
the water, four long laps
in cold emerald light—
an elegant, rich mile.
I want to sit alongside
Barton Springs and talk
to my friends, the swimmers
who have been meeting here
for years, new swimmers,
water people whose eyes are
clear as emerald, and true.

I want to ride the currents,
draft the swimming god,
smooth the jagged edges
of me that shred any hope
of serenity. I want to disappear
into the water, no seams.
I want to ride the currents,

not always fight them,
kick back and stretch,
swim further today
than I could yesterday,
and faster because it makes
me strong, because
it calms me down.

—2001

*   *   *   *   *   *   *   *   *   *   *   *

PAUL RUFFIN
The Storm Cellar

All thy billows and thy waves passed over me.
                                        —Jonah

for Walt McDonald

Those green summer afternoons
when writhing fingers dance
across the Texas plains
my family will huddle here.
We gave up an apple tree and pear
to have this maw of concrete and steel:
It waits obscenely, its raw
back a gray hump on the lawn.

When green waves of wind fling
against the ribs of our house
and dash the heavens down,
our fate will lie in that damp belly
where we will be swallowed and saved
for a brighter day: thrown up
weak and short of breath, wet
with fear, but glad of this gray beast
and what is left to be counted and kept.

—1987

*   *   *   *   *   *   *   *   *   *   *   *

WALTER MCDONALD
After the Random Tornado

Harvest won't save our barn from twisters
on plains as flat as the moon. A keg of nails
can't make old rafters safe for owls
and heifers mild as saints. The last tornado

smashed the church a mile away like match sticks,
sinners saved by grace. Lucky for cows,
the twister froze, veered off
and left their calves alone. Our barn's a maze

of tin and splinters, nothing to do but tear it down
and raise one better for bumper crops.
Fat cattle are in our fields, all fences tight,
a pasture of calves all spring.

But watch the stingy cirrus clouds for signs—
buzzards circling the gate, angels prowling
in the shape of funnels, beggars needing to be fed.
Pray that our gates bring strangers.

Give away grain overflowing the silos,
press beggars in from the road and clothe them,
send riders to warn our cousins
beware of angels seeking work.

—2000

WILLIAM D. BARNEY
Mr. Watts and the Whirlwind
(Andre Watts Recital, TCU)

On Cantey Street a visitor came by
doing a dervish dance in the parking lot.
But we didn't know. We were listening
to Mr. Watts play the *Appassionata*.
(I almost thought it was old Ludwig
softly applauding, but it was thunder,
faint as the sirens, off-stage.)
Beethoven would have approved, though.
The hands that delicately touched
Scarlatti now smote the stays
and timbers of the Steinway
until it moaned with joy.

We had known, of course, there was danger.
Before Mr. Watts came from the wings
a third time, a messenger appeared:
"A tornado has touched down not far—
it must be determined whether
we ought to proceed to the basement."
But we were safe; and Mr. Watts began.
At intermission we learned more—
The twister really had come by, and we
all left to see the destruction.
Autos on top one another or shoved aside
as by an impatient hand, canty
off Cantey Street, you might say,
if only a few. It was all random.
Not at all like that perfect storm
Mr. Watts cleanly and powerfully
struck on the keys and strings.
Maybe it heard and was jealous. It was
a fairly minor tornado as winds go.

But we who had ears will remember
how the two touched down all at once,
a finger of terror from the skies,
those hands of unthinkable skill.

—1999

* * * * * * * * * * * * * *

ROBERT A. FINK
Drought: Sure Signs in Merkle, Texas

The Farmers' Life insurance agent
washed his company car three times this week,
parked it in the driveway overnight.
Come Monday and no thunder,
he'll wax the pickup.

My next door neighbor forgets to close
his back porch windows when he leaves for work
and the retired couple up the street
started yesterday to paint their house.
They claim they're bored with last summer's color.

Ten miles west of here, Jimmie Ruth's father
shot a rattlesnake and hung it from
the top strand of his barbed wire fence.
He noticed small birds walking backwards.
An owl flew over the house at noon.

But I.M. Richards and Mr. Petre
down at Miller's Feed & Seed farmed here in '52.
I.M. shuffles the dominoes
and spits into a box of sand,
swears this ain't nothing:
"The sky's still blue.

Nobody's seen a buzzard in the street.
And Truman's rheumatiz is acting up.
Pull yourself a chair and play this round.
We'll tell you when it's time to call the preacher."

—1989

* * * * * * * * * * * *

PAUL FOREMAN
Impressionist

Paint outdoors?
      In the summer...?
         In Texas?!

No, I would rather
sit in the shade
      of this chinaberry tree,
smell the smell of milkweed,
      let my tongue
fall asleep on leaves
      of prickly ash,

And watch the sun,
      A welt of bright Reason,
burn each thing to its core.

—1976

* * * * * * * * * * * *

CAROL CULLAR
Heat

The interminable heat of summer lies over
the desert a little longer each year
as old age leans more heavily on creature comfort.

Ask a young man what he wouldn't want
to have to live without and he won't hesitate:
it's sex, and he looks at you funny
because he doesn't dream of other options;
but ask an old man here in the desert,
ask him the last week in August;
and five out of seven say air conditioning—
with a fervor in their voices
never there when the boys spoke of sex.

    —2002

FREDERICK TURNER
110 Degrees in Dallas   Sep 4

A few vague clouds in the insane blue sky.
The rabbits on the grass are stunned and tame.
A milk-green mantle chokes the shrunken stream.
A hackberry, heat-shocked, begins to die.
The summer suburbs give off one long hum
Of worn compressors fading with a sigh.
A parched cicada shrieks and then falls dumb.
The grackles march, beak gaped, with deranged eye.
The summer's now so old it's lost its mind.
It's quite forgotten what's the way to rain.
The sun sees everything, except it's blind.
The sky, as we begin, is still insane.
This is the test of all that life can stand.
And being, being presses on the land.

    —2000

JAS. MARDIS
Good-bye Summer

With the blaring Texas sun beating down against my bent back
I am waving good-bye to Summer with my spine

    I am waving good-bye
by arching that spindled thread of bone
   and warm, pulsing blood
  as the last offering to this Pompeii of a season

    Bending it
      gracing the face of this heat monger
   gracing the face of this too long visitor
this too long stayed relative
       from both sides of the family
  whom no one can remember
    having invited

I am waving good-bye to Summer with my bent back
    my curved spine
      my chaffed and scarlet, naked ass
   to avoid her seeing my face

I am hiding
     bent and red with the heat of this Summer sun on my back
   and I am pounding my fist into the parched earth
  calling out the damnation
   carving out the dry land with my fingers
  as my proof
that it is time for the sun to go

and there is a chorus of brown flowers
    with their stems long turned to wilting
and there are young summer grasses
    never known to our eyes as green

and there are panting dogs
      with tongues dragging the pavement
      and there are drying water holes
      with the catfish and bass
        flipping on their sides
        gasping for air, then water, then air

And I am here to say good-bye to Summer
   and to tell her that I will have no more of it

That I am sick and swollen red enough with her beaming
   sick of her constant blushing
  that draws some under its spell
   and drives them madly into   stripping their bodies free of clothes
and lying for hours under her gaze and torment
   until their skin
  is baked into the red-brown singe
     of madness

I am here to say good-bye to Summer
   and to save the singed ones from her torment
   I am here to rid the land of her callous stare
    that leans the grasses into kindling for fire
in these months when the rain hides itself in the Midwest
   and like some frightened school boy
wets the land like his pants

   And so I say, Good-bye Summer
Kiss My Ass
   and let this Texas town
know again: a cool gust of wind in the noon hour
or   the late-night whine of chilled breezes through barely open windows
or   the damp footprints in the sand after a morning rain

Move on Summer
    and make way for the cool days and nights of the next season
    with its bland days of blue skies and gray clouds
    and birds heading North

Make way Summer
    for the damp brow, late season, last picnics of the lovers
        who found themselves while cowering from your wrath
    and those children
    who hunger to know their last days of freedom
    with school already started

    I am here to say goodbye to Summer
and her tattered blanket of heat and heat and heat
        all the day and night long

    I am here to say a shallow-voiced "Good-bye"
because I know that soon
    I will be calling her back
when the rain and wind have me gripped by the neck
    and there is snow
or just the biting winter wind blowing through my clothes
    or
    my toes have turned blue
with my fingers
                frigid and flirting with frostbite
    I will be among the first to scream her sacred name
but until then
        I am saying good-bye to this Texas summer
    with my face hidden
and my back turned
    hoping that she doesn't recognize my voice

    —1993

4

Blessing the Animals

"Oh, yes," he answered. "And the words I repeat are a prayer to the Lord to bless each animal to the end that it may fulfill the purpose for which it was created."

John A. Lomax

JAMES HOGGARD
Oil Field Road off Clyte Escarpment

Ground squirrels dart among
the prickly pear, larks
warbling morning in as hawks
ride rising waves of heat,
and on the split-topped ridge
yuccas prong the slate-blue sky.

Like a shadowed vision of dust,
a coyote loping across the road
disappears in mesquite brush,
and I wonder: when will it break
hard into a run, to roll a rabbit,
rip open its stomach and lungs?

Past noon the heat's a weight
whose whipping winds feel
like catclaw cuts, and your legs,
turned heavy, want to drop
halfway blind, you're dizzy,
the world's so full of mirages.

Then night, when it comes,
if it comes, settles in
with a moon-washed breeze,
and the scorched clay cools,
and a sidewinder glides
toward a mouse in a ditch,

but with eyes in its hair
the mouse bounds off,
its black-tipped white tail
guiding its kangaroo leaps

toward a shadow, the slit
between two sandstone thighs,

but the rattler slides inside there, too.

—1989

VAIDA STEWART MONTGOMERY
To the Rattlesnake

Old Rattler, we have known each other long—
      Both natives of the arid Texas plains—
Where hate is hate, and friendship's ties are strong,
      And red blood flows in every creature's veins.

In infancy I lay upon my bed
      And did not fear that you would do me harm:
I saw you coiled, I saw your swaying head
      And heard your buzzing rattles give alarm.

My father clipped your head off with his gun,
      My mother pressed me to her, strangely pale,
He turned your shining belly to the sun
      And cut the dozen rattles from your tail.

Old Rattler, it is part of Nature's plan
      That I should grind you underneath my heel—
The age-old feud between the snake and man—
      As Adam felt in Eden, I should feel.

And yet, Old Rattlesnake, I honor you;
      You are a partner of the pioneer;
You claim your own, as you've a right to do—
      This was your Eden—I intruded here.

—1930

PAT STODGHILL
Rattlesnake Roundup

*(The Sweetwater Jaycees sponsor an annual rattlesnake roundup in Sweetwater, Texas.
No firearms are allowed and the snakes must be brought in alive. Gas is used to drive
them from their dens.)*

I

Seeking fresh air
they crawl out of the den
curving slowly, hibernation stiff…
crooked brown scaly ribbons,
diamond etched,
wrinkling over the rough rocks.
Their spade heads rise,
eyes staring, forked tongues flickering.

II

The hunters wait,
armed with nooses, wire cages, forked sticks.
It is March, but the men sweat,
sweat as the snakes coil…
dung heaps with heads raised, tails rattling.

III

Bringing innate fear, the people come,
armed with legends…
mystic powers of evil, sex, fertility, rain, immortality…
to sit on the hard benches under the lights and girders
in the Nolan County Coliseum,
to stare back at alien eyes,
to watch ten thousand snakes wind around each other in the pit
forming one brown mass of moving…
heads leading, slowly sliding,
curving under and around, tangled together,

winding and unwinding…
even after the lights go out.

—1970

WALTER MCDONALD
Hawks in a Bitter Blizzard

Hard work alone can't drive blue northers off.
Nine blizzards out of ten blow out
by Amarillo, nothing this far south

but flakes and a breeze to make a man
in shirt sleeves shiver. Every few years,
Canada roars down, fast-freezing cattle

in the fields, dogs caught between barns,
hawks baffled on fence posts. Stubborn,
hawks refuse to hunker down in burrows

with drowsy rattlesnakes and rabbits.
They drown in their own breath-bubbles,
crystal as the sheen on barbed wires

freezing in the rain. Wood carvers driving by,
grinding on chains down icy roads,
see them at dawn and envy, tempted

to haul the fence posts home and burn them,
nothing in oak or juniper they carve
ever as wild and staring as those eyes.

—1989

A.C. Greene
A Hawk Over Inwood Road

High in the clouds on this gray day
Circling and sailing,
As if to stoop on prey,
A wide-winged, feathered plane
        of feathered power.
What brought you here
Above a crawling line of traffic?
Above a paved and cold asphalted
        world?
Would you strike the chimneys and
The sidewalks and the neatly trimmed
Hedges and trees?
Would you fall on some besheltered
        poodle or a Siamese in ribbons,
Here in this wilderness you do not understand?
This prairie is where the wild things scurry about
        in raincoats?
Fly, great red-tailed hawk, so beautiful, so wild.
Fly, my lovely wind-held phantom proud.
Our attraction is death; our excitement pain.
Fly, when we point and when we exclaim.
What we can never be, we capture.
What we can never tame, we kill.
And we can never tame a hawk.

—2001

WILLIAM D. BARNEY
A Rufous-Crowned Sparrow Seen Loitering below
Possum Kingdom Dam

That dry inhabitant of clay,
of postoak copse and sandstone cliff
comes to the fence as though to say
he'd no valid objection if
we kept a distance reasonably trim—
we'd make no difference to him

if we did nothing startlinger
than gawk admiringly at one
with a red pate and black whisker.
No use to think comparison:
he knew himself to be unique
from round of tail to wedge of beak.

Why anyone so fashionably dressed
would live aridly, in seclusion—
the cause is better left unguessed:
rare things come scarcely in profusion,
I told myself, growing profound.
(He cocked his head, the rufous-crowned.)

   —1969

ROBERT BURLINGAME
After Bird Watching near the Mexican Border

I am slow moving.
Like Mexico, the land we walk next to.
But we're not, in truth, lazy. I gaze west, south.
Mexico, always.

I feel passionate music grip my thighs. I sing.
I feel purposeful as milk in a summer breast.

All morning, in this bosque, we watched birds.
Birds irreverently flying across the uniformed border,
ruled line guarded by balloons, patrols, or by
worms with eyes hidden in their genitals:

      Painted bunting, yellow billed cuckoo, borrowing owl,
grackle, air-widening swift, small finch. We watched them,
elegant trespassers of man's ignorance.
We drank from our canteens. A heron flew crazily into Mexico,
Mexico—white wall beneath the shadows of ascension.

Birds dovetailed, broke apart in a scattering of seconds;
vivid as women at the moment of spasm, they delivered
themselves from the green caves of June.
We are denied their adventure. We must imagine,
      So tell me, my friend, where is the woman with our coffee,
      that one with a smile like a deliberate, slow wing.

—1991

* * * * * * * * * * * * *

J. Frank Dobie
Vanitas

San Antonio, Summer

At morning the jackdaws creak and chatter
      Of the day they're going to spend;
They fill the trees with their busy-ness
      and caw at yesterday's end.

At noon the palm-leaves lift to follow
      The breeze that quickens them;

They dream beyond as they fan at their tether—
     Fixed on a fix-ed stem.

At night the palm-leaves dream no longer;
     Their wind has died away,
And the jackdaws mute in the idle trees
     Have spent another day.

—1940

* * * * * * * * * * * * *

WILLIAM D. BARNEY
Mr. Bloomer's Birds

A man needs something animal
to be attached to, thought Mr. Bloomer,
a cur, a nag, a wench. The rumor
of a soul requires a body of fact.
Therefore, nothing is more logical
than that I grant these birds a pact.

And that was how the grackles, boat-
tailed, interior-becandled eye,
took over Belton. Bloomer was why:
he welcomed them with open ears.
The timber-creak in any oaken throat
musicked him more than chanticleers

or nightingales, or even thrushes
(none such in any town he'd dwelt in).
The way those old cocks swaggered spelt in
Bloomer's book, the mark of the elite.
He wasn't one for holy hushes;
he liked a gabble, settling down to eat.

Lord, how he loved those tails! though what
they had to do with boats he never
was able to guess, not being clever.
Nature endowed with plenty to spare—
he watched them waggle in a strut
and he admired more than men dare

on most street corners. Birds can be hatched
in any town, but the boat-tails knew
a platform when they found it. You
might say they hungered for an audience.
True artists need someone attached.
And there was Bloomer in his innocence.

    —1969

       *   *   *   *   *   *   *   *   *   *   *

DEL MARIE ROGERS
Great Blue Heron

Perfectly balanced, he bends in shallow water.
We're on him in a truck before we know
such a creature could stand where the Limpia spills
across the roadway, rain-swollen. The heron, the phoenix
are the same bird except for a myth begun
when the heron rose at dawn from a lake's dark corners,
from a nest of sticks, improbable as an angel,
gray, ghost-white in the sun's thin glamour.
He rises, grand, blue-gray, we know him.

But he can't be in grassland where birds are seldom enormous.
He's trying to fish, though fishing's in question
for a stream that's a sudden mountain runoff,
rock creekbed chalk dry half the year.
I was surprised by another great blue, long legs
in the roadside gravel near dust-driven Saragosa,

and the cotton gin that litters
a ten-mile strip of desert white.
That bird had a lake in flying distance.

Turkey vultures, black above us, soaring,
met close are blood-eyed, ragged, rust-feathered;
fill a dead tree like blackened fruit.
The heron watches the thickest strand of water,
dammed narrow with dirt to keep it from gnawing the banks.
Startled, he flaps a few yards as if fishing could resume
in our path. We have a second chance to watch,
drive slowly toward him. Earthbound, awkward,
he rises at last.

    —1994

<hr>

JAMES CODY
Whooping Crane

At the outer edge again
     of my universe
in the Canadian North.
At the end of my journey, in Vancouver,
I could turn North again
and leave my past.
But I will go South
not knowing where my soul goes,
and what, or if, it will accomplish.
But South I must go to Texas again
like the reason of no reason
in the head of
a whooping crane.

    —1993

<hr>

CHIP DAMERON
Banding near the South Texas Coast, Late April

      Beak
by wing and weight
by band, oven bird
by chestnut-sided
warbler, forty birds
were netted, numbered,
noted if by chance
someday they're found
in Maine or Manitoba
or Manhattan.
      Better
than small science
was the vireo's white-
eyed stare, the female
cerulean's sea-green
skullcap.
      Best was
Mandy, age thirteen,
letting loose a bunting,
blue flash of life
gone so soon into thick
brush just across the
road.

—2000

*   *   *   *   *   *   *   *   *   *   *

CYNTHIA HARPER
Water Birds
for Steve

The crane is not indigenous
to South Texas rivers, you said,

it probably escaped from the zoo.
They do that, you know, birds
just fly away. I thought
of the lions and tigers,
how they were really trapped.

The crane didn't look
like an escapee.
Cream colored, he
stood stock-still
on one long dark leg,
held the other as if
to keep a secret.

In the light of a full
moon you stood ankle deep
in black water, exchanged
stares with the crane
wild creatures, alone
in the river pool, too
wily for cages.

Hours later I lay
my breasts in the curve
of your silent back.
Long tan legs stretched
to the end of the bed,
you turned, bent one
leg at the knee,
tucked it under
your sleeping form.

I stroked your hair
damp with river water;
you let out a long
shimmering sigh,

like the sound of the crane's
wings when it disappeared.

—2002

*   *   *   *   *   *   *   *   *   *   *   *

BOYCE HOUSE
A Mocking-bird

My friend, the football coach in San Antonio,
And I were talking about his team, sitting on the little
     porch in the edge of town at sundown,
When from a tree across the street there came a song
As though rainbows and silver-edged waves and Persian
     fragrances had been woven into throbbing sound.
I knew what it was though never before had I heard the
     singer.
But, to make sure, eagerly I asked my friend.
"It's only a mocking-bird,"
And he kept on talking about long punts and forward passes,
And how the quarterback forgot to use Number Forty-seven
     last Saturday.

—1950

*   *   *   *   *   *   *   *   *   *   *   *

BETSY FEAGAN COLQUITT
Duet

On this April afternoon as Texas heat revs up,
curtains and windows open as the turned-up radio
carries the Met's La Bohéme into the yard.

As the soprano begins her aria
    Si. Mi chiamano Mimi,
    ma il mio nome é Lucia.
    La storia mia é breve

the only outside sounds are live oak leaves
moving in concert with the slow breeze,
but as her song continues,
another singer listens, likes
Mimi's melody, and modestly—
       he's no professional—
does a fast warm-up, a little vocalize,
a bit of *solfége*, and though not a tenor,
turns Mimi's aria into a duet.

He's a quick study, good at timing,
follows her tempo, melodic line
taking it down a 3rd, a 5th, even a 7th
to show his range. Knowing no Italian,
he sings unworded notes,
loves harmonizing—
       even tries a bit of *vibrato*—
and is as smitten as Rodolfo.
He's joyful, amazed at what two singers
can do, at how "music" fills
this quicksilver air
her song and his.

As Mimi sings *Sono la sua vicina*
       Che la vien fuori d'ora a importunare,
and clapping and bravos break the spell,
his interest fails before non-music,
and as mockers do, he goes his way,
no looking, thinking back, no lament
that his addenda to Puccini
is unscored and beyond transcription.

    —1997

Martin S. Shockley
Armadillo

Ambling across aeons to my backyard,
she pokes her little snout into my mind,
ancient cousin from my dismal past.

The dinosaurs were gone, the reptiles going,
when this mammalial experiment was designed:
armored against the menace of the world,
warm-blooded mother, leaving no cold eggs
to hatch in the hot sand,
she severs flesh from flesh
and suckles it, presaging me.

Cornered beneath my juniper, she digs,
and in a moment burrows out of sight.
I grasp her scaly tail and pull;
she holds in tight;
I have to dig her up.
Trailing zoology, she ambles off.

I, tool-using primate, hold with my spade
dominion over armadillos.

—1967

* * * * * * * * * * * * *

Walter McDonald
In Fields of Buffalo

Granddaddy waited while men with spades
dug a maze of trenches to test the treasure maps.
Skulls wedged up like onions on his farm.
Diggers from Austin brought along charts
of slaughter on the plains. By 1880,

buffalo hunters had aimed long rifles
where he plowed. Thousands dropped like manna
for horseflies, hides worth their weight
in silver in St. Louis.…I remember the truck,
the loading ramp, crates of bones dollied aboard.

I hadn't known buffalo roamed there,
never dreamed his dirt was home to anyone
before Grandfather's father. Cotton
was all I'd seen on his rows, those skies
my only horizon. At night I listened hard

and heard far in the distance the howl of coyotes,
the thunder of summer storms. Lying still,
I felt an earthquake rumble, a herd
stampeded by rifles, miles of humpbacks
galloping, about to disappear.

     —1993

★   ★   ★   ★   ★   ★   ★   ★   ★   ★   ★

ROXY GORDON
Living Life as a Living Target

(This was written as an introduction to a book of drawings and poems my wife, Judy, did a couple of years ago. She was watching some TV show about prairie dogs and realized there are a number of us living targets. So I came up with this poem to help explain the concept. The book is called Living Life as a Living Target.*)*

The idea came from prairie dogs.
Prairie dog towns used to stretch
all over West Texas. Prairie dogs
are funny little animals that stand
on the dirt mounds by their burrows
and bark like the devil when
something threatens.
Prairie dogs have no real defense but to
head underground
        (just like human beings)

and even then, they are likely to
be followed, dug out and
            eaten (just like human beings).

Prairie dogs seem
born mainly to furnish
            nourishment.

Living life as a living target,
living life waiting for
            the ferret
living life waiting for
            the fox
living life waiting for
            the coyote
living life waiting for
            the hawk
living life waiting for
            the white man—

            running always, offering
            a moving target,
            fighting like the devil
            to stay alive,
            but keeping others alive
            by dying.

Prairie dogs are an endangered
species now, except up on the
high northern plains and
the ranchers up there would
like to see them that way.
But we expect they'll survive—
            in name and in fact. Because

the world still needs those who
          die
for the survival
of the races.

And then on the other hand,
there are those moving targets
that move so fast
they just never get caught.

          —1989

*   *   *   *   *   *   *   *   *   *   *   *

JIM LINEBARGER
Coyote

Sunday afternoons
my father would idle our '38 Chevy
across the rutted prairie of West Texas,
a fine rifle cradled on his arm.

When we were lucky, we'd see one of them.
He would end up hanging from bobwire,
unravelling in the wind.

Last month, asleep here in my house
in what they call a development,
here where my neighbor's stationwagon
brags that he's a country squire,
I woke to a wild yelping.
The dogs had cornered something.
Next morning, Old Casey showed up
with a neatly-clipped ear
and whined and favored a foreleg.

This morning, I looked out

and saw him shy away
as the coyote calmly trotted
toward the food-scraps in the yard.
Pointed muzzle, scraggy tail, mottled coat.

Camera in hand, I eased the door open.
He bolted. I missed him.

Dad is nearly blind. Casey seems resigned.

I hope you're here to stay.

—1989

☆ ☆ ☆ ☆ ☆ ☆ ☆ ☆ ☆ ☆ ☆

GENE SHUFORD
The Horse in My Yard

In the morning of my manswarmed days
the night breaks open as I come and find
a horse grazing in my yard.
                              The sun
burnishes his winter coat and he throws his head
high in the dawn's burning, aflame on the wick
of night. He has lifted the wire, walked through my fence,
ignoring the barbs. And stands four-footed, firm
as stone, a great shaggy stone horse
planted immovable against the smoking sky.
But then, moving slowly, with immense dignity,
lifting his long muzzle, he stares at me,
at trees green-fired with spring, at passing birds.
How many of us find our fences broken,
our spiked strands ignored, big footprints
inside our barriers? He lets his long
mane whip in the dawn like some wind-flown flag,
rippling in graceful, soundless arpeggios of light;

moves the way thought moves, or dreams, or music;
hunches his big muscles, lowers his head,
and resumes eating. The grass is his business—
my grass—snipped with unbroken rhythm.
You'll say it's Texas—that horses come into yards
in Texas. I'll answer there's no yard where a horse
may not enter, walk big-hooved out of the dark—
no fence where the barbs may not be lifted, strands
thrust apart, snapped if need be.
                                        Of course
this is Texas. A land where the heart lives,
sky is infinite, wind blows forever,
and the distance from here to there stretches past
the atom's core. It's more than big hats.
Or six-guns. Or rusted spurs. Or hanging trees.
Or dreams jet-flown from Texarkana west—
clear to El Paso—smell the dust. Or drives
of cattle north to past's remembered green.
Or sun spinning between now and what has been.
Tomorrow's the answer sought and not yet read.
This business of the fence. Heel flies send
a cow across, through, under wire,
ripping it apart as though cobwebbed
by patient spiders—a gangling, lank cow
bawling her glazed bellow, galloping drunk,
leaping beyond the horizon. The horse comes through.
Like a man, he lifts the wire, walks in,
stands now four-footed against the sky.
It all goes back to land, to the time when horses
thundered across unfenced prairie, the heart's land
beyond all fences, where the grass is green,
where all the stallions come, where mares foal
in spring and colts leap above the sun
and there's a long running no wire can stop.

I did not come to this house alone. I came

booted in spirit, jingle-footed to the music of you.
I came inside the oaks, behind the trees,
to the hill's battlements against the endless sky.
I shut the door behind us, but not the door
against the wind. It blows forever in Texas,
whipping the dust of now to the dust of forever,
spiraling between earth and heaven like a bird
that sings the endless music of eternity.
Yet Texas is not a here, or even a now,
but a place where all men ride, the place they come
to face the end of things. How many of us
find it in our hearts—gunned down by time,
sprawled in the past's muck to the tin-pan tunes
from a corner saloon? We lie death-lidded, eyes
staring sightless at heaven. There it is,
stretching endlessly above us, far beyond
the birds. All we have to do is see—

  —1969

 ✳ ✳ ✳ ✳ ✳ ✳ ✳ ✳ ✳ ✳ ✳ ✳

JAN EPTON SEALE
Big Bend: Lion Warning
(a found poem)

A lion has been frequenting this area
It could be aggressive toward humans

If you see a lion
    Pick up small children
    Stand together
    Appear large
    Wave hands and shout
    Throw stones or sticks
    Report sighting to ranger

Do not

Show fear
Crouch down
Run away

—2000

* * * * * * * * * * * * *

BERTA HART NANCE
Cattle

Other states were carved or born,
Texas grew from hide and horn.

Other states are long or wide,
Texas is a shaggy hide,

Dripping blood and crumpled hair;
Some fat giant flung it there,

Laid the head where valleys drain,
Stretched its rump along the plain.

Other soil is full of stones,
Texans plow up cattle-bones.

Herds are buried on the trail,
Underneath the powdered shale;

Herds that stiffened like the snow,
Where the icy northers go.

Other states have built their halls,
Humming tunes along the walls.

Texans watched the mortar stirred,
While they kept the lowing herd.

Stamped on Texan wall and roof
Gleams the sharp and crescent hoof.

High above the hum and stir
Jingle bridle-rein and spur.
Other states were made or born,
Texas grew from hide and horn.

        —1931

WALTER MCDONALD
Wind and Hardscrabble

It's wind, not rain, dry cattle need.
Vanes of windmills spinning all day
        turn lead pipes into water.
Wind makes metal couplings sough
like lullabies. As long as there is wind,
        calm steers keep grazing, believing

there is always water. On still days
            steers are nervous,
        lashing their tails at horseflies
always out of reach. They stomp
flat hooves and tremble, bleeding,
and thrust their dehorned heads

between barbed wires. When it blows,
                steers don't need heaven.
                wind is mystery enough.
They rasp dry tongues across salt blocks,
            eyes closed, and wind brings
            odors of grainfields miles away.

            Even in drought they feast,
the curled grass crisp as winter stubble.
        Parched, they wade still pastures

shimmering in heat waves
and muzzle deep in stock tanks
        filled and overflowing.

—1985

* * * * * * * * * * * *

NAOMI SHIHAB NYE
Thinking About Cows at Ten O'Clock in the Morning, Abilene

The marker reads: "Western Cattle Trail"
for a second you remember Western movies,
dust rising up around hooves,
the wild driven look of their faces

Now it's tires
Sky Hawk, Gremlin,
a stampede of Rabbits and Pintos
in appropriate lanes

Lately my favorite absolute involves cows—
wherever you go, cows are eating

Across Texas, their slow bodies punctuate fields
You can depend on their bowed heads,
the little ones close by the mothers

When I didn't eat meat
I could look a cow in the eye
Now I say
Forgive us
for using you
to drive ourselves
where we think we need to go

    —1973

VAIDA STEWART MONTGOMERY
Funeral

Out on the prairie the small owls call.
The cattle are holding a funeral.

They mill around a stack of bones,
And grieve their dead in plaintive moans.

Each must sniff at the carcass there—
A hunk of hide and horn and hair.

He was their brother, before he fell,
A victim of drouth, or of stampede's hell.

Now he is dead, and they bleat and bawl,
While over the prairie the small owls call.

—1930

★   ★   ★   ★   ★   ★   ★   ★   ★   ★   ★   ★

PAUL RUFFIN
Burying

I found him stumbling about when the mother
died, an otherwise healthy calf, and fed him
by bottle until another cow came due, then
moved him in with her for suckling.
Third night she broke his neck.
It was a right and natural thing to do:
She reasoned her milk was for hers alone.
I found him barely breathing, head thrown
back, unable to rise for the bottle,
his eyes already hazing over; I could see
myself fading in them, backing into fog.
I brought the pipe down hard, twice, the

second time in malice: not for him or her,
but for the simple nature of things.
Blood came from his nose, his body
quivered. I dragged him from the barn.

The hole in the winter garden was easy, quick,
and the calf fit properly; but when the
first shovel of dirt struck his side,
he kicked, with vigor. I watched the flailing
foot strike against air. Nothing else moved.
There were no considerations: I did what
needed to be done. A few more scoops clamped
the leg and the earth stilled. I mounded
the grave and turned away, looking back once
to see that nothing heaved. I felt neither
fear nor sorrow, love nor hate. I felt
the slick handle of the shovel, slid
my thumb over its bright steel blade,
breathed deep the sharp and necessary air.

—1986

*   *   *   *   *   *   *   *   *   *   *

JOHN P. SJOLANDER
The Last Longhorn's Farewell

I hear a sound, like music through the gale,
Of kindred calling down the old-time trail.

The morning winds, for many, many morns,
Have pulsed with tramping feet, and clashing horns.

And in the burning noons of summer days,
Above the dust I've seen the heat's blue blaze.

And centaur spirits flash before my eyes,
Swifter than meteors through starry skies.
And voices far and faint ring in my ears,
Now soft to soothe, now shrill to waken fears.

I see, I hear, I feel, for through me runs
Tempests of fires and floods, and stars and suns.

For there, beyond the hemming fence and hedge,
I see where earth and sky meet edge to edge.

And all the world between that bound and me,
My kindred once possessed, and roamed in, free.

There bone and sinew, and pure hardihood,
They strove with Nature in her every mood.

Hunger and thirst, these did they understand,
And flood and fire that swept the sun-scorched land.

And these were guarded by the earth and sky
Locked edge to edge, letting no foe come by.

And Nature's gifts they took, and understood,
But Man's they scorned—shelter, and care and food.

They knew the wild. There freedom was at flood,
Its spirit flowing high-tide in their blood.

But they are gone. There must be plains somewhere
Without Man's proffered shelter, food and care.

For I can hear the lowings of my kind,
Soft and content, come flowing down the wind.

And in the night a loving voice and low,
Inquiring wakes me—just like long ago.
True to the past, our common fate I face—
Death—unsubdued—the last one of my race.

—1928

*   *   *   *   *   *   *   *   *   *   *

DAVID C. YATES
Washing the Cow's Skull

Most people, I suppose, would rather not wash one,
would not even think of washing one, would leave
it lying there in the pasture, its chalky
white bone baking in the summer Texas sun.

My son Scott found one lying under a mesquite
behind Ed Greenberger's abandoned ranch house.
He cradled it in his arms and I had a recollection:
Ed riding along the edge of his pasture,

his '41 Dodge pickup bouncing over ruts,
Ed eyeballing his cattle, watching them graze
fat on rich Coastal Bermuda, Ed smiling,
his tan face wrinkled, his Stetson tilted forward.

Daddy, let's wash it, wash it clean again!
I look at Scott's deep brown eyes, radiant, alive,
then stare into that skull's deep, empty sockets,
and the sun washes the sky pink as it elbows

its way off the edge of the prairie, and I shudder
at that dirty old hunk of bone with its hollow ear-
passages and yellowing jaws laced with yellow teeth
set loosely in bony yellow gums so they

click like dice when Scott runs his fingers
along their moldy crowns. *This skull once had
a tongue in it, and it could moo once*, Scott said,
and I knew, then, that washing the skull

was what we were going to do. Scott held it
in his lap as we drove towards West Beach,
and we stopped at a U-Tote-M for a scrub brush, a can
of Ajax, some paper towels and two tooth brushes.

That night, while the waves lapped against our legs
and the moon reflected on the water, we washed
that cow's skull till it was as white as a gull's
belly, and it seemed to smile as we brushed its teeth.

    —1982

  *　　*　*　*　*　*　*　*　*　*　*　*　*

5

This Stubborn Soil

They had seen the land and knew it would raise good crops. I had not seen much of anything but the long walk to and from the well.

★ William A. Owens

MARTHA ELIZABETH
The Way of Words
for Mary Vanek

Outside Amarillo, you think you will never get anywhere:
the grazed prairie rolls before you, soothing, or boring,
until you are grateful for cows,
trees so rare they evoke form like sculpture. Then,
sudden as jackrabbit
you see the full range of sunset—
land so open to sky should be loved.
All that dust,
infiltrating the windows and dulling the windshield
now becomes a million million prisms,
and the sunlaced clouds
crystals in a sky-cut geode—you forget
that there is anywhere you were going, that night
becomes a tunnel, words seem bigger, or louder,
uncertain as finding that full glass of water
on the bedtable in a new motel, in the dark,
alone, where is the light switch, where
is the water, what if it spills?

—2002

* * * * * * * * * * *

Starting a Pasture

This far out in the country no one is talking,
no rescue squads row by in boats to prairie land
so dry the Ogallala water table drops
three feet every year. The digger rams down
through dirt no plow has turned. In the heat
I let my mind run wild. For days I've thought
the world is ending, the red oaks turning red
again, the last geese there could be
stampeding from the north, surviving
to show us the only hope, the tips of their
arrow formations pointing the way. So many birds,
if the world doesn't end, this will be for Canada
the year of the locust. I shake my head
at my schemes, and sweat flies: cattle
on cottonland. The market for beef
is weak, the need for cotton constant.

I might as well raise goats and sheep as cows,
or trap for bounty the wolves and coyotes
that claim my fields at night. I might as well
rent a steam shovel and dig a lake deep as an ark,
empty my last irrigation well to fill it
green enough for geese on the flyway
both seasons. I could raise trout and channel cat,
horses and bees, gazelles and impala imported
from other deserts, two of each kind
of animals in a dying world.

                    Sun going down,
the last hole dug, the last post dropped
and tamped tight enough to hold three strands of wire,
I toss the digger in the pickup between bales
of barbed wire ready for stringing, the calves

I bought last week already overdue, the feedbill
mounting. My father used to say a man could lift
a bull if he'd practice on a calf each day.
Pulling my gloves back on, I lift the first bale
out and nail the end, uncoil the wire and nail it
tight to the posts. And while it turns dark
I go on stretching and nailing until I don't care
how many neighbors drive by with their lights on,
honking, sticking their heads out the windows
   and laughing.

  —1985

Robert Burlingame
Walking Past the Dugout of Felix McKittrick
(Guadalupe Mountains, West Texas)

Halfway up
or halfway down in this sparkling canyon
I see the dugout you gouged after the Civil War

rude hollow beneath the mountain
grown over with gray oak,
sotol and juniper

—these days a new trail
misses your doorway
by half a hundred feet—

once you lived here
summer into summer in leaves' loneliness
when you couldn't stand more

you went down to raw
whiskey bars and tit-flashing girls
then gathered the face you'd spilled

you took it back to your home
spooned it coffee in long, careful sips
you healed yourself

in that leafy place
the Apaches forgave you under
the limestone cliffs—somewhere, nowhere—
lit by moons as immense as suns.

—1995

* * * * * * * * * * * *

STEVEN TYE CULBERT
Van Horn

At the foot of Old Hill
a black cat with a broken leg
has been watching traffic
all night long. In the cafe
two old men know each other
well enough not to talk
at all.

In the Mountain House motel
horns of antelope pierce heaven,
still hard with purpose,
meeting in the twain…
At The Antlers, beauty and blubber,
muscle and misery
dodge the whisper
unsuccessfully.

But about it all, melody
mounted like the hills
by boots and sky, hooved,
the tune at the edge of town,

the little word in the cat's eye
still counting, still measuring up,
perfectly round.

—2000

* * * * * * * * * * * * * *

Ray González
The Prison, San Elizario, Texas

Billy the Kid broke a man
out of this adobe jail.
It still stands with barred windows
and deep, black cells
a tourist attraction,
historical place of confinement
for the souls of dead prisoners.
Does this monument make them angry,
or have they finally escaped?

When one prisoner died,
in July of 1880,
they dragged his body out of
the subterranean cell
and threw it into the 112 degree sun.
The flies competed with
the shimmering waves of heat,
but neither claimed the body when
the wagon took it away.

Dozens of yellowjackets
have taken over.
Their mud nests are
the new population,
bringing life out of
these walls for a change.

With the warmth of this October,
the eggs will hatch and
each new wasp fly out of
the cracks, leaving
the empty rooms behind,
constant buzzing rising
between bars in the windows,
keeping anyone from opening
the giant, black-iron doors.

—1976

✶   ✶   ✶   ✶   ✶   ✶   ✶   ✶   ✶   ✶   ✶   ✶

ROBERT BURLINGAME
Desert, Not Wasteland

Squaw-thorn, devilsclaw, and Joshua;
Sunray, bullhead, and Spanish bayonet—
These are the plants of the desert,
A hard, curt, unpretentious poetry
Put down in the margins of bloodshed.
They need at most an inch this side death
To teach the rude drop hidden like love's wink
Inside a trim pelvis, perfect but unlavish.

They prevail. Each root a beak, each pore
A womb, each stem and leaf thorn-arbored
Beneath a sky blandly immaculate.
Here love is solemn, a strict icon of thirst;
And birth a blind tear in a sun-chiseled font.
Here no sound but wind scales the dry heights.

And what, one asks, can man's damp brain
Take from such wealth speared without greed
To this light-cisterned land? What parable?
Nothing. Against lip old peace engods first silence.

Soundless, rock ripes on rock.
From beardtongue's flame no speech—save flame.

In grails of heat life guards its grace, quiet.

—*1981*

* * * * * * * * * * * * *

ALBERT HUFFSTICKLER
Travel Note

In case nobody ever told you,
it's a long way to El Paso.
It's a long way to El Paso
from *anywhere*.

—*1994*

* * * * * * * * * * * *

RAY GONZÁLEZ
Paso del Norte

in the bar,
I float in tecate.
the whore belongs outside.
I grow old and fat
in the desert
without desire to die.
summer is an illegal alien
clinging to my arms.
thinking of comfort,
I see the rio grande
cares for its mud.

—*1976*

* * * * * * * * * * * * *

Carol Coffee Reposa
Dawn in El Paso

Above the cinderblocks
Pocked sidewalks
Beer and Pepsi cans
Lined up along the streets
Like soldiers
Light slides down
The Franklins
In a ragged progress
Drops sun
In charcoal pockets

Purple clefts
Colors shifting
On the mountain face
Like crumpled taffeta
As early morning

Ripples down the rocks
Peels night
From patient stones
In acts
Of random grace.

—1998

Cherie Foreman Spencer
from Desert Symphony

Night

See how the sage brush slants before the wind,
A mad wind crying for the slim witch girl
Shadowed against the moon. The broom weeds bend

And now the sand imps have begun to whirl
Out of the dark in frantic ecstasy.
The cactus devils! There!…the silhouettes
Against the white sand, reeling drunkenly!
The stars are gone, but still the lone wind frets.

The dark has walled us in. El Paso's lights
Are blotted out, and only sand is here,
Pale sand that keeps the secret of these nights,
Too ghostly beautiful to harbor fear.
The grasses shiver at the lonely song
The mad winds make, a nocturne of despair.
A gaunt-limbed coyote's howl echoes along.
The witch girl in the moon lets down her hair.

—1929

* * * * * * * * * * * * *

BOBBY BYRD
Things You Can't Do in Albuquerque or Santa Fe, #11

The metal blue sky, the sun
with its 104 degrees
raked across bleak Concordia Cemetery,
those acres and acres of graves
scattered like seed
among the weeds and salt cedar,
tombstones tumped to the side,
a burrowing owl poking up
from her cave in the dust where
the heart and soul of Rosa Gutierrez
was laid to rest in 1916—
that's where we found
the grave of John Wesley Hardin,
gunfighter,
shot in the back of the head

in downtown El Paso, 1895.
John Wesley was 10 feet south of Rosa
and just across from the stone-walled entrance
to the Chinese plot.
Confucius waved at us and said Hello,
but he wouldn't say a kind word
about this ancestor of ours,
except that we're all better off
that he's dead. Instead,
Confucius pointed us to the L&J Cafe
in an adobe across the street
where the ladies make
fresh lemonade every morning,
squeeze the lemons themselves, they
serve it in big tall
brown plastic glasses of cracked ice.
The L&J is dark and cool inside.
Their enchiladas con queso are delicious.

     —1992

*   *   *   *   *   *   *   *   *   *   *

RAY GONZÁLEZ
The Head of Pancho Villa

The rumor persisted that the head of Pancho Villa
disappeared on its own before they buried him,
found its way across the Chihuahua desert to El Paso,
where he killed several men and kept women.
The head floated across the Rio Grande,
snapping turtles diving out of its way,
the brown mass moving on its own, his thick hair
and mustache shining in the green water.

The skull of the general evaporated in the heat,
only to reappear at the church door,

the early man who came to pray startled by
the bullet holes between the closed eyes.
He stared at the head, then ran.
When he brought the sleepy Padre to look,
they only found a wet spot on the ground
before they bowed and crossed themselves.
The rumor ran that the head became
the mountain surrounding the town.
Others said it was the skull that sat for years
on the highway west to Arizona.
It was true because my grandparents lived there,
told their children the skull glowed
on the roads, until my grandfather died
and his family returned to the other mountain.

I see the head of Villa each time I drive into El Paso.
It rises off the setting sun as the evening turns red.
By now, I am convinced the eyes are open, the hair longer.
After all, the moon is enough when I turn and take a look.

 —1999

Pat LittleDog
crossing the river to juárez

Past the bananas and mangoes,
past the piñons, the bins of frijoles,
the baby chickens' yellow flurry,
the bursts of paper flowers in the rafters,
I can take my friends past
the butter and the cheese and the warm tortillas,
I can lead them down the dark stone stairwell
deep in the market
down the steps crowded
with bright funeral wreaths
and shrine flowers,

I can show them where touristas can't take pictures:
the herb stalls in the moldery fragrant gloom.

"See the bits of mirrors? They ward off witches.
See the jars of shells? The iguana
and the stuffed fox with marble
where his eyes once were?
This with the white flower
and feathery leaf in manzanilla;
see the snakeskins? They cure cancer,
The herb man grinds one first in a metate,
puts the powder in a newspaper cone."

I show my friends the stalls
(the herb dealers bow politely);
I speak in Spanish—one peso
for a cone of yerba buena for my friend.
Then we dance again up the stairs
past the funeral flowers,
swollen red gladiolas,
past the blackened stones.

In the newspaper I read some days later
too much gordo lobo killed a baby
        gordo lobo

I know it for its thick grey leaves
and furry stem.
the next time I will tell my friends
about gordo lobo;
I will ask for a one-peso newspaper cone.
After our shopping, across the bridge
and safe at home, I will steep a very small handful
against the cool evening

to sip as the shadows of Juárez
clamor at the foot of our mountain
in the late afternoon.

     —1982

* * * * * * * * * * * *

Sarah Cortez
Attempt to Locate

Be-bopping into Juarez
hot sun on our heads,
Mary, Raul, and I are walking
fast. Me in front, Raul
almost keeping up, courtesy
of Army Reserves twice monthly. Mary's
lagging because she's not yet fit
after her on-duty back injury.

We're joking about being three
police officers walking into
a country not famed for justice
or mercy, when I see in the front
window of a shop, beside a lavender
lace bra and an infinite array
of sheer, pastel, nylon panties,
a clothing item I can't figure out.

Huge silver sequins cover
two triangular pieces of fabric.
A delicate beige band holds it
all together. I think BRA—
a Border version! I reach for
Raul's arm as he breezes by,
buzz-cut hair obstinately forward,
growling, "I don't do lingerie."

By now, Mary has caught up and I grab her
instead, also just now figuring out
this is a garter belt. "Look, Mary,
there are sequins, so the guys can
find it in the dark."
We each see our dark
triangle framed by huge, round, silver sequins,
illuminated in reflections of neon
Border lights, on top of a strong man
in a hotel room, flushed and sweating.

Then my 4'6" friend, who entered the Marines
when no girl did that, who now raises a son
alone after two spent marriages,
who lives with her mom, who goes to Church
cada dia, and is taken seriously on the streets
in uniform, says, "you know, most of those guys
need lights and sirens to find it too!"

  —2000

✴ ✴ ✴ ✴ ✴ ✴ ✴ ✴ ✴ ✴ ✴ ✴

LESLIE ULLMAN
The Way Animals Are

Sometimes I'm startled to find myself
in this white skin, this blankness,
time's drawings erased
the way highways have leveled
the land's natural drift.
I'm distracted by the history of rain
in a single cactus. I wonder
how heavy the mountain is.
Sometimes I feel the earth tilt
on a great magnet while I sleep
and a man with a history of his own

leaves his wife's body parts in boxes
all over town, while a building is blown up
in another state and 20 children die,
now 30, now 95, not just children, some
still missing, and the numbers
flash across the world in slender cables.
Yesterday I walked the border bridge
into Juarez, where time had stopped—women,
children, begging or selling candy,
their bare feet tough as roots
and their skin streaked with weather.
Such patience in their faces—
the shadow of the Andes,
broad cheek and burnished braid,
rain over terraced slopes,
the breath of childbirth and sorrow
keening through bamboo. Across the river
the windows of my city gleamed.

I stepped into a cathedral
where matrons one by one knelt
by the altar, their privacy
a brief and deepening well,
to speak with someone I wish
I could love. Or fear. Then they rose
and returned to their used bodies,
vessels shaped to gentle fullness,
broken and mended again and again

Across the blowing litter
of Avenida Juarez, an old man
sat on a curb playing a violin—
a tuneless song that fed
on its own exhaustion.
Once he stopped and put his head
in his hands. Traffic rushed

between us. My eyes touched him
but I didn't cross the street.
This morning he is slow rain
passing through me, waking in the same
grey clothes, tightening his bow
and still I try to sing
in any language I can,
sing to you one at a time
which is all I can do;
there's a slow tongue that some days
runs through me unbidden,
in rhythms I am part of
the way animals are, even when
they're standing still.

—1998

RAY GONZÁLEZ
The Angels of Juárez, Mexico

Sometimes, they save people from drowning in the river.
Their faces are the color of the water,
wings soaked in the oil of crossing
keeping them from leaving the border.
The oldest angel is a man from the last century
whose white hair hangs to the ground.
He floats above the water each time he saves
a *mojado* who tries to cross in the raft,
falling into the current to be somebody.

The angels of Juárez look over the *colonias*,
nibble on the cardboard shacks like the rats
they never fear because rats have their own angels.
When children fall into the poison waters,
the angels dance above the glowing waves,

pull out the chosen child with a kiss,
toss him on the bank for others to find.

These angels know about revolution and dying,
prefer to hover over the Rio Grande,
where the bodies move at night,
fighting for air some angels mistake
as a grasp toward heaven.

The angels of Juárez sometimes hide
from the desire to cross,
to take a chance and send a chant
over the dirty waters, the latest
drowning victim wondering
why the tired old man he was told
to look for never extended a hand.

The angels appear in the night,
listen to the crush of water as the course
of the border tightens with searchlights
and the hidden green cars of patrol.
They swim over the electricity,
wings humming to create a magnet
that makes it easier to cross.

The angels don't know
something is going to end.
They don't appear near the churches,
the missions, or the kneeling altars.
They are not part of the prayer,
the ritual, or the escape.
They know the river is moving faster,
churning toward the horizon
that accepts fewer souls each year.

The angels hover to make sure
the water keeps flowing,
mud of the barefoot moving
to the other side of the river where
no angels dwell because this side
was cleared of faith long ago,
waiting streets of El Paso never
mistaken for the place of angels.

—1999

* * * * * * * * * * * * * *

BENJAMIN ALIRE SÁENZ
"I Wouldn't Even Bleed"

He appeared, white as any angel:
"¿Me regalas un cigarro?" Not his
native tongue.
          I handed him the pack:
"All yours."
          He grabbed at them
and stuck one in his mouth.
"English is good. You don't look
American."
          "Tell me what one
looks like."
          He smiled, "You want
we should grab a beer?" Nothing
of a beggar in his voice, nothing
of a boy.
          "Don't know you," I
turned to walk away.
          He grabbed my arm:
"Just got out," he said
pointing at the Juárez jail's wall.

How long
you been in there?"
A couple
years, or maybe three. Doing time
is doing time
not counting it."
How'd you
get yourself in jail?"
"I took the rap—"
he stopped himself,
"Don't want to talk 'bout that.
I burned that bridge."
"Where you from?"
"Texas."
"Big state," I said.
"Yeah, big state," he said, "you wanna
grab a beer?"
"Look," I said, "You need
some cash?"
"No money, man, just
buy my beer."

We drank—not much, ate
food. He swallowed fast, then asked
for mine. He was hungry still
after the plates were licked. He talked,
his words like steps in an old abandoned house.
He spoke about a girl who'd made him feel
as though he might stop breathing, as though
his heart would stop at any minute.
"What I did, I did for her." The table
shook beneath his pounding fist.
Even in the light his eyes were dull.
I thought they'd once been blue
but something faded them

like a book left out—forgotten—
in the unforgiving sun of Texas summers.

I drove across the border, and when
the *migra* asked where we were born,
it took a while before he said "American."
He looked so white and Texan, they
let us come across.

"You're home," I said.

                        "Texas," he said as he spit,
"ain't nothin' but a grave." He looked at me,
then laughed. "You got a knife?"
I shook my head. "Too bad." He laughed
and laughed. "If you cut me up,
I wouldn't even bleed."

     —1993

THOMAS WHITBREAD
Alpine, Texas

Alpine is a fresh lust,
Undesiccated steer,
Air of a spatial dust,
Discovery of Coors beer,

Place where eroded rocks
Are seldom touched by rain
And local saddlejocks
Seldom meet a train,

Yet Sunset Limited
Can intersect full moon

Rising, as if a dead
Man met himself at noon,

And a man can go from there
Down to Big Bend, then back
There, and for six days swear
He has no inner lack.

—1981

ARTHUR M. SAMPLEY
South Rim: Big Bend National Park

From this sheer wall the Indians watched the plain
And saw, as I, the Rio Grande bend
Southward to Mexico, and saw it end
In mountain ridges, fathomless terrain,
Then reappear and slash two thousand feet
Across a mountain's face and carve a land
In wounded rocks and bleeding veins of sand
Until it ceased where sky and mountains meet.

Far as the bending river sweeps they saw
The leagues of stricken ranges north and south,
And they exulted in that zone of drouth
That lay about their mountain like a law,
Nor dreamed that far beyond that river's mouth
Came ruin from which no desert could withdraw.

—1948

SHERRY CRAVEN
Chalk Draw Ranch

On a ranch down near the Texas-Mexico border,
at the mouth of Big Bend, I saw
the chalky white of a bleached cow skull
lying on the desert floor, deserted,
and felt the days descend through my heart,
exploding old memories into soft, silky dust.

Wild turkeys strutted like my
soul, vainly, bravely telling
their tale to the wide and empty skies.

Deer looked woeful, expectant,
all at once, wondering, too,
why I was there.

High up the side of the rocky hill
caves echoed lives much like mine,
separated by centuries but little else.
Ancient tribes scratched life onto walls,
in the red burnt sienna of iron oxide.

Pictographs pictured lives like scorecards,
pots to pour, arms to hold,
weapons to protect, suns to rise
and moons to mark the days,
one after another.

I found myself sketched on the rock by
the brush strokes of the ancient artist
in the woman bearing a child, as if
the baby floated from her body, dreamlike,
two spaceships merely visiting the earth.
Standing in late-day sky striped orange and purple,

at the top of the world I prayed and watched my words
float south to Mexico and settle softly on the dusty earth
while below me in the creosote the herd of javelina circled their prey,
like the stories wind round our lives and go on and on.

—2002

* * * * * * * * * * *

ROBERT JAMES WALLER
Three Poems

#1

Wearing a floppy hat,
the summer ran
as if it were afraid
I might catch it
one more time.
The border collie
and I,
by the south fence,
smiled
at such innocence.

#2

In the canyons,
nature
runs things
with an iron fist
and no quarter given.
I hear cries at night,
step over bones
a month or two later:
 Death
 in the short grass.

#3

The cowboys,
a few of them
stay behind
while times
change.
Sam,
Apache,
Monte,
Dogie and Vince…
           they drink
           at the Crystal Bar
           telling the old lies
           on which they all agree,
           hearing the sound
           of distant trains…

           …like passengers
           left at the station.

—*2001*

* * * * * * * * * * * * * * *

David C. Yates
Century Plant

For over twenty years you prime
for your one grand entrance.
You do your poetry-straining, sucking
life from the baked slopes of the Chisos.
When it comes—your exquisite poem—
exhausted, you die, as if
Beauty had raped you at the roots
and advertised its conquest
in golden pannicles perched

high in goblets, their nectar drawn from
your proud bronze stalk.

In your death lives the
enchantment of the Chisos.
You overshadow the cacti,
piñon pines, junipers.

From your death your debris,
your brown lifeless stalk—
like a crucifix—
adds a spirit to the rock slides
of Casa Grande.

In your death there is poetry,
for as in life, you are
a part of the Chisos,
where death…and life…
never really matter.

—1976

* * * * * * * * * * * *

DEL MARIE ROGERS
Near the Rio Grande

An iron-blue line of hills—
lightweight milk-blue and sand mountains
on the other side.
Sand flows silently
to the brush knotted at my feet.

I was born under a spell.
My skin holds a tight darkness.
When another human
touches my side, I will wake up.

A star is buried underground
somewhere close to this place,
so that the whole earth shines.

—1982

✦　✦　✦　✦　✦　✦　✦　✦　✦　✦　✦　✦

BERTA HART NANCE
Rio Grande Hills
(A Pioneer Speaks)

When I rode south at twenty,
Then first I saw them stand.
The little hills of Mexico,
Across the Rio Grande.

I have seen taller hillsides,
But none that spoke to me
Of love and welcome danger
And all that came to be.

The years have bloomed and faded,
I'll never ride again:
The bugle of adventure
Must sound for younger men.

But still they seem to beckon,
Across the yellow sand.
The little hills of Mexico,
Along the Rio Grande.

—1933

✦　✦　✦　✦　✦　✦　✦　✦　✦　✦　✦　✦

ROBERT BONAZZI
Changing Borders
Laredo/Nuevo Laredo

Bridge at noon
shadow underfoot
I cross this sultry divide

—*Rio Grande*—
boundary of passage
a long gray ribbon
of floating debris

Brief holiday sheds habits of logic and limb
overtaken suddenly by the spectacle
of an articulate face

Silent allegory of elegant elders
inhabiting a stone bench
lyricism of shared glances shattered
by a blaring horn

Energetic ink of memory
delicate forgetfulness
lies in this instrument
who writes

  —1992, 2002

 ★ ★ ★ ★ ★ ★ ★ ★ ★ ★ ★

SUSAN BRIGHT
Makes Them Wild

When I grew up there were 4 elements, seed stayed where you planted it,
earth was deep, black, moist and stayed down—where it belongs. In
West Texas, on the Caprock, earth, air, fire and water blow around together

in vast confounding walls of wind. It howls through window glass and comes up through cracks in the floor. Wind, it gets so dark sometimes the chickens go to roost. Wind, the old people say it has a nasty breath, they say you know you been in a wind if there's no paint left on your car, if you got sand between your teeth, under your tongue and on the backs of your eyeballs, if you want to inhale water, or stay in bed all day with a papersack over your head. Wind, it blows through your ears and makes you crazy. You'd swear you're on another planet. At night the stars come down so close the Milky Way sloughs layers of solar dust on children sleeping, makes them wild. You wonder how the farmers know whose land will bear their seed. Women, men, children and even pets move slant to the ground. Sparkling eyes and jokes blare out from the dust like miracles, nothing is like it seems. There is one town called Earth. The rest is alien. Space ships land there often. Almost everyone has seen one, they say the Caprock is a magnet. In the middle of Earth is a sign that says: SHOP EARTH. One man from Pampa rents the wind from his cousin and sells power to the electric company. People say he's so crazy that he might be brilliant. They say his cousin is no fool either.

—1983

* * * * * * * * * * * *

BETTYE HAMMER GIVENS
West Texas

Where is the beauty
In a world of steel tractors,
In an icy blue sky
That shines like a silver ball?

Where is the beauty
In white concrete elevators,
In skinny stunted trees,
A run down fence,
An unpainted barn?

Where is the beauty
In the barren, silent sky,
In space affluent with distance?
Beauty is the oneness with the greyness,
In the earth filled with promise
For all that underlies.

Hale Center, Texas 1983

    —1985

* * * * * * * * * * * *

CHARLES BEHLEN
Windy Day/Slayton, Texas

I kick the earth.
The dust, a ghost,
leaps at my face,
reminding me
with gritty tears
of lovers, whores,
friends and kin,
gone to the ground
before I was born.

    —1973

* * * * * * * * * * * *

NAOMI SHIHAB NYE
Site of the Indian Fights of 1871, Abilene

little purple flowers under out feet

it's hard to imagine
the Indians finding one another
in this huge space
and having something to fight about

     —1973

*   *   *   *   *   *   *   *   *   *   *   *

DAVID C. YATES
Sex

I think about it
everytime I'm in Mentone, Texas,
way out there in
lonely Loving County
where those West Texans
punch oil wells
all over the Permian Basin
and where the land's
so dry and harsh and naked
sometimes the sky
gets kind of tired
of looking at it,
so she takes in her breath,
sucks real deep,
holds it for several days
as she hovers above,
kind of still and mean
and menacing,
her belly getting grayer and grayer
until she finally
lets it all out

in a long moaning howl—
half joyful and half painful—
trying with all she's got
to blow the desert away.

—1979

* * * * * * * * * * * *

WILLIAM VIRGIL DAVIS
I-35, South of Waco

The Ford pickup, painted red but rusted, straddled
the center line. Both back fenders were dented in.

It was almost noon in Waco. The truck stalled in
the sun, in time, in Texas. As if in a dream, it
began to move forward slowly.

There were three of them in the cab; two men and a
dog. One was brushing his teeth. One was drinking
from a brown bottle. The dog was driving.

—1979

* * * * * * * * * * * *

PAUL FOREMAN
Brazos de Dios
for my father and our river

The river winds perfect in the moonlight,
        stretching out over gravel bars;
magic laughter echoes from water ripples
        to the willows that crowd the banks.
In the mud, in the shallows, the raccoon
        slaps his paws, digs for mussels,
delights in tough sweetness of white flesh.

Holy God in the cedars; sweet smell of cedar
on my lips, wet sand between my toes;
as fish swim for minnows, I swim for fish.
I thy fish. For his sake, partake of my flesh
for it is good and fit for all to eat.

Down cross the rocks, lifted by the wind
the sound of human feet, sprung
from the dead past, quickening the line image;
all those thirsty German tribes
on the march across Europe, swept up
in the great stream, the wake of Christ;
Christ woken and marching across Europe!

Holy angels sing in the tops of Elms;
the memory of a beautiful girl from Mexico,
the flash of her brown eyes, passionate and sad,
as she sat in the chapel; the strains of Saint
Cecilia fall on the mantilla, cover for her head:
cover our heads and bless our ears
till they blush red, serve sacred our music,
O musician!

The river runs as quicksilver, laps at its banks;
warming their hands around a driftwood fire.
Far from man's constraints, this testament to life:
the father and four sons dry their lines.
Bundled for the night's sleep in thick quilts,
the boys' eyes bury their cares in the deep of space
their hearts open, and the father unfolds
his story from out the memory of his race.

the Babylonians climbing the Tower of Babel,
Confucius teaching the Chinese love of family,
the Greeks with stoic laughter to refute
gainsayers, the Angles and Saxons

struggling for land with the druid Celts,
   for whom the oak is holy. . . .

Tears filled his eyes as he spoke of how the Germans,
      heavy with the mantle of their newfound Christ
cut down the great sacred oaks, crowned with mistletoe.
      As the night waned, the moon went down;
between the river's talk, the stir of air,
      the rustle of woods, and the magic voice
of their father harkening to the past,

   their hearts were made glad
      and their heads, nodding,
                     touched the stars.

—1976

⋆　⋆　⋆　⋆　⋆　⋆　⋆　⋆　⋆　⋆　⋆

WALTER McDONALD
Losing a Boat on the Brazos

Downriver rocks were rapids. Believe me,
even fish have ears. Sweating, we coasted
too far out on a river we've fished
for forty years. I swear it's never
been this low, but two old cousins
can't keep the Brazos full forever.

Sharp rocks are death to aluminum boats
harder to split than wood. We're safe,
spitting out mud and minnows, but alive
after months of drought and a soaking.
Bury the boat and forget it.
We could have drowned any wet year

under tons of the Brazos flooding
downhill to the dam. We could be food
for alligator gar and catfish.
That rip is wider than the lies
we'll tell for months, the size of bass
that got away, the granddaddy cat

we finally caught that flipped
and disappeared through the hole
of the boat, going down. Let's sit
on the bank and laugh at why we let
eight hundred dollars of rods and tackle
sink and saved a shell worth less

than beer cans we crush for salvage
every day, two old fools splashing ashore,
dragging a gashed boat out
as if dry land could save it,
like old bones mired in mud we've proved
can rise and walk again.

—1987

JAMES HOGGARD
Anniversary Trip

It was not evil, though it looked that way,
the copperhead wrapped around a branch
four feet from our eyes by the Brazos,
a river once called Arms of God

After beaching our canoe for lunch
we had lain on a slope on the bank
then moved to a clearing for shade

where a breeze, sliding coolly now
through our loosened clothes,
fingered its way across us,

a salt cedar brake and scrub oak mott
screening us from public view

Letting skin see in its own oblique way,
I let my gaze drift, but my breath
disappeared, my eyes now locked
on an oddly long knot

twisted on a branch twisted before us,
and the dark ragged bands were not wood,
and the shotlike red eyes did not blink

Look straight ahead, I said, *don't move*

And fingernails now biting blood
from our palms, we rose,
and the brush seemed to watch us,
as slowly we moved away

in a way we have not always done,
memory saying we'd see that snake
everywhere we looked the rest of the day

    —2000

  *   *   *   *   *   *   *   *   *   *

LARRY D. THOMAS
The Red Raging Waters

For weeks on end it has rained in Texas
Sending the Brazos miles beyond its banks
Where it rises even now under dark Texas skies

Over the wooden floor of a bottomland Baptist church,
Floating creaking pews shaped with aching buttocks
Of generations, the wild Brazos rising higher yet

To the stained-glass robes of the Apostles,
Soaking the feet of Jesus and lapping the elbows
Of His uplifted arms, creeping up the pulpit

On whose open Bible coils a fat diamondback,
The red raging waters of the Brazos
Bringing to sweet communion the serpent and the saint.

—2001

* * * * * *

WILLIAM VIRGIL DAVIS
On Lookout: Guadalupe River Ranch

Someone said the place had been the secret
hideaway of Olivia de Havilland. The way in
led through lonely, narrow, twister roads,
past markers placed to measure the depth
of rising water. We traced our way through rain,
then sudden sun, and arrived late afternoon.

The "view" was from a small wooden platform
at the end of a short dirt path near the main
house. We stood above an elbow in the river,
on a high cliff near small stone cottages,
and watched the muscled arm of water wind
slowly through the cypresses. We saw the water

seem to pause, seem to turn against itself
in the late afternoon sun, then run on again
around a lake of land, the huge flood plain
that lay beyond the cliff and river.

We wondered, when the rains came heavy,
several years ago, when the river suddenly rose

and caught the campers (there to ride the river
all along, but live to tell of it) how high,
how quickly, the water advanced upon this hill,
how quickly it carried them, how far downstream,
to death? Across the river, on the wide flood
plain, a herd of cattle grazed peacefully.

We watched them for a while and talked quietly
among ourselves of nothing much worth memory:
how the weather had so suddenly turned around;
how peacefully, now, the river flowed. Tomorrow
we would return home. As we left the lookout,
"They aren't real cows of course," someone said.

—1992

* * * * * * * * * * * * *

JOSEPH COLIN MURPHEY
Lake Austin Diorama

The waterfowl, the cedar brakes
and the shimmer of the river still
maintain a wilderness façade.

The rocks on the high cliffs
enable one to shade his eyes
and imagine what it once was

ignoring the suburban cut
and trim of lawns and shrubbery
The buzzards in the high sky

still roost in the ragged tree-
snags on the ridge, wheeling
over the new paradise with

jaundiced eye. Their silence
is unchanged, their diet is still
death. They lend an ironic stare

to the bill-of-fare flashing
below in BMW and Mercedes which the
undertaker always cheats them of

    —1996

Karle Wilson Baker
from Some Towns of Texas

Austin

She leans upon her violet hills at ease
At the plains' edge: innocent and secure,
Keeper of sacred fountains, quaintly sure,
Greek draperies fluttering in the prairie-breeze.
She stands tiptoe and looks across the seas,
Where older lands and richer shrines allure,
Wistful, that she is young and crude and poor—
But secret-sure that she is proud as these.

Her sons bring delicate plunder home, to grace
Houses discreet, and gardens sweetly walled—
She is enamored of the fit and fair.
Far-gathered treasures in her love find place:
White peacocks where the prairie-schooners crawled—
Italian roses in her sunburnt hair.

    —1929

   renting

the rumor is Kate is a full blood Tonk
but she was raised by a dallas millionaire
that's why she is so weird and
rides around town in that 52 ford truck
with that damned Doberman in the back

lately she's been making her bucks
cooking vegetarian meals for the rich
in their homes up northwest
she used to be a book buyer at the Co-Op
and before that she sold popcorn at the State

my friend Bart speaks a little Tonkawa
and sees himself a scholar of Indian lore
he thought he was in love with Kate
and talked her into moving in with him

they went on canoeing their first weekend together
on the san marcos and when Bart took too long
over his morning coffee Kate thumbed a ride
back into Austin

at the end of the month
Bart was fuming and making fists
just at the sound of Kate's name
and when she ran up a 300.00 long distance
phone bill Bart threatened to kill her

Kate called up a few Oklahoma braves
they surrounded the house in south Austin
and shot through the windows
filling the walls with decorative holes

the landlady just wouldn't believe
it wasn't Bart's fault
so he never got his deposit back

    —1984

*   *   *   *   *   *   *   *   *   *   *   *   *

WILLIAM BURFORD
South, Southwest

Justice is bright; the State is luminous;
Who cannot see the dome flooded with light?
Glowing, almost translucent, like alabaster
Tonight? Hardly a shadow to let us think
It was ever dark, or blunted and twisting—
Walking toward it through the elms, sitting
On benches with its influence overhead.

It is like white salt we come to eat,
Take into our eyes, our thin or thick hides,
Let our spirits lick. This was cattle country,
And now we have come to sit at the dome,
To wait. At midnight the sprays are turned on
That keep the grass green—which touching us
Feel suddenly sweet, but then whip us away

Grabbing up sacks, shaking our wet clothes,
Scrambling surprised. Still the dome does not change:
There it gleams. Only, it is distant again,
As we leave, fade toward the town, forgetting
But not wholly, past the Governor's house
Its pure columns lighted too, like snow
Though it's summer, that slaves hauled the logs for.

179

But we have a new place! Though in the end
They say we keep our own tastes: Crowded shacks
We can smell our acid sweat in an embrace,
Make love like cats with savage clasp, and so
Multiply. The young break plate glass
Snatch shiny rings that make their eyes wide
And run with them in panic through the streets

From the jangling bell. We are animals.
But who's to tell? We live in a tale
With our opposites, separated yet the same.
Tomorrow it will be day again.
The great dome we came for will be gray.
We'll go in, see what they're giving us.
It was like white salt, what we came for.

—1966

* * * * * * * * * * * *

ALBERT HUFFSTICKLER
October 31, 1981

Winter, Austin. 1964.
Bright windows steam-fogged
in coffee shops around the Drag,
love a mist rising from damp streets
to fog the air as,
chilled, you trudged homeward
hunched in your coat,
having sat anchored
in shop after shop
(The Night Hawk, Hank's
The Rexall, The Pancake House)
sipping your coffee,
reading messages in the air
of those bright, warm rooms

and others in the lights
on winter streets as,
burrowed in your coat,
you peered out, animal-like.
Cosmic. It was all cosmic.
You see that now
walking those same streets,
the buildings just buildings,

      the pavements flat black
      flashing no messages
      in the lights of passing cars.
      It was.
      Now it's gone.
      And you sit sipping your coffee
      hunched and forlorn
      like an old drunk seeking refuge
      from night's violence
      and winter's cold.
      God!
      Was love really here
      and we missed it?
      Or is it somewhere farther on?

      —1982

★ ★ ★ ★ ★ ★ ★ ★ ★ ★ ★ ★ ★

CHUCK TAYLOR
Winterdirge

in winter
your streets
turn cold and haggard
like any prairie town

petulant shoppers
walk hugging hated bodies

while varicose trees
mark the gloomcast sky

and the grass turns grey
on development lawns
as if to match the gods.

Austin my citylove,
you then are no longlegged woman
enfolding with bosom warmth
of sustaining thighs—

your lips are lean
and tightfitted:
what spirit remains
is buried among record albums
in armadillo caves
among the drugged and lost,
who have forgotten
the unnamed hope
of thaw.

       —1976

CARMEN TAFOLLA
San Antonio

San Antonio,
      They called you lazy.
they saw your silent, subtle, screaming eyes,
      And called you lazy.
They saw your lean bronzed workmaid's arms,

And called you lazy.
They saw your centuries-secret sweet-night song,
      And called you lazy.

San Antonio,
      They saw your skybirth and sunaltar,
      Your corn-dirt soul and mute bell-toll,
      Your river-ripple heart, soft with life,
      Your ancient shawl of sigh on strife,
      And didn't see.

San Antonio,
      They called you lazy.

—1976

* * * * * * * * * * * * * * *

CAROL COFFEE REPOSA
Alamo Plaza at Night

Even now, tourists come
To gaze up at the chipped façade,
Weathered double doors
Oaks twisting into dark, floodlights
Trained along their branches.
Cameras flash against white limestone
Pocked with centuries
And gunshots long ago.

Within the walls
And Roman arches
Heavy with their bars
Are tidy gardens:
Boston fern droops languidly
Toward fresh-cut grass
and copper plants.
Goldfish wallow in their quiet ponds.

Outside people talk about the mission,
Where to go, what to eat.
Visitors brood over maps
And time-lapse shots, children peering
At old plaques, words lost
Within a diesel's whine, the clop-clop
Of a horse's hooves, wind rising
In dark trees, voices gathered
Finally
Into the stones.

—2002

* * * * * * * * * *

BRYCE MILLIGAN
San Antonio Nights

Away from the literate river
where I can still hear
Lanier's flute
and his rattling cough,
where Stephen Crane leapt
to save a pretty face,
where O. Henry watched
the tuberculars coughing, dying
like the frontier itself.
Away from the literate river
where Frost mourned
and Kerouac drank.
Away from the Alamo
where heroic ashes
still burn the nostrils,
where history has a meaning
but time does not.

Away from all
the charms of anecdote
I am caught
by a moment in the long dark rain
when my heart catches
at a child's cry—stills
to listen, to identify
to search my own house.
The cry summons me away
from the safety
of fire and book,
calls me into
the streets
to seek
a face
to match
the pain.

—1993

* * * * * * * * * * * * * * *

SANDRA CISNEROS
Black Lace Bra Kind of Woman
for la Terry

¡Wáchale! She's a black lace bra
kind of woman, the kind who serves
up suicide with every kamikaze
poured in the neon blue of evening.
A tease and a twirl. I've seen that
two-step girl in action. I've gambled bad
odds and sat shotgun when she rambled
her '59 Pontiac between the blurred
lines dividing sense from senselessness.

Ruin your clothes, she will.
Get you home way after hours.
Drive her '59 seventy-five on 35
like there is no tomorrow.
Woman zydeco-ing into her own decade.
Thirty years pleated behind her like
the wail of a San Antonio accordion.
And now the good times are coming. Girl,
I tell you, the good times are here.

—1994

CARMEN TAFOLLA
Aquí

He wanders through the crooked streets
      that mimic river beds Before,
      and breathes the anxious air in traffic
      filled with tension left from wooded crossroads in attack.
      He shops the windows, happy,
      where the stalking once was good,
      and his kitchen floor is built on bones
      of venison once gently roasted.

"It's a good place for a party!" he concurs
to friends now dressed in jeans.

      The ground was already beaten smooth
      and festive by the joy of ancient dances.

He feels the warmth,
and doesn't know his soul is filled
with the spirit of coyotes past.

—1993

STEPHEN HARRIGAN
A Poem Of Adulthood

The alligators have left their home
in the hotel lobby,
they have died,
they have lumbered away.
Beneath the palms
their chickenwire cage is dry
as a wrenched heart.
Soon it will be seen as useless
and removed.

It seemed to me once
that that cage
was the Menger's engine,
that the creatures inside
kept the old hotel from swaying forever
into the vault of its own reverie.
They were durable, a fact.
I could not know that the building itself
would someday absorb them,
as it is said
the living must absorb the hollow
places of the dead,

as in fact I had done
that same afternoon
across the street at the Alamo,
where I had covered enough ground
to make an honest claim
that I stood where Crockett stood.
I looked up at the chandelier
which I believed then
that Bowie had ridden
to his death.
I felt my lungs drift, sky-blue.

Today, at the Menger,
above the mesh of that empty pit,
there are two of us carrying our
childhoods to the altar.
In your mind, maybe, is a tornado,
maybe the idea of long-parted grass
on your prairies.
Above us the lobby
is grounded, staked down
like a tent.

As it billows out I search
for the space once occupied
by that historical boy,
wonder what he and the alligators
have grown to,
whether they have commingled
in this man,
this woman,
this listless hotel.

—1980

NAOMI SHIHAB NYE
The Lost Parrot

Carlos bites the end of his pencil
He's trying to write a dream-poem, but waves at me, frowning

       I had a parrot

He talks slowly, his voice travels far
to get out of his body

a dream-parrot?
No, a real parrot!
Write about it

He squirms, looks nervous, everyone else is almost finished
and he hasn't started

It left
What left?
The *parrot*

He hunches over the table, pencil gripped in fist,
shaping the heavy letters
Days later we will write story-poems, sound-poems,
but always the same subject for Carlos

It left

He will insist on reading it and the class will look puzzled
The class is tired of this parrot

Write more, Carlos
I can't

Why not?

I don't know   where   it went

Each day when I leave he stares at the ceiling
Maybe he is planning an expedition
into the back streets of San Antonio
armed with nets and ripe mangoes
He will find the parrot nesting in a rain gutter
This time he will guard it carefully, make sure it stays

Before winter comes and his paper goes white
in all directions

Before anything else he loves
gets away

     —1982

*   *   *   *   *   *   *   *   *   *   *   *   *

CARMEN TAFOLLA
Allí Por La Calle San Luis

West Side—corn tortillas for a penny each
     Made by an aged woman
      and her mother.
     Cooked on the homeblack of a flat stove,
     Flipped to slap the birth awake,
     Wrapped by corn hands,
Toasted morning light and dancing history—
     earth gives birth to corn gives birth to man
     gives birth to earth.
Corn tortillas—penny each
    No tax

—1976

*   *   *   *   *   *   *   *   *   *   *   *   *

CYNTHIA HARPER
Día de Los Muertos
(the day of the dead)

It is today you will come,
press your ancient bones
against my back, whisper in
my ear, *Mija, I love you.*

In my dreams you will be
young again and strong.
We will swim naked at
sunrise, giggle over
pan dulce and coffee.

My skeleton will cry out
to you, *Be patient*
I will come to you
when she is through
with this living.

We will dance again
on the flat earth
at Market Square,
our bleached bones
glistening in the
moonlight.

  —1994

☆ ☆ ☆ ☆ ☆ ☆ ☆ ☆ ☆ ☆ ☆ ☆

JAN EPTON SEALE
Subtropical

The southeast wind brings the smell of Gulf.
The orchid tree blushes a hundred blooms.
The cactus can't decide, pink or yellow,
all the while hiding its fruit like a girl.

I walk the circle, where the setting sun
and a cluster of palms plan a postcard.
It's a street with escape routes,
but who would want them?

Someone needs to tell the woodpecker
it's evening, time to knock off.
A crowd of starlings is making
Susan's cottonwood shiver.

Homeward, I drag two dried fronds.
In the alley, a dead grackle,
still vain in his amethyst feathers,
discovers me and grins.

I fold him in the fronds.
They are two of a kind,
a small funeral mound
against this excess life.

     —1990

     ✳   ✳   ✳   ✳   ✳   ✳   ✳   ✳   ✳   ✳   ✳   ✳

Mayme Evans
Song for a Baby on Padre Island

Go ahead, baby.
Howl to the sky,
The neighbors can't hear you,
Cry, baby, cry.

Fill your lungs, darling,
With good ocean air,
The sea gulls won't shush you,
The sand crabs won't care.

There're no "adults only"
Signs on the dunes,
No fussy old landlord
To throttle your tunes.

There isn't a human
In sight for a mile,
Just Mommy and Daddy,
So yell, honey chil'.

Daddy's a fishing,
Mommy's close by,
It's a great day for crying,
Oh cry, baby, cry!

—1955

* * * * * * * * * * * *

ISABEL NATHANIEL
Galveston

We keep the shutters drawn all afternoon
against the sun. It's the custom here.
Light filters through, wavery as water.
The sun's the enemy to beat. We trust
the seawall to hold the gulf, but drowning
is our fate. Be careful on these stairs.

I must catch my breath. It's the steep stairs
and the heat. I lie down in the afternoon,
the quiet so close it feels like drowning.
This climate robs all strength if you stay here
too long. When I arrived I was a trusting girl whose only fear was the water.

That's your room, rose-papered and a water
view. How young you are to take the stairs
two at a time! You'll visit me, I trust,
in my room across the hall. Each afternoon
I rest from three to five. It's not uncommon here
to find solace in a dim room, drowning

until dinnertime. Of course the drownings
no one forgets were long ago. Water
swept the city down. Six thousand died here,
their bodies were stacked high as stairs
and burned. The foul smoke turned afternoon
dark. To rebuild after that was a trust.

I've picked gardenias for your bedside. Don't trust
their scent. Breathed close, you will be drowning
in languor. A trap set to steal your afternoon.
Would you like refreshments? Rosewater,
perhaps, or wine? There's no one on the stairs.
Brandy, chocolates? We're quite sequestered here,

our rooms a refuge from the crowds here
in high summer. Port cities can't be trusted.
In this fancy street more than one stair
led to a brothel, nomad sailors drowning
in unimagined pleasures and watered-
down liquor. But this is *our* afternoon.

Here is your treat. Brandy in the afternoon.
You trusted our complicity on the stairs.
In this watery light we lie down as if drowned.

—1996

★　　★　　★　　★　　★　　★　　★　　★　　★　　★　　★　　★

THOMAS WHITBREAD
Whomp and Moonshiver

Whomp and moonshiver of salt surf on sand,
Beer cans, rocks, seawall: Galveston night vision
Anyseawhere hear- and seeable, incision
Cut into land, incessant dentist's hand
At drill, letless force, without countermand

Order thump order order thump intermission
Thump order thump thump thump order No Permission
For surfers Danger Deep Holes yet all how grand.

Palls the heart, yet how go on without? Within
Gyrates the heart, at such terrific. If
Heart is the essence of a humane being
And life love, let heart leap to share its thin
Pump with the din about against the stiff
Photograph that succeeds the act of seeing.

—1982

ISABEL NATHANIEL
The Coast of Texas

If it's appendicitis, you're in trouble
out here on the *Isla de Malhado.*
Despite bright stars there are disturbances.
It's three o'clock in the morning.

Ashore on the *Isla de Malhado*
the shipwrecked Spanish came to no good end.
It's three o'clock in the morning.
If it's not an emergency, go back to bed.

The shipwrecked Spanish come to a bad end,
lost and unlucky in the New World.
If it's not an emergency, go back to bed.
The balcony is drifting out to sea.

You're lost and unlucky in a new world,
four hours till it lightens to a morning.
The balcony is drifting out to sea.
You heard a bosun's pipe above the tide.

For hours it is lightening to morning.
The pain on your right side is a warning
as was the bosun's pipe above the tide.
Your nightgown is white batiste and lace.

The pain on your right side is warning,
and the red aureole around the moon.
Your nightgown of white batiste and lace
is in reckless windborne flight

toward a red aureole around the moon.
The wretched Spanish huddled on the beach,
their barge in windborne flight
toward still further shores of darkness.

You see the wretched huddled on the beach.
Despite bright stars there are disturbances
and still further shores of darkness.
If it's appendicitis, you're in trouble.

—1992

ROB JOHNSON
Reverse Engineering

The nose cone of a rocket
Washes up on Mustang Island
And causes more commotion than
The Statue of Liberty did buried in the sand.
NASA and the Feds are on-site
Skinny black ties flapping in the prevailing
Winds, glasses fogged.
Whose rocket is it lost its nose?
It's not one of ours.

I know who lost his rocket. (Inside information).
Deke Slayton, retired from the Astronaut
Corps because of high blood pressure,
He's going to bypass NASA
And start his own Rocket Launching
Company. He picks Mustang Island
A stretch of sand in the Gulf of Mexico
And from that precarious
Point of shifting ground
And variable weather
He shoots rockets into the sky
At dawn, when the sun rises over the
Gulf and the oil on the beaches
Just starts to heat up in the sun.

While NASA snoops and wonders
Who owns Space
A local with a pickup hauls off
The nosecone under NASA's nose.
He takes it home and reverse engineers:
Now he has a hot tub.

  —2002

✳ ✳ ✳ ✳ ✳ ✳ ✳ ✳ ✳ ✳ ✳

PAUL CHRISTENSEN
Driving Toward Houston

The miles are more like time than anything—
disks of prairie turning
like clocks in either window

in each of them a cow stands
or a horse nods itself to sleep
a house darkens against the distance

We are the present moment tangible as
breeze but no more, shifting the boundary
between east and west, this crumbling wall

of north behind us, sealing as we move
into the dissolving south, its unmade history
gushing like springs before us

    —1999

*   *   *   *   *   *   *   *   *   *   *   *

ROBERT BONAZZI
Houston's Adolescence

I

Houston's adolescence was my adolescence
murder capital of the world
when I turned fifteen

Bobby Clay's mom shot at a prowler
his dad swallowed fumes in a locked garage

Howard stabbed a girl of fourteen
because she wouldn't
or so we were told—
but after silent years in the pen
we learned he'd been set up to be robbed
this kid who never spoke
during our games at the gym
except with his deadly jumpshot

II

I have stitches in the arms I didn't break
also stitches in the other arms

My brother stuck a dart in the side
of my skull at forty paces
said he wrestled a knife away from me once
I don't remember that

Lawrence could catch a football
with on hand more gracefully
than anyone with two

III

Best view was the rooftop sunset
twenty years ago these backyards were neat
now they're cluttered with dog houses
chicken coops and toolsheds
old truck tires hanging
from the lowest limbs

Snake bayou's filled in
little hills leveled
clumps of trees we called the jungle
just an empty parking lot
Plaza's Saturday Fun Show
were serial afternoons for a dime
now it's skin flicks at five bucks a head

IV

In 1962 I returned home from San Francisco
it was 102 degrees at the train station
I was the only one getting off
the old Santa Fe which is gone

But dad didn't recognize me
with my shaved head
I recognized him
he's the Italian boy in New York
who walked ten miles to school in the snow!

—2002

ROBERT PHILLIPS
Houston Haiku

The frozen rain drop,
          dozing on the death-black twig,
dreams of hurricanes.

—2002

SYBIL ESTESS
Sunset on the Bayou
for the Challenger Seven

Now dusk is on Houston: flat and breastless.
Not on Seattle, red-hilled Greensboro,
nor Concord, Kona, old Jerusalem—
those subtle or volcano slopes they could have climbed.

It's the last of January, virginal
until last Tuesday. It's 5:30,
six weeks past winter solstice.
Soft southern deadness, broomstrawed and brown.

Sun, setting we say, is red placenta, edging
the child's promised sky not yet night....
Walking one block from my house,
I'm by the concreted, graffiti-marked bayou, circling this city,

churning rain debris, turtles, trash, tires,
unfound trapped bones—a woman's who drove off
in last year's rainstorm catastrophe.
Stars, boats, babies, all that goes forth here
will travel again—down, down such dark canals.

—1987

* * * * * * * * * * * * * *

LORENZO THOMAS
Downtown Boom
Houston ca. 2001 A.D.

There are no gospel singers
Anymore

On the corners
They held down for Jesus
Valets park cars
At restaurants for fancy people
On expense accts or dates

So many times
People come up to me
And say, Billy
Hey wait a minute
You not Billy!

You can see the new ballpark
Just past the Courthouse

But which way is redemption?

—2002

* * * * * * * * * * * * *

PAUL CHRISTENSEN
from Houston: An Ode

Prolog

Cubic and rinsed,
       in a soft, mild foam
       of light, its glinting
       edges soar in thin planes
       of diamond sparkle,
        so crisp in its footings,
        and jointed orange bones.

Ions pebbling the air,
     the blue tension of electric
     rites, the om-thrum
      ozone air.

—1983

* * * * * * * * * * * * *

ERIC MUIRHEAD
A Reflection on the Paintings of Mark Rothko's Chapel

A heart is there—
The dark blood of the art
Bared unto itself, and waiting:
A woman bare and in a dark hold,
Her woman's breasts
Held tight in her own hands,
Within a frame of flesh and blood
An art bare unto itself,
Pondering, pondering—
The blood tight in the breast,
The womb growing.
Within the frame is eternity there,
And deep the dark blood;

Outside the frame is wall,
Binding the woman's bare and fragile flesh,
Where her breast held tight in her own hands,
Pondering, pondering,
She awaits the new birth.

—1976

* * * * * * * * * * * *

LORENZO THOMAS
Liquid City

I

This morning wakes
Sun all around my head
A small confused attempt with memory
All urge to pry
Out
Dusty leaves and shelves a song
On Nottoc mart tram cotton no
Song
Not grand relic remains in Houston
Of a derelict glory
La Carafe, sure
Glatzmaier's lunch Old
Market Square blazing in sun
A dream of builders

Hush
As Juke Boy sang
It's going to be a long lonesome ride back home
It's going to be a long, long
Lonesome ride back home
As Juke Boy sang, something seemed wrong
Ain't nobody even missed me
All the time since I been gone

No song

A little sun,
White as a cotton bloom,
Rounded a boll or blossom
To blue dawn
Ripens to gold, and all blues
Green to noon
By fires at night, by clouds at day
No song

No song

Bring us, O givers
From towers stilted in this ancient bayou
Merchants and manufacturers
Bring us
Of survey transits, of plumbs
The tools &c intense volcanic sight
Sublime of mud commodity &c
Mud.

Up from the waters, a lush green
From the bayou from the landing
The urban the lush geology lapidary layers peel
First banks   then markets   horizontal
Shops   hotels   then Banks
In constant replicate year by year

With dreams of songs just waking
Piano player tinkle plunk tinkle Louisiana sound
Come 5th Ward, Texas
Silver Moon Cafe busy streets downtown
It's raining in the barren parks
The city first a dream of New Yorkers
By Abe & Pappy's

A city marching proud away
Shining from its countenance
Shining

No song

II

> *And yet i cannot find my own face.*
> *James Wright*

No song
Sounds like eavesdropping at a cocktail party
Chit chat from strangers
About someone you'd rather not know

Facades of shining surface, blinding glass
More than a pile of stone and steel
Walls of mirrors stilted underneath
Rising above the green twine of the bayous

All brokedown W. Dallas porch
A freedman names Jules Verne invents
A century complete with all we have
A place of material dreams

Look like upper class people
Don't care how the lower class of people live
Too poor to have a song to sing
When you gave all that you could give

III

No song
To expand his unconsciousness
As he sees each one
Like you look at them this way

So much like another
Can't quite come to mind
And they stretch, pout so charmingly then
Along graceful lines.

                            Graceful lines
Glimmering among each others' shadows
Socially.

                    She watches coolly
As ornate old-fashioned lines
Flex through distortions
It comes between Splendora and splendor,
News from east Texas Dallas Alice
From Manhattan from Midland
From home
Soft eyes then and sudden
Hard mouths

Chit chat from strangers
Or neighbors,

Yes, they stretch out so charmingly then

IV

Glass is a shifting liquid
        stunned by flame
    and passersby;
      a shame
Nobody understands
Shy glass. Embarrassed buildings
Houston's pride
The city first a dream of New Yorkers
In a pickup near the icehouse
A Cajun named Jules Verne invents

A century complete with all we have
The 1950s realized at last
Views from Cody's fashion-cluttered roof
Only the most recent bent
That Graettinger & Kenton and Associates
So fervently outlined
Of Transco beacon light and boomtown press
Now and then, stinging as a Blues guitar
Muted and wan as April's palest rose.
City of glass

Glass is a shifting liquid
In disguise, bearing its panic with more grace
Than any man could ever understand
More delicate than any nervous sparrow,
Stronger than any girl's soft, yielding hand:

Here, for who wants to see it
(Though nobody asked for a sign)
Triumph of Dubuffet's "Phantom" seen
Through hurricane of Duchamp's chance
Stressed in the glass of Milam's pyramids

City of glass, a place of material dreams
Bestowed in plain sight and transparently denied.
A town where high school children on the bus
Discourse on architecture. Would-be boyfriends
Mew, "I like that new one there. You like it, too?"

Old songs from radio, ancient courting poetry and fancy talk
Magnetized here by stone striking the eye
While set designers for the TV Evening News
Frantically paste new photos on the anchorman's backdrop,
More harried than the station managers who wait for ratings

"When you show houses, you always find a way

To drive the client there along an esplanade,"
So my friend tells me. CENTURY 21 is here, unfolding.
The 1950's realized at last
An awesome isometry of reflection

Facades of shining surface, blinding glass
Where the desperate mother, the unemployed man,
The brutal or blundering thief in the night
The crazies of Main Street who wander by night,
Homeless and dazed, are vanished from the frieze

Of commerce. If they were present, would be but rendered small
Glass shadows. Vampires and victims are not reflected at all.

No song

V

Those in these houses only are allowed.

This is but a gift, well-meant. This isn't gossip
Of invention, not malice.
Brightest intention, really
Something to expand
And why not what's unconscious
Since we don't know where light starts anywhere,
Just its most recent bent

There is no brilliance of subtropic sun
Today. Unseasonal. So cold, so calm.
This Gulf the radio reports so roilsome.
No gleam reflected from a murky thread
Of tainted bayou,
No brilliant humor jostling on the street
No hope, no dream coming to "save the day"
Unless you want one.

Builded in mud, proverbial shifting sand
      Sand fired stands still
  Long enough to qualify as glass
Banded with steel and concrete, it can touch the sky,
     A miracle.

In all this glass, when every face is seen,
These mirrors will hold conversations with the sun

We,
Chortling from babyhood to grandest dotage, sing.
Each egotistic we
We sing to each awakening "Good morning"
We shout through disappointments in loud restaurants
Sleeping, we sing to ourselves.

And still
Can neither speak nor sing
What space we share or crop into coherent beauty
Here
But shards of reflection, but glimmers of shadows
No schedule but chance of annoyance,
Distracting refraction
A petulance designed of light rebounding—languid, liquid.
There is a gulf between us and ourselves
A missed perception

We need a song that all of us can sing
A true reflecting. A moody, bright, expansive song.
In all this glass, when every face is seen,
These mirrors will hold conversations with the sun.

—1987

JANET LOWERY
Houston Heights

I have decided not to forget these little houses,
these tiny cottages, these small frames of brick
and clapboard and stone, these roofs of silvery
shingle and green tile. I have decided not to forget
the pastel colors of the jaunty homes: mauve
and peach, sage and lavender, pale pink
and bleached periwinkle blue. Nor the smooth
scallops of gingerbread peaks, the fresh white
trim of picket fences, nor the spiked tips
of black iron gates, the neatly groomed lawns
and beds of bright flowers: pink candy impatiens
and frothy azaleas, velvet-mouthed pansies, lace
periwinkle, crepe canna lilies, the ragged lips
of scarlet hibiscus, pots of pink begonias, pots
of marigolds, pots of geraniums and portulaca.
And the carved statuary figures, the frill
of window dressings, the painted shutters,
the sidewalk borders of feathered monkey grass,
the yard sale signs, the tropical mossy air,
I won't forget rows of ornamental pear trees,
the sweet cloy of wisteria, the sycamore-lined streets,
the arbors of live oaks and their knotted roots,
the fragrant magnolia blossoms flagrantly arranged
amidst dark waxy leaves, the smooth sleek-skinned
bones of crepe myrtle, the slender leaves of pecan
trees, the bleached white hide of silver birches.
I have decided not to forget these tiny side streets
tunneling toward the tracks, the wide boulevards,
the neat avenues and cracked sidewalks. Here,
on the notebook page, I will remember everything
promising about these streets: the sleepy cats
and fat wagging dogs, the nests of blue herons
atop neighboring trees, girls on green bikes,

boys playing catch, and the brave grey squirrel
spit one noon from a truck's underbelly of ragged steel
that died in a fit of violent twitches, a fireball of flesh
and fur and ricochet spins, stunned by a ruthless
nick of time, the jagged sweep of gutter winds.

—1994

✳   ✳   ✳   ✳   ✳   ✳   ✳   ✳   ✳   ✳   ✳   ✳   ✳

SARAH CORTEZ
Interlude

I watch a handsome young female
heifer along a ditch line, tramping
down knee-high weeds, tail swishing. Ears
outlined against the blaze of car headlights
at 60 miles per hour on FM 1960. She's free—
she's an 800 pound potential traffic hazard.

An off-duty cop pulls up in a shiny, red,
one-ton, extended cab pickup. Shirtless
because he's been mowing fields on a tractor.
She's too spooked to come to his horn
or be roped. He tries to help me out
but the cream-colored, good-looking heifer won't respond.

Waiting for the Livestock Office, we talk
standing. He crosses his arms over
his bare chest, deepening the crease
between his tits, the beckoning seam of dark hair.
I focus on his eyes, chin, moustache—
anywhere higher than his chest.

Anywhere safer than the tanned stretch
of smooth stomach sliding into dark green twill
shorts. He gives me his name and shift,

days off, cell phone, pager, extra job
location. The owner of the cow arrives,
Marlboro dangling inside the smooth sweep
of her burgundy Buick. I disregard the Livestock
Officer. The cow gets roped, her adventure
ended. He leaves grinning on the other side
of his naked chest, briefly lit by speeding headlights,
a scant outline against black twilight's pliable face.

—2000

*   *   *   *   *   *   *   *   *   *   *   *

VASSAR MILLER
Whitewash of Houston
with thanks for the title to Mary Jean Irion

Who would have thought of her as mother small
town raunchy with cowhands coming and country
girls and boys not knowing Dr. Freud but
Moses well enough as big-nosed Bach pumped both
organ and wife scattering music even
more than her cattle safely graze those meadows
of midnight and darknesses presences surrounding
her with cloud by day and night also going
before her where she only stumbles in
imagination fearing that they are
only dry holes reverberating with
some ancient terror tutored by none
but teachers' voices like a piece of chalk
scratched white across the face of midnight breaking?
Who would have thought of her as mother sleek
big-butted like black cars that bulging slickly
swim over pavement and pothole splattered with
delicate bone and gut of squirrel none
except poor folk afoot or else on bike
would ever notice much less mourn on grounds

as female as the moon her sons trimped on
galumping ghosts crumpling that most dainty
fingernail of poetry into a
fist fondling their rod that flaunts their flag
dribbling oil and slime and muck that ooze
from under her armpits as she stuffs her mouth
with garbage drooled onto her front until
she drops dead in her tracks to bed hot for
that prick and prong of sleep's sweet long and hard?
Who would have thought of her as mother gunning
down eerie corridors of her dark self
dented and bent the shape of truth no meaning
can measure and that has no end but life
to cradle whether for its good or ill
nobody knows however life may teem
with fact outwearing pint-sized brains made all
who ought to stand up straight behind her shame
before the world that tossed her to the dogs
as innocent as she once seemed with knowing
what shadow loops its coil about her legs
quickened with light and slowed to dusk on seeing
her terror driving all her children dumb
down the long chute of death and safely home?

II

Who would have thought of her as mother mad
at morning and mad with mourning and merry
as the scissor grinder's whistle blown far dodging
February currents and her memories
bouncing it up and down like a fey bell on
her cars as keen as gray chill cuts and leaner
than Lent has stripped away the clover blossoms
long ago vanished with the honey bees
the horny fingers of the rain uncoiled
March and April meandering across

the vacant lot of Easter and back home?
Who would have thought of her as mother fed
and fudged till fattened on her lentil vigils
as open as her covert cesspools ripe
with the rich grain of avarice and April's
froth of green and dogwood's lace hung over
the land and greening all her lawns until
she lies down with her apron smelling of summer?
Who would have thought of her as mother light
could lift into corn cribs to lie until
curious as a calf she grows and swells
with moonstruck offspring pushing all awry
who have not known the hollow of her womb
more hollow than the opening leading to it
to gobble down her shacks and spires till time
has hulled them all like winter's dried pecans
dropped to her earth leaning and lurching fawnwise
mulched with the sunshine long since loamed with darkness?

—*1984*

* * * * * * * * * * * *

Eric Muirhead
Closing Time

*(On Hempstead Road, headed northwest out of Houston, stands a
small motel in a lonely line of warehouses and freight depots, called
"Paradise." It is a favorite resting place for roughnecks, cowboys,
working men in town for a few days.)*

Just another joint:
Men all stare
Over beer pools in glasses
Scattered and long neck bottles;
A worn but friendly woman serves,
Trying to look a bit sexy
In a short red cowhide skirt.

Men stare at the dark walls
Merging in a delirium of haze,
A bit of stink, and dreams—
Listen to the juke box
Whimper hurt tomes of unrequited
Love for them. Hysteria breeds
In undertones of choked
Hurt. Burning flesh points
Of cigarette mouths
Float drunk in raw smoke.
A woman serves,
Trying to look a bit sexy.

2:00 a.m. Time to close.
Law requires.

The lights out.
Juke box
Quiet, unplugged.
Hysteria—contained
In shadows, harmless.
A cowpoke's the last to leave,
Called a taxi;
Slips in beside the driver:
"Paradise, please Sir."

  —1976

 ✳ ✳ ✳ ✳ ✳ ✳ ✳ ✳ ✳ ✳ ✳

BOYCE HOUSE
Beauty is Elsewhere

Truly, there is no beauty in Fort Worth, no song;
Only the clamorous, glad cries of the sparrows in the trees at
  the City Hall;

And the little pool at Rock Springs that tall poplars seek
        jealously to hide, with the graceful willows trailing their
        bending boughs in the silver water;
And the smoothly rolling hills to the west, like those of
        Palestine,
And beside the Public Library on a January day, if you are
        fortunate, you may see the bushes sheathed in ice,
Each slender limb all wrapped in cellophane.
No, there is no beauty in Fort Worth—
Just sunsets, and rainbows, and the slanting rain;
And, I nearly forgot, the same moon that shines on Venice…
The same stars.

    —1949

* * * * * * * * * * * *

ROBERT TRAMMELL
A Nightclub
on the Jacksboro Highway

waitin for Jimmy Reed
You got me waitin, Yeah
I'm waitin for you…   I mean we
could get shot, sitting & waitin for you.   On the
Jacksboro Highway on Saturday nite Ft Worth men
maybe the Cecil Green Gang liked to
go to these bars to hunt
Dallas people. We had to walk
our best walk & get
tables right up near the dance floor, in the light.
Lucky once Jimmy
Reed showed up 3 hours late mumbling
Mama Reed whispers, he layed
on his back in front of the stage & sang: I got women to

the right of me.
the left of me.
all around me,

       —1989

I got women to
I got women
but I ain't got you.

* * * * * * * * * * * * *

DAVE OLIPHANT
Dallas

encircled by freeway loops
has wished itself a Roman arena
styled more after Texas Stadium
where gladiators   this time
Christians from Abilene or SMU
take on Lions Bears Rams
while the lawyer-merchant class
spies down night & day
from box seats or tinted glass
spots the animals in goal-line stands
or last ditches along skidrow
below
       too are those looking for his-
tory   staring at tobacco stains on
Federal Building walks   visitors in from Boston
wondering
Is this where our hero bled?
buying his souvenirs   windows Xed
in snapshots where Oswald took his aim
his bullet granting one more wish

such carpet rides lift powerlines
overpasses skyscrapers high
rises hopes of masses   recall
how they were raised for
days   driving here as a family when fall

trips to the State Fair were long & hard
where at last in Sears would try
the cowboy boots had wanted so   like Gene's
or Roy's but with narrow feet
dad said no   they didn't fit
nothing in Dallas ever does
it's Texas but then it's not
it isn't the West it never was
would have it moved to an eastern spot

partly this comes out as
the talk of a Cowtown boy   Fort Worth-Dallas
called twin cities yet rivals from the start
the real Texas   with cattle & horses
rodeos at Will Rogers Coliseum   versus
the Airport

typical of towns grown near   the closest father & son
are born to carry a rivalry on
Darío's red head sticks
out in any crowd
can be a pain   yet will claim him any time
like all of Texas   or so would rhyme

Big D's a sore thumb too
though giving credit where credit's due
both share winning points
this city can boast of parks & lakes
are a blue-green sketch
for him to sit & draw   match
with watercolor or tempera paints
outdo this description   make a papa proud

carry him back to creeks shaded
by pecan & peach   running clear & cold
over smooth & green-furred rocks   fresh

by willows   in summer a cool conversing   traded
for memos typed at the Apparel Mart   to baskets sold
beside the bridge   their priceless wrinkled pits
brown-black nuts fallen at feet once bared to ripples   rainbow perch   a movement Darío can better catch

need for that his art   need his love
needed Love Field too   a where to land
& seek for him athletic fun   a higher flight than had on fleetest jets   a swimming hole for deeper dives than
dips on tollway drives   a where to buy
western boots for the skinny kid
right for walking streets can still recov-
er that magic word will trim shed blood
like a genii whisped
back inside an olym-
pic lamp overrubbed

     —1976

  ✴   ✴   ✴   ✴   ✴   ✴   ✴   ✴   ✴   ✴   ✴   ✴

DAVID RUSSELL
State Fair

From counties far and wide the people come
Bringing in pride the tokens of their labor,
Spreading their wares for all the world to see,
Vying for honors neighbor with proud neighbor;
Fruit that would tempt the palate of Croesus,
Grain that would grace the table of a king,
Wealth that the sweet rich soil of Texas
Has fashioned forth to make the quick heart sing.

With them they bring their music and their
      laughter,

For youth comes with them and the strength of
      mirth,
And men of good will walk in pride together
Because they know the blessings of the earth;
People who know a heritage of valor,
Joined in a bounty widely understood,
Thankful for all, and now come forth united
To gain a vision of tomorrow's good.

For even as they boast abundant harvest
And stroke their handiwork with rightful pride,
They turn their dreams from this admired be-
ginning
To richer dreams that will not be denied,

Knowing themselves as people in a pageant
That moves in splendor through a vast domain,
Ever increasing, till its golden bounty
Has made an Eden of this flowering plain.

    —1946

★   ★   ★   ★   ★   ★   ★   ★   ★   ★   ★   ★

FREDERICK TURNER
Texas Eclogues

ONE

Now there's a pause in the journey, the journey to carry the epic,
Carry the good news, the future, to those who have almost forgotten:
Episodes out of the story, not told because not important,
Not in the line of the argument, remembered nevertheless.
Consider the prince in his exile, his grief, his constant anxiety,
Constant inner euphoria; dreaming, addicted to dreaming,
Walking among the farmers, as a woodcutter earning his bread
Incognito, known only to one or two faithful disguised Counsellors,
Just so am I, the deposed one, the king hiding out in the country,

Mad duke, sly fox missing a foot from the trap, the escapist.
Just so I have been dreaming, plotting the means of my triumph,
Waiting in silent joy for the time of my fresh revelation,
Chuckling and waiting, the craziness sometimes too clear in my eyes, too
Obvious, seen in the scrap of mirror I packed in my exodus.

This is the landscape that nobody wants. It's my cup of rejection:
Driven to this unformed scraggly ignored backlot, this not-quite
Prairie, not-quite thicket, not even natural corner of
Texas, the hardscrabble left butt of a demoralized nation,
It is my choice and my pleasure to cherish this haphazard wilderness.
No, it's not even "wild." —it's a neglected product of artifice.
Come, let us walk by an improvised lakeshore, to be given a vision:
Beaches of black dust, beautiful white ghosts, this drowned forest.

TWO

I walk by Lavon Lake in the indian summer,
By the satiny-silver bones and skulls of the trees,
Where I find half-buried in crumbly sable gumbo
The great greenblack shell of a dead snapping turtle,
A tiny convolvulus, a violet-throated, enweaved
In its gaping orifice; a foam-rubber cushion choked
With the lake-silt, bearing a miniature garden of clubferns,
An ant's-nest, a gauzewinged azure surefooted dragonfly!
The caked and powdery beach is curiously pure:
Even the halfburied Budweiser gleams in the sungold,
And bronzy-black grasshoppers evolve to scavenge this newness,
And archaean footprints of North American marsupials
Cross with the dog's, the crane's thin cuneiform
Stalked by what must be the paws of a feral cat.
The seeds of willows have made their way here, have grown
Into little sallowy arbors of halfshadow green
Where the shore is spongy, prairie aquifers spring
To the surface, lagoons, with tussocks of buffalo-grass,
Groves of exotic bamboo, impede the footsteps.

And the lake, lit by the glowing skeletons, green
In the unnatural light of my sunglasses, turns to light blue
And mirrors, fantastic, the miniature hills of the shore,
Gold-brown in the early fall, with woodlands,
Radio-beacons, real-estate development.

How young the world is. I am its oldest inhabitant;
I was there at its white condensation, I am here, I shiver,
I hear overhead the whimpering whoop of the geese,
Two-year-old ghosts of this, the new dispensation,
In their plunge southward over the edge of the planet.
They do not know where they are going; I drink them,
Swallow their great raggedy flightline into
The inner sky of my spirit, the divine southland
That dreams in the web of the human software, the fold
That the shepherd has made by the side of the still waters.
And the sky is so blue! The outlines but not the substance
Of brilliant clouds sometimes appear in its firmament,
deflecting the sunrays to cast a shadow of azure
Over the breezed, hazy perfection of heaven.
This place of bones is a province of ancient Pangaea;
I am the large land mammal of the Pleistocene,
My food is the turbulence caused by the jut of consciousness
Into the flow of world-information, the swirl of spirit
Boiling about the point where nature, transfigured,
Breaks and shivers into the glow of the supernatural.

    —2000

* * * * * * * * * * * *

JACK MYERS
The Gift

Remember Father's Day, the banner says.
But I can't give my father what he wants
much less name it, so I get him a golf machine
that pops the ball right back.

If I can't give him what he wants
I can get him what seems wrong.
It's the thought that counts, he'd say,
not having caught the exact misses
I sent past him into interstellar space.

I'm telling my wife how she looks super-good
in this flouncy purple maternity suit,
though in truth it looks like her behind
is in front, when I suddenly think
I'm going to be a father! and I remember
my own two kids who don't live with me anymore
and I get quiet in order to receive their thoughts.

But instead I think about those poor Black kids
I took for a ride through White North Dallas
and how one little six-year-old beauty
leaned over my shoulder and shouted to the wind,
"How do you get to live like this?"

　　　—1986

*   *   *   *   *   *   *   *   *   *   *   *

BRIAN CLEMENTS
Historia

Forty degrees from yesterday's argument for sun,
Bradford pear and daffodils fooled into bloom
　　　　(Here they call them buttercups:
　　　　the asphodel of Homer,
　　　　Dr. Williams's green for love),
the swimming pool a mirror of pin oaks
pitiful with leaves like lost notes, leaves like afterthoughts
　　　of the wind,
hardly four hours since the first signs of drizzle
　　　patterned my windshield
like news from another world, undecipherable,

223

the first day of March sends weak signals from my breath
ahead to the places I'm going, where someone is looking
        for smoke.
The troubles in Ireland have quietened for now,
and the voice that comes through the static and rain
        from the BBC
half-sings of corporate bail out, investment disaster
two days after the Dow crossed 4,000;
culprit suspected of sailing Pacific.
According to this side, something has happened
        in Chechnya
that we can't understand, an unexpected uprising
like spontaneous combustion of the brain,
the body confused, flailing to find its way back
        to the world.
Meanwhile, I drive to work, looking for signs
to tell me where I am and where to go,
sorting through street names and arrows like messages
        from the dead,
the rapid report of an assault rifle echoing off the windows,
my speakers screaming like a woman who sees
        her daughter shot,
exactly like that. My wife is at work in West Dallas
where the second largest housing project in the nation

is being demolished. Two blocks from her school,
the abandoned site of a lead smelting plant
smolders like Berlin's Wall. Nearby, the Trinity River
divides the projects from Commerce, Royal, Main,
a little Rio Grande. I would like to think there is a story,
terrible and rational, which explains why, crossing LBJ
into white North Dallas, downshifting past a Swiss
Bank disguised as a school, I think of Oak Cliff
        and The Bottoms,
their names darkened like Wounded Knee,

their cottonwoods and live oaks thick as bison.
Perhaps the Mayor could spin a respectable parable—
        why this city sprang up
like pine trees stuffed with birds of paradise
        in the middle of the prairie,
why this early in March the low supply of sun
        off bronze towers
translates into travel written plain in the low waves
        of half-choked White Rock Lake,
why the wood duck's semaphore means go
and this drizzle reflects the airborne dust, a vision
of vision's shroud falling evenly on the living streets
        and the dead.
Near work, I look forward to smoke—the physical plants

repairing, construction crews churning out houses
like missionaries sending out scouts
        into the undiscovered lands.
Behind my apartment, a facsimile of paradise
about to overtake a chain-link fence gives refuge and oasis
        to Mexican
birds fled north for summer. When I get home, I will open
        the blinds
and watch for the pileated woodpecker
which hammers a blackjack for ants outside my window.
He is there for maybe half a day, feasting and resting
half upside-down, alert to grackles outside my window
        at work,
the grackles make their racket for hours, strut and pose
on the electric lines that connect me to a net
of information I hack at each day, looking for clues
in machine language, in databases of cyberspeak,
in Spanish, in sign. I'm looking in the woodpecker's
        dumb Morse,
in the mistaken tongue of ancient asphodel,
in the prattle of pin oaks and the interstate's gibberish

for a story one could live by without drowning
        out the news,
no need to search billboards, *The Times*, radio dial, sky

for the key to a message no one gets.

        —1996

* * * * * * * * * * * *

ROBERT TRAMMELL
Light Forms

Batting averages
flashed on
the tallest
buildings in
Dallas for
Oak Cliff Benny
who died.

An old drunk.

Why did
I not
give him my
History of the Texas League?

        —1971

* * * * * * * * * * * *

JAS. MARDIS
Perseverance
(Oak Cliff, Texas   Remembrance #12)

   When he was drowning
having found the city seaweed: algae
     in that overflow creek behind the paper plant

filled with waters: rain water, polluted street run-off water, chemical leaked waters from
        the paper plant

    run now to a clear strain over the rocks and down through the cutting blades of grass
until it found the rebar jutting like dreadlocks out of Mother Earth

and spun round the spirals of that metal before falling finally
 drop and burping slivers at a time
into the depth   hungry dirt pit from years ago

    he did not think to kick free of the heavy jeans: Levi's
still so new that the blue dye begged itself free in spools through the cool
Summer waters

    he did not think to hold on to his savior's grace
slip into the calm that prayer brings
        in moments like this that demand control and patience

    he did not think to shut his open, useless mouth beneath the waters
that he knew from swimming   *always* filled in the gaps
        and so he swallowed bellyfuls of the unknown, bitter-sweet liquid

before I could reach down with the fallen tree limb
    that he had to get naked to climb out on
  because of the snapping turtles pulling, holding on to the jean legs

and he was like a dog then
  pulled from the depths of some new despair and left whimpering
 and shitting on the bank of the creek paying some near-death dues

    while I stripped down to my underwear and went into that safe danger
to claim the dignity of his heavy pants
        that would almost dry   waiting for him to stop regurgitating that water

and when we did finally   climb the rock wall back toward home
he stopped three times to beg me to keep his swimmer's baptism secret
    and each time I said, "yes"

   we walked the longest way home
and he did not think about the legacy of being saved by me
    and like in the movies: he now owed a small portion of his new life
    or that he could have easily paid me back in a similar moment of strength
when my sister came to his window after hearing my twelve-year-old's secret
    and wanting to see it for herself that he was all right

   he was not thinking about the short distance between him and death and me and the limb
when he lay my sister beneath the blue light above his bed
    later that same night
when they were both sixteen, safe and he was filling with sperm that could
 indeed,

swim

   —*2002*

★   ★   ★   ★   ★   ★   ★   ★   ★   ★   ★   ★

TIM SEIBLES
What It Comes Down To
for James Mardis

Eyes shining in that half-sane stare,
T-shirts ripped with sweat—Dewey and Zack
one-on-one in Zang Park: a second ago
they climbed the air, new Nikes
laced loose, dark blue, stole three feet of sky,
and Dewey spit, "Gaah-damn!"
when his finger-roll spun off the rim.

August spins the breeze to wool, the late sun
melts like butter. Somebody says, "Zack gonna,

Zack gonna bust the bottom out now,"
and a car radio thumps bass, but the real
beat is a basketball banging concrete
and two tall brothers blowing hard.

All summer they'd been *talking that talk*
about who had the moves, who ruled the lane,
who had the angel's kiss on the shot—
this was the championship of the park.

Just one more bucket, just one sweet J
and Zack goes home with the game
like a jewel in his heart. "Yo, Dew,"
yells a boy with a penny's worth of hair,
"you know Z ain' nothin' but money
lef' side a'the key." Across the street

three men play poker: one hums
a slow run from a blues and, seeing
the two boys glistening sweat, remembers
when he could glide the air, could
"damn near rub his nose on the rim,"
those summers spent under the trees
cooling between games, how the fellas
used to call him "Sky," and the girls
used to call him sweet—right there,
right there in the park   while

the ball bounces back   back   and back
with Dewey flexed low, one hand on Zack
the other pawing toward the dancing rock.
Night makes its move, its smooth black hand
palming the earth.

Sometimes, everything you want
comes down to one shot, one perfect play

on a street where forty years
can steal your legs and leave you holding
two wrong cards. Sometimes
the only thing that makes sense
is the right kiss of fingertips
against a ball too sweaty to grip,
when your body aches like a wish
above the city and a splash of fire
opens your eyes. All over the Southside
brothers lace their sneaks and smolder
for a little luck to see by: Zack

                              fakes right
                  skips the pill left   spins
                  rises   pumps hangs
                        and falls into the dark, shooting.

—*1992*

* * * * * * * * * * * *

DAVE OLIPHANT
Denton

like every other place
is Janus-faced
take its dreamed of campus Kenton blessed
near where an only brother bled to death
on his final trip from picking up a remaining group
of Green Beret reservists the last to parachute

delivered them safely then flipped his truck
on a narrow curve   his stomach crushed
between the driver's seat & the steering wheel
have grieved for years with that lonely feel
of his young life slipping away

three months after graduation two weeks before his
                    wedding day
talked Aunt Sis into taking a pilgrimage to its
                    hallowed sounds
in a summer heat to its celebrated tree-cooled grounds
a home to festivals a division of Columbia Records pressed
a where to buy this treasured album has stood the test
though so scratchy & filled with cuts by imitative combos
a true aficionado would not confess he even knows

much less still listens to this Euel Box Quintet
on "Toddlin'" or "Woodchoppers Ball"   the only regret
never to have caught them in live performance
here in this town for that final chance
for afterwards the valve-trombonist-leader would graduate
see his sax & trumpet his bass & drums all go their separate

ways to public schools where jazz is seldom heard
to some a discouraging word
few on the road with a Herman or Stan a record date with those
neither first nor last chair with East or West Coast studios
can only hope wherever they went
each made music on his chosen instrument

their talents might have been or maybe not
the equal of a fellow alum's like Giuffre whom none forgot
from here Jimmy had gone to join those idols' bands
to star with Shorty Rogers on Atlantic's *Martians*
Come Back   his name mentioned on liner notes
with the likes of a Mingus   his tune set off in quotes

his famous "Four Brothers"   left now with not even one
on the outskirts forever of marriage & the job he'd won
never to share with his bride-
to-be a game of golf at the Country Club laid out beside

the Trinity River   to practice on his trap set for another gig
as drummer to roughnecks off an oilfield rig

—1995

* * * * * * * * * * * *

Martha Elizabeth
On the Porch—Denton, Texas

Let us live the slow way,
watching the light
while the rail-posts shadow us
with lengthening stripes.
The hours have our own momentum, a pace
logical as cloth.
Fossils from a local creek,
and stones from travels, unpolished.
Cowskull, cholla skeleton.
An oak stump, partly hollow,
where a glass leaves rings.

No more movement than to lift a wet glass.
Skin glossed with sweat.
Cool shininess
like a mirror glancing back at the sun.

Let us turn the rule of time
to pleasure, the hours
measured by design,
tailored for fullness.

Taillights blaze and dim
to the west horizon avenue.

A wasp returns to the stump and enters it,
filling the hole where the heart was,
making itself at home.

     —1995

  ✳   ✳   ✳   ✳   ✳   ✳   ✳   ✳   ✳   ✳   ✳   ✳

ROBERT TRAMMELL
After Hours

after the Country Tavern & all the bars in Gregg County
were closed, we headed back to Tyler
with a bottle of whiskey looking for
a Private Club, a party, some girls, a friend, anything.
The Galaxy top down I decided
to trick Clinton while he drove I climbed
over into the backseat, counting on
him being so drunk he wouldn't notice. I crept
out onto the trunk & he still didn't see
me. I thought I
had a good hold on the back edge
of the convertible top well. He would think
I'd disappeared into the night right
out of the front seat just vanished in a drunken cloud at
60 miles an hour but my hand slipped. He looked for me &
I *was* gone. He glanced into the rearview mirror in time
to see me crashflipping, rolling
head over heels down the highway away from his Galaxy &
wondered where I'd stop maybe back in Kilgore. I landed
sitting up in the gravel by the side of the road. I checked
to see if my new Christmas watch was broke, wiped the blood
off my face wiped off the watch which
kept on ticking.

Later when it was time for the cops they said: What
in the world happened to him?

Clinton said: He fell down some stairs so
they arrested me and let him go.

I met a guy in jail who said he'd lost his knife.
I asked him where.
He said: In the last man who asked me that question. I asked
him: Do you want the top or bottom bunk?

   —1989

* * * * * * * * * * * * *

BRENDA BLACK WHITE
Tolly Masters
(*Tale from Red River County*)

Tolly Masters sat on the porch
smoking his pipe,
listening to the hogs' high-pitched squealing.
Reba, his sandy-haired, seventeen-year-old
daughter was ripe,
the midwife said, and was in hard labor. Kate
Masters was kneeling
beside the bed asking for mercy and forgiveness.
She prayed
the child be stillborn. It wasn't.
She bade
Tolly come to the kitchen table where it lay
kicking on its back
flailing its arms, crying lustily. It was
healthy and black.
So, Reba had lied. Tolly remembered the night
he'd seen Jim
in the yard and Reba slipping into the house.
It was him.
Well, Reba was ruined. And the rest of them
would be disgraced.
But, by God, Tolly could salvage his family's

decency. He embraced
the newborn, still wet from the womb, and
carried it down the hill.
Returning to the porch he nodded, satisfied
at the old sow's greedy squeal.

   —1988

* * * * * * * * * * * * *

KARLE WILSON BAKER
Nacogdoches Speaks

I was The Gateway. Here they came and passed,
The homespun centaurs with their arms of steel
And taut heart-strings: wild wills, who thought to
        deal
Bare-handed with jade Fortune, tracked at last
Out of her silken lairs into the vast
Of a man's world. They passed, but still I feel
The dent of hoof, the print of booted heel,
Like prick of spurs—the shadows that they cast.

I do not vaunt their valors, or their crimes:
I tell my secrets only to some lover,
Some taster of spilled wine and scattered musk.
But I have not forgotten; and, sometimes,
The things that I remember rise, and hover
A sharper perfume, in some April dusk.

   —1929

* * * * * * * * * * * * *

Roger Jones
Strata

In these wrinkles, bared
when the county gouged and blew
this blacktop road from sheer
hillside, we see the story
of our own ground etched
in lines of red iron, nickel,
sandstone. Like stripes
on a flag, these colors
unfurled to the warp
and writhe of the world's
upheaval, thousands
of eons' pressure crinkling
above and below sea, long
before any human mind
came near to set it all down.
Now, the sun's work done,
slide and buckle of earth's
distortions slowed to faint
immeasurable crawl,
it bares itself on a cold
sunny day in mid-December,
the shady face of a hill beside
a roadside in eastern Texas,
capped with deciduous trees,
underbrush, deer run,
with fence posts and half-
rotted wire, and one crumbling
wooden sign warning off hunters.
Here, this close to home
where we have stopped,
an oak root cants over

the coppered gully, an ooze
of water trickles down
the stone face, staining
the rock with a green slur,
wandering down the visible
ages of earth's early times,
which read now like the wide-
lined pages of tablets
where, as children, holding
pencils big as clubs,
we shaped the wobbly letters
of our first alphabet.

—1993

Susan Wood
Carnation, Lily, Lily, Rose

Mornings we walked on air, moments
our stilts cut a wide path
through clouds of grass. I think
of a grandfather who lived by his hands
carefully planing the boards to make
those wooden legs. He knew children want to be
lifted up. We wanted to rise above our small

selves, as though knowledge equaled
height. We'd climb the body's ladder any way
we could, even scale a tree's green cliff
to watch a pair of lovers say goodnight. He was
taller, and stronger, but when she raised her mouth
to his each face opened to the other
like a door. Late that night we climbed out,

forbidden, onto the second-story roof, as high
as you could go in Commerce, Texas.

For a while, it was enough just to sit out
our secret, everyone in town asleep
but us. Down below, in the dark, the garden
ran wild, like the one in Sargent's painting
of two girls, who don't know anyone
is watching. From that distance, among flowers
and the names of flowers, it's what the eye
picks out. Their white dresses, lilies-
of-the-field, all that roots them
amid such overwhelming growth. What rooted us?
High in our high house, everything
seemed possible, that even

if we held our breaths, the flowers
would go on blossoming.

—1990

* * * * * * * * * * * *

CYD ADAMS
River Road

Humid July drive-in nights
we swigged Webber's root beer,
the 50 cent gallon jug beaded cold-sweaty,
scrapped among our selfish selves
for the greasy paper bag
of burnt, salty popcorn,
and frayed the Belair's backseat
slick and sagging.

Huge Sabine mosquitoes whined and dined
on restless sweaty flesh
as 40-foot heroes rode Technicolor horses
down from the clouds of the hills,
and over and over recycled the *Iliad,*
adapted Armageddon.

They sculpted our absolutes,
boldly strode the streets of our dreams;

and we left Dirgin,
left the work, the sameness,
left the dim kitchen,
the hot, crowded beds in the room added on,
the cold water tub on the floor
that buckled,
shrugged off the seedticks,
the cattle and their screw worms,
the coiled water moccasins
truculent and still,
and pushed our horizons
out beyond the walls of the trees.

> *—1993*

* * * * * * * * * * * * *

ALICE EWING VAIL
Coons in the Corn

Had me a corn patch, back o' my place,
In the Big Thicket, off Coushatta Trace;
Dogs started yappin', an' wife hollered,
    "Lynn!"
Them coons is raidin' our corn agin!"

I waked up cussin' them coons in the corn;
I grabbed me my gun an' my powder horn.
Grabbed me a pine knot out o' the fire.
Coons kited up a tree, higher an' higher.

Raised up my knot, an' what did I see?
Coons' eyes shinin' like a Christmas tree!

Coon eye candles! It amazed me so,
I felt like prayin', and I let 'em go.

—1979

* * * * * * * * * * * *

JERRY BRADLEY
How the Big Thicket Got Smaller

First they got the panther,
then the bear.
The pigeon flocks
went with the wild timber,
and oil,
plain crude,
drove out dens of all sorts.
Roads did in the plants.

There are still some trees
though now they stand
in a slaughterhouse of saws,
and iron rigs,
black as poachers' kettles,
bob like chained birds
drinking from the earth.
A life ordered and lubed,
hard as blacktop,
a tax supported legacy
for the mechanical world
where the ivorybill
once tapped its confused code

and big cats screamed
like frightened women in the dark.

    —1991

＊　　＊　　＊　　＊　　＊　　＊　　＊　　＊　　＊　　＊　　＊　　＊

    JAMES CODY
    Big Thicket Words

Full Moon
Rises
over tops
of Pines.
Yellow
from the red
left
by the Sun
just passed
clear
from the woods
on our right
from the car.
In the East
Ikemetubbe
rising
from the fog
over the lake.
White
Sky.

    —1976

＊　　＊　　＊　　＊　　＊　　＊　　＊　　＊　　＊　　＊　　＊　　＊

6

Love is a Wild Assault

Let me say right off, watch out for the young man with heroic face and hungry hands—with the look of lost dreams in his eyes and a great need.

Elithe Hamilton Kirkland

Mirabeau B. Lamar
Carmelita

I

O Carmelita, know ye not
        for whom all hearts are pining?
And know ye not, in Beauty's sky,
        The brightest planet shining?
Then learn it now—for thou art she,
Thy nation's jewel, born to be
By all beloved, but most by me—
       O Donna Carmelita!

II

But woe is me thy love to lose,
        Apart from thee abiding;
Between us roars a gloomy stream,
        Our destiny dividing.
That stream with blood incarnadined
Flows from thy nation's erring mind,
And rolls with ruin to thy kind,
       O Donna Carmelita!

III

'Tis mine, while floating on the tide,
        To stick to love and duty;
I draw my sabre on the foe,
        I strike my harp to beauty;
And who shall say the soldier's wrong,
Who, while he battles with the strong,
Still softens war with gentle song,
       O Donna Carmelita!

IV

I soon shall seek the battle-field,
  Where Freedom's flag is waving—
My Texas comrades by my side,
  All perils madly braving;
I only grieve to think each blow,
That vengeance bids the steel bestow,
Must make thee mine eternal foe,
  O Donna Carmelita!

V

Full well I know thy pride will spurn
  The brightest wreaths I bring thee;
Full well I know thou wilt not heed,
  The sweetest songs I sing thee;
Yet, all despite thy scorn and hate,
Despite the thousand ills of fate,
I still my soul must dedicate—
  To Donna Carmelita!

VI

Then fare the well, dear, lovely one—
  May happiness attend thee;
Ten thousand harps exalt thy name,
  Ten thousand swords defend thee;
And when the sod is on my breast,
My harp and sabre both at rest,
May thee and thine be greatly blest,
  O Donna Carmelita!

—1857

JERRY BRADLEY
For a Texas Beauty

Wherever you sit
the Alamo lends
      its shape to each breast
and rescues a race, a flag;
eyes blue as bonnets,
cleaner than all the rivers
in this state.

      Consider this just a theory
of liberation then, a canon
where a morning in San Antonio
becomes a mission, a monument
to revolutionary love
which rises for you now
like the cottonwood moon.

     —1991

  ★   ★   ★   ★   ★   ★   ★   ★   ★   ★   ★   ★   ★

FRANK DESPREZ
Lasca

I want free life, and I want fresh air;
And I sigh for the canter after the cattle,
The crack of the whips like shots in a battle,
The mellay of horns and hoofs and heads
That wars and wrangles and scatters and spreads;
The green beneath and the blue above,
The dash and danger, and life and love.
And Lasca!

      Lasca used to ride
On a mouse-gray mustang close to my side,

With blue *serape* and bright-belled spur;
I laughed with joy as I looked at her.
Little knew she of books or of creeds;
An *Ave Maria* sufficed her needs;
Little she cared, save to be by my side,
To ride with me, and ever to ride,
From San Saba's shore to Lavaca's tide.

She was as bold as the billows that beat,
She was as wild as the breezes that blow;
From her little head to her little feet
She was swayed by her suppleness to and fro
By each gust of passion; a sapling pine,
That grows on the edge of a Kansas bluff,
And wars with the wind when the weather is rough,
Is like this Lasca, this love of mine.
She would hunger that I might eat,
Would take the bitter and leave the sweet;
But once, when I made her jealous for fun,
At something I'd whispered, or looked, or done,
One Sunday in San Antonio,
To a glorious girl on the Alamo,
She drew from her garter a dear little dagger,
And—sting of a wasp!—it made me stagger!
An inch to the left, or an inch to the right,
And I shouldn't be maundering here to-night'
But she sobbed, and, sobbing, so swiftly bound
Her torn *rebosa* about the wound,
That I quite forgave her. Scratches don't count
　　　In Texas, down by the Rio Grande.

Her eye was brown—a deep, deep brown—
Her hair was darker than her eye;
And something in her smile and frown,
Curled crimson lip and instep high,
Showed that there ran in each blue vein,

Mixed with the milder Aztec strain,
The vigorous vintage of old Spain.
She was alive in every limb
With feeling, to the finger-tips;
And when the sun is like a fire,
And sky one shining, soft sapphire,
One does not drink in little sips.

The air was heavy, the night was hot,
I sat by her side, and forgot—forgot
The herd that were taking their rest,
Forgot that the air was close oppressed,
That the Texas norther comes sudden and soon,
In the dead of the night, or the blaze of the noon—
That once let the herd at its breath take fright,
Nothing on earth can stop its flight;
And woe to the rider, and woe to the steed,
Who falls in front of their mad stampede!

Was that thunder? I grasped the cord
Of my swift mustang without a word.
I sprang to the saddle, and she clung behind.
Away! on a hot chase down the wind!
And never was fox-hunt half so hard.
And never was steed so little spared;
For we rode for our lives.   You shall hear how we fared
        In Texas, down by the Rio Grande.

The mustang flew, and we urged him on;
There was one chance left, and you have but one.
Halt! jump to the ground, and shoot your horse;
Crouch under his carcass, and take your chance;
And if the steers in their frantic course
Don't batter you both to pieces at once,
You may thank your star; if not, good-bye.
To the quickening kiss and the long-drawn sigh,

And the open air and the open sky,
            In Texas, down by the Rio Grande!

The cattle gained on us, and, just as I felt
For my old six-shooter behind in my belt,
Down came the mustang, and down came we,
Clinging together, and—what was the rest?
A body that spread itself on my breast,
Two arms that shielded my dizzy head,
Two lips that hard on my lips were pressed;
Then came thunder in my ears,
As over us urged the sea of steers,
Blows that beat blood into my eyes;
And when I could rise—
Lasca was dead!

I gouged out a grave a few feet deep,
And there in Earth's arms I laid her to sleep;
And there she is lying, and no one knows,
And the summer shines and the winter snows;
For many a day the flowers have spread
A pall of petals over her head;
And the little gray hawk hangs aloft in the air,
And the sly coyote trots here and there,
And the black snake glides and glitters and slides
Into a rift in a cotton-wood tree;
And the buzzard sails on,
And comes and is gone,
Stately and still like a ship at sea;
And I wonder why I do not care
For the things that are like the things that were.
Does my heart lie buried there
            In Texas, down by the Rio Grande?

—1882

JACK E. MURPHY
I Dreamt of Lasca
(Inspired by the poem "Lasca" by Frank Desprez)

I camped one night in Lasca Land,
Not far from the storied Rio Grande.
I bedded down by a water hole
And laid my head on my worn bed roll,
    And thought of Lasca.

Lulled to sleep by murmuring trees
And twinkling stars of the Pleiades
I felt secure with my pinto near
He'd sound alarm if he felt fear;
    I dreamt of Lasca.

She walked to me through the river mist;
Her raven hair was moonlight kissed.
She wore serape and bright-belled spur.
Just as her lover had told of her.
    Yes, it was Lasca.

We sat and talked as the bright moon paled,
While gray owls screeched and coyotes wailed;
Her eyes grew sad as she talked to me
About her love from across the sea
    I wept with Lasca.

When I awake with the rising sun
I looked for tracks but I found none;
But she'd been there I have no doubt;
Her vibrant spirit seemed all about—
    The spirit of Lasca.

I shall return to Lasca Land
Down by the flowing Rio Grande.
I'll camp again by the water hole.
And lay my head on my worn bedroll.

And wait for Lasca.

—1983

* * * * * * * * * * * * *

PAT LITTLEDOG
love letter sent south

yes I am a border crosser
extra out of ordinary
legal into illegality
me into your skin
bringing you back
in a bottle
with a worm on the bottom

all those borders
don't you love to cross those waters?
listen to the moon flow
in the day-glo
souvenir stands for
a gringo

and I tell you right out
that I love to smuggle in
a little contraband
and have learned how
a word or smile or invisible hand
will find the bridge that
will cross whatever

yes north and south do
like to mate
if you don't believe it
show me where
one starts being the other

just take a look at
these two desert lands
stretching lips out to kiss
the Rio Grande
their banks sometimes
even touching each other
oh lover lands
aren't you embracing
under that river?

there are so many borders
and i can't even see one
without some education
or reminder from authority
that will make a map reality
with a scrap of paper or
gun in a holster or
some electrocutional wire
made just for us
still that kiss kiss kiss
just naturally comes across
where north meets south and
love is boss

—2002

* * * * * * * * * * * * *

LEXIE DEAN ROBERTSON
Memorabilia

Five things glimpsed unexpectedly
Have filled my heart with singing gladness:
A sudden hillside lake of Texas bluebonnets;
A winding forest roadway in the golden haze
Of an autumnal sunset;
An ice-sheeted apple orchard,
Dazzling under a brilliant moon;
A slanting line of nile-washed turquoise sky
After an April shower;
And your love-awakened eyes.

—1928

* * * * * * * * * * * * *

WALTER McDONALD
All the Old Songs

I never knew them all, just hummed
and thrummed my fingers with the radio,
driving a thousand miles to Austin.
Her arms held all the songs I needed.
Our boots kept time with fiddles
and the charming sobs of blondes,

the whine of steel guitars
sliding us down in deer-hide chairs
when jukebox music was over.
Sad music's on my mind tonight
in a jet high over Dallas, earphones
on channel five. A lonely singer,

dead, comes back to beg me,
swearing in my ears she's mine,

rhymes set to music which make
complaints seem true. She's gone
and others like her, leaving their songs
to haunt us. Letting down through clouds

I know who I'll find tonight at home,
the same woman faithful to my arms
as she was those nights in Austin
when the world seemed like a jukebox,
our boots able to dance forever,
our pockets full of coins.

—1993

SHERRY CRAVEN
Garden City Diner: Loving Back

There's a diner in Garden City
where a white house used to stand,
a white house turned to a store,
then turned to empty and to nothing
but a vacant lot on which a hastily built,
cheap diner sits today, invisible to the cars on Highway 158,
hurrying to someplace else, someplace bigger, more important.

But if you look hard enough you can see
through the film of thirty years' haze
the old white clapboard store with the hand-painted
sign announcing it is owned by "Roy."

There a white Ford pickup out front, and
a cowboy with pale blue eyes, like a Scotsman,
and a white forehead from years of wearing a hat,
called Son driving. Son wanted me to have a horse, my size,
he said, for a small city girl like me. An Arabian seemed fit.
Had to be white for his little girl.

I drive on through the one stop light
that makes an X in Garden City
where the two highways cross,
but in the rearview mirror I see my past more clearly
than I see the future through my windshield.

I never was very good at riding that small
white Arabian, but I got damned good at
loving Son for loving me.

 —2002

 *   *   *   *   *   *   *   *   *   *   *   *

FAY M. YAUGER
County Fair

I got me dressed for going down
   To Teague, the County Seat,
With half my savings on my back,
   And half upon my feet.

My father said, "Be careful, son."
   My mother said, "Be good."
My sister said, "Bring me a ring
   The way a brother should."

The leaves were in the ditches
   And haze was on the ridge
The morning I stepped through our fence
   And crossed the trestle bridge.

Oh, chimney-pots were smoking.
    And flags were in the air
When I came heeling into Teague
   To see the County Fair.

I stopped a peddler-woman
  And bought a box of corn
That had a small tin bird inside
  For blowing like a horn.

I guessed at pebbles in a jar
  And had my fortune told
And learned that I would meet a girl
  That day, and find her cold.

The cards were right, for very soon
  I crowded through a swirl
Of people near a platform
  To watch a dancing girl.

And sure I lost my senses
  Right there upon the street
From seeing how she tossed her hair
  And shook her little feet.

And "Never will I take a wife
  To share my roof and bed
Or spend my gold, unless it be
  This dancing girl," I said.

But she—She looked me thru and thru
  When I had caught her glance
And said, "I think the hicks have come
  To clutter up our dance."

And then—"Get on, my fellow,
  And see the cattle shows,"
She said, and snapped her finger-tips
  Just underneath my nose.

I got me from her curling mouth,
  And from her scornful eyes,
And never stopped to ask if I
  Had won the guessing prize.

I cut the miles to home by half,
  Straight up a mountain side,
And "Hope to God I never see
  That girl again," I lied.

My father let me in at dusk,
  My mother looked distraught,
My sister lay all night and wept
  The ring I had not bought.

My father questioned me of mares,
  My mother spoke of lace,
But I had not a word for them—
  I'd only seen a face.

They tell me now I am no good
  For sending to a fair,
And do not know that only part
  Of me came back from there.

They do not know my hands are here
  And here my heavy feet,
But that my heart is miles away—
  In Teague, the County Seat.

—1935

Brenda Black White
Country Boy, City Girl

She was from Fort Worth, just out of high school
and going to college in the fall,
he and his pal Tom were working the
Johnson place. He was broad shouldered and tall

and brown as a walnut from working the hay
fields six days a week in the Texas sun.
She was strawberry parfait, pink and white ribbon.
Tom told him, "Look here Frank, don't jump the gun

and get carried away by the charms of a city girl.
You're country bred and country raised,
and you don't know nothing 'bout what it's
like to live each other's ways."

"No use talking, I'm hell bent to have her.
She's different. Not like country girls."
"That's just my point. Too different. You'll
never make a paired team. You're worlds

apart in experience. It'll be as hard for
her to live on a farm as for you to live in town."
"We're getting married Saturday. Will you be my
best man?" Tom grinned. "Frank Foster, you hound

dog, you haven't heard a word I've said.
Yes, I'll stand up with you." And so
they were married by the justice of the peace
at the court house in Baird, united for a life of woe.

—1988

CHARLOTTE RENK
Mistletoe Kills

Miss Nettie was mystery to me at nine
her hat brim trimmed by a blue cotton band
that snugged seven red-tipped matches and
seasonal sprigs of bloom against the straw—
wisteria, azalea, dogwood, honeysuckle, rose.
Mama said, "Nettie works magic on whatever grows."
"Minor miracles" in sandy clay hills,
claimed or framed by live oak and pine—
Cherokee County, universe of mine.

Her "Just as I Ams without one plea"
seemed somehow real to a kid like me.
One Sunday, she wore mistletoe tucked in the band,
and I dared to ask if she'd ever kissed a man;
she frowned at my dare, and she began to rasp,
"Mistletoe kills the tree it clasps."
Her eyes dazed distant and somewhere wise.

We'd pass her place, a shack in the shade:
I thought of the garden and the bow she made
as her hat bent to shoulders that also bent
in a semi-circled loop leaning on the hoe
surrounding certain silence and sweat she spent.
"Woa now, Lizzie, you slack-brained nag;
Hold that row! Now come on back!"

At ten, I never saw Nettie's hat again,
nor heard her bellow at Lizzie, her friend.
I saw her stable lean as we drove past.
Her yard grew lilies and larkspurs; her garden,
bull nettle and Johnson grass. And then I saw
the oak, claimed by mistletoe. Somehow, that
seemed important; now I think I know.

—1994

LILLIAN WRIGHT
West Texas Suicide

Jim went north to Maine
      And brought a wife back.
The days were dry that summer,
      The plains burned black.

She pined for fresh green hills
      And cool blue skies.
She looked for rain clouds every day
      With wide, sad eyes.

The drouth stayed on and on
      Day after fevered day.
She grew to weep hysterically
      Or kneel and pray,

Until she was too weak, and then
      She lay like dead.
Jim said he'd send her home
      When she could leave her bed.

The long spell broke at last.
      The lake filled up that night.
Jim slept, but her dark eyes
      Were wildly bright

With beauty all unbearable.
      She left the little room,
And in the blinding pour of rain
      She seemed to lift and bloom.

The miracle of water
        Made her body ache.
She threw her arms wide to the sky
        And walked into the lake.

    —*1937*

＊　＊　＊　＊　＊　＊　＊　＊　＊　＊　＊　＊

SANDRA CISNEROS
I Am on My Way to Oklahoma to Bury the Man
I Nearly Left My Husband For

Your name doesn't matter.
I love you.
We loved.
The years

        I waited
by the river for your pickup
truck to find me. Footprints
scattered in the yellow sand.
Husband, mother-
in-law, kids wondering
where I'd gone.

        You wouldn't
the years I begged. Would
the years I wouldn't. Only
one of us had sense at a time.

I won't see you again.

I guess life presents you
choices and you choose. Smarter
over the years. Oh smarter.
The sensible thing smarting

over the years, the sensible
thing to excess, I guess.
My life—deed I have
done to artistic extreme—I
drag you with me. Must wake
early. Ride north tomorrow.
Send you off. Are you fine?
I think of you often, friend,
and fondly.

     —1994

    ✶   ✶   ✶   ✶   ✶   ✶   ✶   ✶   ✶   ✶   ✶   ✶

R. G. Vliet
Penny Ballad of Elvious Ricks
(c. 1927)

Elvious Ricks grew up in sunlight
and shade of a hackberry tree.
He ate his mama's spoonbread
and played on his daddy's knee.

Sometimes on the way to school
and sometimes in the night
Elvious saw a certain something
that gave him a terrible fright.

It was an angel singing
in a black-branched tree.
The angel said to Elvious,
"You must follow me."

Elvious went to high school.
He wore a black bow tie.
He parted his hair down the middle
and never thought to die.

The angel sat on the clock
of the Stockman's City Bank
Where Elvious came to work
with his lunch in a sack.

The angel hovered by the steps
of the Ranchman's Family Hotel
when Elvious came from work
in time for the supper bell.

The sun went by high in the summers
and down low in the fall.
Elvious' hair grew thinner.
He slept with his face to the wall.

There's a girl in this story
with black, bobbed hair
wore a white dress to her graduation,
a white dress on her bier,

wore a white dress to the dance hall
down by the riverside
and to spark in her daddy's flivver
where she and Elvious died.

Her boyfriend caught them spooning
and shot them one dark night.
Elvious fell out of the left door,
Lorena fell out of the right.

They buried her in Comfort, Texas,
and Elvious in Privilege,
stone lamb over her grave,
stone angel over his.

—1980

Fay M. Yauger
Planter's Charm

Slowly Nan the widow goes
Up and down the furrowed rows.

Corn-bags chafing her waist, her hips,
As the kernels fall from her finger-tips:

> *"One for the buzzard—*
> *One for the crow—*
> *One to rot—and—*
> *One to grow!"*

Once she had dreamed (but not of late)
Of another life, a kinder fate:

Of quiet streets in foreign towns,
Of dancing tunes, and men, and gowns.

But all her dreams were dreamed before
Tim Slade drew rein outside her door.

"One for the buzzard"—Tim was dead
With a bullet hole through his reckless head.

Tim with his cheating ways and words,
Marked from the first for the wart-necked birds,

Tim who had left her sorrowing days,
The farm, and a pair of sons to raise.

Lon was her first-born: "One for the crow!"
Where had he gone? She'd never know

For there was a price upon his head—
"A chip off the old block," people said.

Then "One to rot!" Her thoughts go back,
Like hunting-dogs on an easy track,

To the girl she's been before she came
To love Tim Slade and bear his name.

And something as stinging and hot as sand
Slides down her cheek and strikes her hand

And she sees the field through a shimmering blur
For what has marriage meant to her

But a heel of bread in a roofless hut,
Or a crawling course through a mouldy rut?

As if in answer, over the ditch
A child comes riding a willow switch:

Her second born, of whom no one
Could say in truth, "His father's son."

For his chin is firm, and his mouth is grave,
And the look in his eye is bright and brave.

And she, remembering farm-hand talk:
"You lose three seeds to get one stalk,"

Stands tall and proud and her pale cheeks glow
As she drops a kernel: "One to grow!"

Slowly Nan the widow moves
Up and down the furrowed grooves,

Peace in her heart and a smile on her lips
As the kernels fall from her finger-tips:

> *"One for the buzzard—*
> *One for the crow—*
> *One to rot—and—*
> *One to grow!"*

—1935

* * * * * * * * * * * *

7

Tales of Old-Time Texas

*A*ny tale belongs to whoever can best tell it.

J. Frank Dobie

Sybil Estess
Mastodon Teeth

Orange Coral, tan sea-cork, fishnets
hang in curves over the formica bar
of his hermit hut, the man from Racine,
a curator who's lived for seven years
on this beach-cliff in south Texas.
He scavenges the coral from the Caribbean,
perhaps Cancun. He shows us petrified wood,
as we fight off troops of mosquitos,
the fields of Texas expanding beyond us,
the "Danger"-marked sea below… .
Three pieces he holds off until the end—
two five-inch mastodon teeth, one mammoth's bone.

The teeth are encrusted with nipple-like cusps
that make them bumpy and ugly and odd.
They aren't at all like teeth of a toy elephant,
or glassed, dated relics in some museum.
No, real mastodon teeth simply lie
in my quaking hands—casual remains of a monster,
picked up on an inaccessible shoreline
near Brazoria. The man keeps them with
a foot-long piece of the old pachyderm's bone.

Dear old beachcomber, you loosed fear in me
on that hot and itchy night under an August moon.
Fangs gnawed in my kneading nightmares,
and I waked knowing this: of all there was
of these beasts, only their teeth remain.

—1966

Carol Cullar
12,000 Years Is Not Too Long

(*conservative estimates of the age of Pecos River petrographs place the earliest ones at 12 to 14 thousand years)

The handprint, small and negative,
forms the eagle's eye,
then clay and grease and blood
smear downward,
sweep into wings up-flung;
out-thrust talons,
bonded with limestone cliff,
poise above the sanguine serpent/hills
that wait for clutch of claws,
might of myth to penetrate
their slow zig zags;
then protracted tongue
can turn to face the foe:
12,000 years is not too long
to wait

—*1993*

* * * * * * * * * * * * *

Violette Newton
The Caddo Mounds

We never questioned what they were.
We played along the gentle mounds
Where grass grew slick and soft enough
To slide upon, so up we climbed,
All laughing, to the pretty crests
And sat and downward went. The domes
Were part of nature, only that.
We never questioned what they were.

We never knew that layered there
The centuries waited, pure and true,
To tell themselves in scattered beads
And bowls and cups and bones, of course;
Old objects that had origins
In earth itself and now returned
To dusty peace. Instead, we slid,
All ignorant in childish bliss.

We never questioned what they were,
And if we found an arrowhead,
A bead or shard of cup or bowl,
We did not think of pain or death
Or love or passion, gone and spent,
Or lives cut short or lives too long.
We were too innocent to read
These pages we can now translate…
We never questioned what they were.

     —1982

*   *   *   *   *   *   *   *   *   *   *   *   *

STEPHEN HARRIGAN
Papalote Creek

If there are wing-shaped stones in the water
where it's too dark now to see them,
then allright.
Allright
if it's 8 p.m. over South Texas tonight,
here is where the loss of history
has a hand in us
like a surgeon rearranging organs.
A quiet red glow on the dashboard:
our generator dies
with the grace of a bird

turning over in flight,
and our car glides down
by the historical marker.
Allright.

We read that the Karankawas
named the creek
for the wing-shaped stones they found here,
named it some other late summer,
some other dusk
when the banks sloped
into Papalote Creek
like dreamers rolling out of bed.

The clouds are flaring up
at the source of Papalote Creek.
There is no wind but the mesquite moves,
and somewhere near here
on an extinct pampas
the Karankawas are eating
alligators and deer shit,
scalding their throats with yaupon tea
that won't ever make them drunk
or alive again.

I'm going to find me a pile
of those wing-shaped stones.
They'll be burrowed
like oysters
in a century of creekbed.
I'm going to take them home
and wear them down
in my hands.

  —1980

Maude E. Cole
Over Texas Hills

Out where silver-blue distance is calling,
And picturesque hills wait the pageant of day,
Satin-smooth roads, rising and falling,
Will carry you on, on and away
Over the hills, while deep rooted silence
Brings from the past a buffalo herd;
A band of Comanches, ready for violence,
And courageous old padres, armed with God's word.

These pass, and comes a slow moving caravan;
The plodding hoofbeats of a road-weary team;
And the cry, "Yonder's water," as eager eyes scan
The silvery curve of a hill bordered stream.
Soldiers of fortune, seeking a mecca,
Burned by the heat, or numbed by the cold,
Dreaming, as did Cabeza de Vaca
And the great Coronado, of treasures to hold.

On westward they go and comes a strange pounding,
And great lines of cattle, some thousand strong,
Move over hills to voice resounding,
"Get along little doggies, get along, get along."
Maybe a storm and cattle stampeding,
Maddened by thunder, lightning, and hail
They scatter and run till cowboys out-speeding
Circle and turn them back to the trail.

—1935

ISABEL NATHANIEL
The Weepers

(In 1528 the shipwrecked Cabeza de Vaca and a dwindling number of armada survivors lived for a time with Indians who roamed the narrow islands of the Texas coast. His account describes their curious ritual of weeping, how as another culture might salute or bow or make the sign of the cross, these people wept.)

This is the island named Misfortune
where Karankawas are weeping
and the sea is wildly in agreement:
sorrow, sorrow.
               From the terrace
how white everything white is in the dark,
simplified and heightened:
parallel lines of waves fixed
as if by brush in titanium white
and the beach a long white stroke
to darkness.
             It would be the same
even then, this edge of the New World.
This sea over and over, this trek of moon.
The wind in this direction,
this smell of salt, of weather.
                 And the weepers
starting up. A half hour of wails
for greeting. How are you? Not too good.
Simplified and heightened.
The castaways were impressed
with such lively sense of their own calamity.
To this island we gave the name Malhado.

Night makes dark mirrors of the terrace windows.
Inside I appear out there, come
so far, castaway from some
                old world.

The weepers are assembled, their lamentation
rising in this direction, profound, insistent,
all the years ahead
come to an end alike forlorn and fatal.

  —1996

*   *   *   *   *   *   *   *   *   *   *   *

ARTHUR M. SAMPLEY
Coronado at Rio Grande Del Norte

The horns and cloven hoof are in the mire,
Webbed in the river flats, and the scorched rock
Smolders, the whetted winds' electric shock
Keens westward, scudding dust like puffs of fire
And fanning the draggled plume of a cavalier
Hawk-nosed and beagle-eyed. The caravan
On specter horses canters toward the Gran
Quivera and the pueblos pitching sheer
In slabs of shining metal. Indians spur
With Coronado, pointing toward the sky
And the silver glimmer of the alkali
Where in the level wastes mirages blur,
And the banner and the cross go sweeping by
The pale, impassioned brow of Lucifer.

  —1951

*   *   *   *   *   *   *   *   *   *   *   *

ALAN BIRKELBACH
Coronado Points

In Blanco County, near Floydada,
the man who lived in a nursing home
kept the chain link glove he had found over thirty years ago
in a box

While probably important, he'd been told,
it didn't prove much of anything. It had less
conversational magnetism than a box of someone else's medals.
It was just something limp lying around.

It wasn't until folks starting finding
copper crossbow points in that same canyon
where the old man had wandered
that someone who knew someone

dropped off a letter to an anthropologist
who right off said, "Coronado. Yes, I'd bet,
by God, he passed this way looking for that place,
looking for Quivira,

where there were huge boats and monstrous fish
and 'las platas de oro.'" That anthropologist,
when he heard, had to wipe his mouth.
"You wait," he said,

"People will be digging there for years
looking for more proof, looking for the trail."
A scanning hawk, that far-off day,
might have seen the falling glove's glimmer

or maybe he flew on, intent on prey in
the next canyon, or maybe that glove fell
across the path of a route-ruled rattler
who, envious, of the fine scales, struck,

and then followed his natural track. Or maybe
someone should hurry back to that nursing home
in Blanco County, near Floydada, and find
that man who's still got the box,
and ask him quick, before he dies,

"Tell me,
when you first saw it lying there,
exactly which way
were the fingers pointing?"

—1998

Carmen Tafolla
Mission San José

The rocks are warm
have had the hands upon them
through the years
with sun to bake in
memories.
Gentle, even with
ungentle missions,
somehow life got through
to Them,
the priests amazed
that rabbit tasted
good,
slowed their passion fervor
one San Antonio sunny afternoon
learned to
lope
a bit
and breathe
with warm brown human flesh
touched the rocks in
tenderness
one time too many,

ceased to call it mission
as it grew to make itself
home
for all of us.

—1992

* * * * * * * * * * * * *

STANLEY E. BABB
Portrait of a Pirate

One summer afternoon old Jean Lafitte
Tramped out along this wide deserted beach,
A dark, spectacular man moving across
The sea's blue dazzle and the skyline clouds.

He wore no cutlass dangling from his hip,
No silver-mounted pistols in his belt;
But round his neck hung by a silver chain
A golden crucifix sparkled in the sun.

And as he paced along his tired eyes roved
Over the beach, across the bright blue sea,
Into the white clouds streaming along the skyline.

And for a moment as he watched these clouds,
He dreamed they were the sails of galleons
Sweeping slowly up from Panama
With ingots of gold and heavy leather bags
Of silver and of jewels from Peru....

And then this old man longed for those bright years
When he had shared the sudden hellish clangours,
The fierce excitements and the tensing terrors
Of long tumultuous battles—

But he was old now, and he realized
His fighting-days were ended, and his dreams
Had gone the way of last night's wind and rain...

He tramped along the beach and scanned the sea,
And the tall clouds coursing up across the sky,
And a great longing kindled in his heart....

There were no ships in sight, not a single ship:
Only the dazzling sea that hurt his eyes,
The seagulls cruising above the beach with shrill
Inscrutable cries, the tide-line on the sand,
His shadow, and the cedars in the dunes.

And then he remembered his brief hours of triumph—
Mornings when he buried bars of gold
On lonely beaches....windy midnights when
His little schooner put out from Tortuga
To harry some great treasure ship...and squalls
Off Yucatan that tore away his sail....
And autumn evenings when he swaggered through
The streets of old New Orleans in the moonlight,

Astonishing the youngsters with his tales
Of his wild raffish Baratarians—
And that slim Creole woman and her kisses....
But these brave days had swept into the past,
And he whom men admired and envied once
Was now a scorned and tired old man wandering
Aimlessly along a windy beach:

And now his schooner was a shattered wreck
Embedded in the sands....his men were gone:
He had few dreams....

And so he slowly walked
Back to his cabin, his bottle and his charts
And to the wench who kept him warm at night.

—1923

* * * * * * * * * * * * *

BRYCE MILLIGAN
Copano, 1834

Aransas was stormy,
the channel churning and full of muck;
it lifted the *Wild Cat* to the south,
the *Sea Lion* to the north,
set down the two schooners
      gently
one in sand, one in mud,
and left them there to rot.

Two ships full of Irish
escaping, escaping
in the black dull days
between the ninety-eight
      and the famine,
escaping to Texas
and more honorable deaths.

The sea receded, placid,
calmly accepting its toll
as the cholera took them
      one by one
until the bay was littered
and the sands of San Jose
became putrid.

The survivors passed on
as survivors do
to the Alamo,
San Jacinto,
and
Comanche moons;
glad to have escaped Eire,
gladder still
to forget.

—1984

* * * * * * * * * * * * *

SAM HOUSTON
Texian Call to Arms

Unfurl the banners to the breeze,
    Come rear the standard high:
Upon our mountains, shores and seas,
    Be liberty the cry

Shout the glad word—and shout again,
    That makes each bosom swell.
Bid the drum beat a martial strain
    Bid it sound oppression's knell.

To arms! to arms! Let each firm hand
    Its battle sabre wield.
The oppressor comes—but stand;
    To tyrants never yield.

And bloody be his welcome here,
    Who would our sort enslave.
His myriad host we cannot fear:
    Who would? Tis not the brave.

On. On! and struggle to be free,
      And battle bravely on!
Our country calls—and who will see
      Her call in vain? Not one.

By our God—by our soil—we swear
      Freemen to live—or die.
And now 'tis done—the standard rear
      Be liberty the cry!

Shall these rich vales, these splendid pines
      E'er brook oppression's reign?
No! if the despot's iron hand,
      must here a scepter wave,
Raz'd be those glories from the land,
      And be the land—our grave.

—1835

★ ★ ★ ★ ★ ★ ★ ★ ★ ★ ★ ★ ★

MICHAEL LIND
from The Alamo: An Epic

Now Crockett said, "You gentlemen are free
      to keep those guns—on one condition, please;
this argument about authority
      has got to end, or else our company's
      departing for a post where unity's
not threatened. Duel or deal, this split must end;
shoot at, or with, each other, gentlemen."

Jim Bowie, in a low and angry tone,
      rebuked the Tennessean: "Congressman,
I think how we resolve this is our own
      concern." "Beg pardon, Colonel, if I've done

offended you. These boys rode to join one
united garrison. I recommend
you gentlemen consider joint command."

"Ridiculous," snapped Travis. "Two in charge?
       That's monstrous as a double-headed calf."
Beneath his visor, Crockett wore a large
       and friendly smile, enjoyed a little laugh.
       Why, sir, that's a mistake, a downright gaffe.
I used to court a fine two-headed girl:
to port she was named Sue, to starboard Pearl.

"Her Pa, he let us stay out twice as late;
       each sister, you see, acted chaperone
when I was with the other on a date.
       When one dozed off, we two were all alone.
       Those twins were very different. Pearl had grown
up liking reels, while Sue preferred the jig;
Pearl was a Democrat, and Sue a Whig.

"Now Sue, she was a Methodist, but Pearl,
       she was a Baptist, the foot-washing breed.
You should have seen Pearl baptized; how that girl
       protested when the preacher dunked her braid
       while Pearl was praying—oh, how Suzy brayed!
They both were baptized, thus, by Brother Lou,
who had three noggins: Christian, papist, Jew."

Despite themselves, the Texans had to smile
       as Crockett spun his yarn. "Well, tell me, sir,"
said Bowie, "why didn't you walk the aisle?"
       The answer: "I was forced to choose 'twixt her
       and her. Which one of them did I prefer?
Well, Sue and I, we wanted to be wed,
but Pearl complained to Pa, who vowed to have my head."

In laughter all the tension was dissolved,
        the way a soggy drought will suddenly
explode in cleansing rain. The foes resolved
        their bitter battle for supremacy;
        each order that was issued now would be
approved by both commanders, who would
share authority. Travis returned to Bexar.

        —1997

⋆ ⋆ ⋆ ⋆ ⋆ ⋆ ⋆ ⋆ ⋆ ⋆ ⋆ ⋆ ⋆

VIOLETTE NEWTON
The Witness, Susanna Dickinson

March 6, 1836

They had chosen their deaths and martyrdom,
They had chosen to stay, and one by one,
I saw them fall—I can never erase
The sight of each bloody and broken face.

Still, through the years, I remember well
How I cowered there in the hours of hell,
For I was the only one left to say
What had happened there on that fateful day.

I was the one who must suffer the pain
Of the story I told again, again.
I was the one who could never forget
But must tell it over to all I met.

And I was the only one left to know
What we lost and gained at the Alamo.

        —1986

⋆ ⋆ ⋆ ⋆ ⋆ ⋆ ⋆ ⋆ ⋆ ⋆ ⋆ ⋆ ⋆

James Gregory Smith
Antonio López and Emily

April 1836

That day as guidons fluttered,
  she did as told
  passing supplies along the wharf at Morgan's Point.

Stomping bare foot
  to prancing mare,
  coffee arms crossed tight,
  she drew inward
  from a fine silhouette upon a Spanish roan.

The rider asked where he was,
  and Emily replied,
  unfolding,
  "This be the place."

Then smiled,
  simply because the wind was blowing
  that sunny day in Texas.

—1993

*   *   *   *   *   *   *   *   *   *   *

Mirabeau B. Lamar
San Jacinto

Beautiful in death
  The soldier's corse appears,
Embalmed by fond affection's breath
  And bathed in his country's tears.

Lo, the battle forms
      Its terrible array,
Like clashing clouds in mountain storms
      That thunder on their way.

The rushing armies meet,
      And while they pour their breath,
The strong earth trembles at their feet,
      And day grows dim with death.

Now launch upon the foe
      The lightnings of your rage!
Strike the assailing tyrants low,
      The monsters of the age!

They yield! They break! They fly!
      The victory is won!
Pursue! They faint, they fall, they die!
      O stay! the work is done.

Mourn the death of those
      Who for their country die,
Sink on her bosom for repose
      And triumph where they lie.

Laurels for those who bled,
      The living hero's due.
But holier wreaths will crown the dead—
      A grateful nation's love!

—1836, 1902

A.L. Crouch
Mirabeau B. Lamar

Mirabeau B.
(Buonaparte) Lamar
Hitched his wagon
To the Lone Star.

With a sword in one hand
And a pen in the other,
He earned almost
Enough glory to smother.

He wrote some verses
And kept a journal,
And jumped in ten days
From Private to Colonel.

When hot lead and cold steel
Determined our borders,
He and Sam Houston
Were giving the orders:

Imperial Texas,
Claimed Mirabeau,
Included all
of Mexico…

Not only that
(The man was terrific),
He dreamed of a Texas
That reached to the Pacific!

—1945

Mary Austin Holley
The Plea of Texas

Admit us—we would deem it shame,
Of other lands such boon to claim,
  For we are free and proud.
But we a mother's love may seek,
And feel no blush upon our cheek,
  Before her to have bowed.

We are thy children; doubt it not—
We've proved our birth on many a spot
  Where cannon thunder pealed.
'Twas Saxon heart that dared the fight,
'Twas blood of yours that gave us might
  Upon Jacinto's field.

Rebels, they say! We learned from you
What freemen could and ought to do.
  Against a tyrant's might—
And what by valor first we gained,
And have for eight years full maintained,
  Is ours by every right.

They call us poor! 'Tis false—the Sun,
A fairer land never shone upon,
  Than this we offer you.
We are no beggars—well we know
The worth of what we would bestow—
  We have not gain in view.

We love your flag, your laws, your land—
Wishing to worship, see we stand
      At Freedom's Temple door.
Admit us now for it may be,
That tost on Time's tempestuous sea,
We part to meet no more.

    —1844

✳ ✳ ✳ ✳ ✳ ✳ ✳ ✳ ✳ ✳ ✳ ✳

MARGARET LEA HOUSTON
To My Husband—December 1844.

Dearest, the cloud hast left thy brow,
      The shade of thoughtfulness, of care
And deep anxiety; and now
      The sunshine of content is there.

Its sweet return with joy I hail:
      And never may thy country's woes
Again that hallow'd light dispel,
      And may thy bosom's calm repose.

God hath crown'd thy years of toil
      With fruition; and I pray
That on the harvest still His smile
      May shed its ever gladdening ray.

Thy task is done! another eye
      Than thine must guard thy country's weal:
And oh, may wisdom from on high
      To him the one true path reveal!

Where'erst was spread the mighty waste,
      Of waters fathoms deep, and far
O'er earth thick darkness reigned, unchased
      By ray of sun or moon or star, —

God bade the gloomy deep recede,
      And so young earth rose on His view!
Swift at His word, the waters fled,
      And darkness spread its wings and flew.

The same strong arm hath put to flight
      Our country's foes, the ruthless band
That swept in splendid pomp and might
      Across our fair and fertile land.

The same Almighty hand hath raised
      On these wild plains a structure fair:
And well may wondering nations gaze
      At aught so marvelous and rare.

Thy task is done. The holy shade
      Of calm retirement waits thee now;
The lamp of hope relit hath shed
      Its sweet refulgence o'er thy brow.

Far from the busy haunts of men
      Oh may thy soul each fleeting hour
Upon the breath of prayer descend
      To him who rules with love and power!

—1844

Teresa Palomo Acosta
For Maximino Palomo

the official history that
traces in pictures and words,
endlessly depicts
in minute detail
the stealing of your honor

the selling of your manly labor,
the pain you endured
as sons and daughters
drifted from you,
met their death in the
hour of thorns and swords
will fail you

just as will history texts
written with the cutting pen of
palefaced brown/stone men who recall 1848
and
forget to tell about
the man who cradled children to sleep,
soothed their damp hair,
told them stories,
played la golondrina on his violin,
and laughed
aloud
at dusk.

*Note: The United States and Mexico signed the Treaty of Guadalupe-Hidalgo in
1848, thus ending the Mexican American War.*

 —*1984*

★ ★ ★ ★ ★ ★ ★ ★ ★ ★ ★ ★

PAT STODGHILL
Traitor
(Sam Houston, 1857)

He had been called many things by many men,
yet the word "traitor" went against the grain;
not when the new ones sneered,
but when old friends said it…
the ones who had been at Gonzales and San Jacinto,

who had voted to trade the single star for twenty-eight,
who now had changed their minds.
He spoke in cotton fields, corn fields,
on riverbanks and hillsides and on courthouse steps
saying, "We must stand by the Union."
They did not hear.
They did not want to hear,
puffed with pride and ambition, boasting
that no "northern states" could tell them what to do.
He warned of bloodshed, civil strife,
and they had laughed,
hurling epithets like stones around his head.
"So long as the flag waves over me,
I can forget that I am called a traitor," he declared,
remembering the sting of stone-tipped arrows,
the musket's ball.
What could the words do that the fire had not?
So he spoke on, ignoring crude remarks;
yet when alone, apart,
the word "traitor," loud as cymbals,
echoed in his heart.

  —1975

  ✩ ✩ ✩ ✩ ✩ ✩ ✩ ✩ ✩ ✩ ✩ ✩

BETTY ADCOCK
Kaiser's Burnout

Jayhawkers, an army, and fire are the reasons
there's a prairie in the middle of these woods
a hundred and twenty years
after the last of the smoke cleared.

Warren Collins and his boys and all their cousins
thought the Union ought to stay, already put together
like it was—like a marriage or a dwelling-house—
and because whatever seam up there had split

was too far away to think about, this deep
in East Texas. You couldn't call them Jayhawkers exactly,
since not much politics was in it. They were just poor
and they had thought it out, living where a panther
could spook your woods cattle, or bear
get at your hanging hogmeat if you didn't watch it.
They thought they wouldn't go this time to war.

And that was fine until Captain Charlie Bullock,
a man pretty nearly local, but out of Woodville,
got sent by a Galveston officer named Kaiser
to do something about it with militia.
The Collins boys heard ahead, and they lit out
for the Thicket where it's tight.
They dug two wells for water to last them
in a place still known as The Union Wells,
and brought in supplies. They'd depend on game
for the long haul. In another war, Sam Houston
had a plan, if things went poorly, to hide
his whole army in the Thicket. Collins figured
his boys could hide from Confederate Texas just as good.

Kaiser's men and the militia boys
with Bullock came from towns,
or from the smooth farms of the better counties.
They weren't good for much, or their horses either,
in country that could turn into a pure weather
of yaupon and vines, a brierstorm
with snakes for lightning.
So after stumbling around in there half lost
with wrong-way creeks and the bad heat,
Bullock decided to make use of a dry summer.
He set a circling fire.

Like most people doing anything, the men
who torched it left one hole in the wrong direction
and right there was where Collins' boys tore out,
beside the running deer and varmints, straight through
the open end of a flaming horseshoe and on home
where they sat down to breakfast like anybody would.
Bullock followed with his men, and there was shooting,
and nobody knows exactly why no man was hit
on either fighting side. The army ended up
with nothing to show but one old man named Lilly
shot dead through the suspenders to the heart,
and him no sympathizer to anybody, being afoot
behind an oxteam on the road, coming to pick up
a new cart. A war will do strange things
even off to the side. But fire is predictable,
and this one ate three thousand acres before it quit.
The whole business went so bad that both the captains
went back to their war and forgot about Collinses.

And their war was over the next year,
nothing changing much one way or the other
here, though more people came to the rest of Texas
from bigger burnouts farther off.
Charlie Bullock stayed alive to get back home,
and Warren Collins stayed glad he hadn't gone
anywhere at all. After a while, the two of them
took to going out hunting together,
firesetter and runner, two old men
and both sides of a story
looking across a campfire at each other
while a pack of hounds mouthed glory after
fox or wolf, and the Thicket closing in
every place but one.

—1988

* * * * * * * * * * * * *

Mayme Evans
Whiskey-Bomb Battle

A story they tell, the people who dwell
In the town of Corpus Christi,
How once long ago, while beset by the foe,
It rained down bourbon whisky.

Fierce was the fray on Corpus Bay
Between the Yanks and Rebels;
The cannons boomed, the rockets zoomed,
And bullets fell like pebbles.

Upon the shore a score or more
Of shells lay unexploded;
Lay (the distraught defenders thought)
With precious powder loaded.

One of the duds fell in the spuds
Of a local politician;
He viewed the prize with frugal eyes,
Being short on ammunition.

He called a slave and orders gave
To rip the bomb asunder,
Sorely afraid, the youth obeyed,
Then stood pop-eyed with wonder.

Inside the shell a hollow well
Was brimming full of liquor;
He took a sup, then drained the cup,
With never a wince or flicker.

The boys around came on the bound
To seek the magic nectar;
And every son lay down his gun
And became a shell collector.

Booze imbued, with hope renewed,
The Rebels charged the raiders;
In a rosy fog of heaven-sent grog
They vanquished the invaders.

Oh, many an eye has scanned the sky
On the Bay of Corpus Christi,
But never again in the memory of man
Has it rained down bourbon whisky.

—1957

NORMAN H. CROWELL
Texas Trails

Trails that wander and writhe and bend—
Mighty trails . . . take them end to end.

Old trails made by conquistadors.
Trails to the far Pacific shores;

Gouged by the tires of the pioneers,
Cut by the hooves of the longhorn steers:

Devious trails where Comanches fled
On moonlit night when their hands were red;

Deep-cut trails through the gramma grass
Where the buffalo herds took a year to pass;

Trails on the sands where the buccaneers
Hid their spoils in the daring years;

Trails to the North where the cattle bawled,
Where the cowman bluffed and the gambler called;

Trails that saw brands on a heifer's hide
Still warm as the brander gasped and died;

Trails that knew the cow-puncher's tune
And the coyote's call to the thin grey moon;

Trails to the West where Kit Carson told
Of mountains laden with yellow gold;

Where long lean men spurred down the way
To the red saloons of Santa Fe;

West to the snowcaps through sand and mud—
A trail of battle . . . a trail of blood;

Where outlaws rustled and bandits killed
And the man who lived kept his right hand filled,

Down this grim trail tall wagons creaked
And stragglers died if their canteens leaked;

Here buckskinned scouts with tobaccoed lips
Slept by their fire of buffalo chips;

And the bullwhacker spat and cocked his eye
As the Pony Express went riding by;

Trails to the hills where the Indian fires
Told of the passing of their sires;

Winding trails to the mighty springs
Whose clear cold water forever sings;

Trails, criss-crossing, cutting deep
Where Texas heroes are at sleep;

Long trails writhing . . . trails that bend—
Mighty trails…take them end to end!

—1937

ROSEMARY CATACALOS
Homesteaders
for the Edwards Aquifer

They came for the water,
came to its sleeping place
here in the bed of an old sea,
the dream of the water.
They sank hand and tool into
soil where the bubble of springs
gave off hope, fresh and long,
the song of the water.
Babies and crops ripened
where they settled,
where they married their sweat
in the ancient wedding,
the blessing of the water.
They made houses of limestone
and adobe, locked together blocks
descended from shells and coral,
houses of the bones of the water,
shelter of the water.
And they swallowed the life
of the lime in the water,
sucked its mineral up
into their own bones
which grew strong as the water,
the gift of the water.

All along the counties they lay,
mouth to mouth with the water,
fattened in the smile of the water,
water flushed pure through the
spine and ribs of the birth of life,
the old ocean,
the stone,
the home of the water.

     —1984

*   *   *   *   *   *   *   *   *   *   *   *

LAWRENCE CHITTENDEN
Old Fort Phantom Hill
(An abandoned fort in Jones County, Texas. Supposed to be haunted.)

To the veterans of the Blue and the Gray

On the breezy Texas border, on the prairies far
        away,
Where the antelope is grazing and the Spanish
        ponies play;
Where the tawny cattle wander through the golden
        incensed hours,
And the sunlight woos a landscape clothed in royal
        robes of flowers;
Where the Elm and Clear Fork mingle, as they
        journey to the sea,
And the night-wind sobs sad stories o'er a wild and
        lonely lea;
Where of old the dusky savage and the shaggy
        bison trod,
And the reverent plains are sleeping 'midst drowsy
        dreams of God;
Where the twilight loves to linger, e'er night's sable
        robes are cast

'Round grim-ruined, spectral chimneys, telling
      stories of the past,
There upon an airy mesa, close beside a whisper-
      ing rill,
There to-day you'll find the ruins of the Old Fort
      Phantom Hill.

Years ago, so runs the legend, 'bout the year of
      Fifty three,
This old fort was first established by the gallant
      soldier, Lee;
And to-day the restless spirits of his proud and
      martial band
Haunt those ghostly, gloomy chimneys in the Texas
      border land.
There once every year at midnight, when the
      chilling Northers roar,
And the storm-king breathes its thunder from the
      heights of Labrador,
Where the vaulted gloom re-echoes with the owls—
      "whit-to-woo!"
And the stealthy cayote answers with his lonely,
      long "ki-oo!"
Then strange phantoms flit in silence through that
      weeping mesquite vale,
And the reveilles come sound o'er the old McKenzie
      Trail,
Then the muffled drums beat muster and the
      bugles sadly trill,
And the vanished soldiers gather 'round the heights
      of Phantom Hill.
Then pale bivouac fires are lighted and those
      gloomy chimneys glow,
While the grizzled veterans muster from the taps
      of long ago,

Lee and *Johnston* and *McKenzie, Gran*t and *Jackson,*
      Custer, too,
Gather there in peaceful silence waiting for their
      last review;
Blue and gray at length united on the high re-
      doubts of fame,
Soldiers all in one grand army, that will answer in
      God's name.
Yes, they rest on heights of glory in that fair, celes-
      tial world,
"Where the war-drum throbs no longer, and the
      battle-fields are furled."
And to-day the birds are singing where was heard
      the cannons' roar,
For the gentle doves are nesting 'midst those ruins
      of the war.
Yes, the mocking-birds re-echo: "Peace on earth,
      to men good will,"
And the "swords are turned to ploughshares" in
      the land of Phantom Hill.

    —1893

  ✶   ✶   ✶   ✶   ✶   ✶   ✶   ✶   ✶   ✶   ✶

BERTA HART NANCE
Old Fort Griffin

Here once the endless wagon-trains
Brought hides of shaggy buffalo,
And brown adventurers raced by,
Trampling the April flower-snow.

Here once that columns hurried forth,
Against the steady southern gale,
Their guides, the friendly Tonkawas,
To find a red Comanche-trail.

The dove calls where the bugles sang,
The cactus-flower lifts a bell,
Where soldiers drilled, mesquites parade,
The mocking-bird is sentinel.

—1931

✴   ✴   ✴   ✴   ✴   ✴   ✴   ✴   ✴   ✴   ✴

CAROL COFFEE REPOSA
At Fort Clark

No one has named the colors
Drifting down those hills
That rise like incantations over Mexico,
Those shades that glaze
The towers in the town.

Old tones roll like echoes
Into earth
While new ones form in stones
Along the road
Or light-filled spaces
Between leaves.

These analogs of blue and green
Or gold and red
Require new words,
Even for the simple things:
Mulberries dropping on the grass
After a rain,
Swallows flying in their changing planes
Sun bouncing off the bells
That sway through the afternoon.

Even night does not obscure these tones.
They float from cloud to cloud
Or star to star
Demanding speech
That none of us can make.

—1992

* * * * * * * * * * * * *

LAWRENCE CHITTENDEN
The Old Mackenzie Trail

Stretching onward toward the sunset,
    Over prairie, hill, and vale,
Far beyond the Double Mountains
    Winds the old Mackenzie Trail.

Ah, what thoughts and border mem'ries
    Does that dreaming trail suggest;
Thoughts of travelers gone forever
    To the twilight realms of rest.

Where are now the scouts and soldiers,
    And those wagon-trains of care,
Those grim men and haggard women?
    And the echoes whisper—where?

Ah, what tales of joys and sorrows
    Could that silent trail relate;
Tales of loss, and wrecked ambitions,
    Tales of hope, and love, and hate;

Tales of hunger, thirst, and anguish,
    Tales of skulking Indian braves,
Tales of fear, and death, and danger,
    Tales of lonely prairie graves.

Where are now that trail's processions
    Winding westward sure and slow?
Lost! —ah, yes, destroyed by progress,
    Gone to realms of long ago.

Nevermore shall bold Mackenzie,
    With his brave and dauntless band,
Guide the restless, roving settlers
    Through the Texas border land.

Yes, that soldier's work is over,
    And the dim trail rests at last;
But his name and trail still lead us
    Through the borders of the Past.

—1893

BERTA HART NANCE
Moonlight

My father hated moonlight,
And pulled the curtains down,
Each time the snows of moonlight
Came drifting on the town.

He was an old frontiersman,
And on their deadly raids,
Comanches rode by moonlight,
In stealthy cavalcades;

And took the settler's horses,
Or left a trail of red —
He came to love the darkness,
And hate the moon, he said.

—1935

WILLIAM WENTHE
White Settlement

Early September, the weather temperate again;
the autumnal, surburban routines in place:
children with bright backpacks walking to school,

and a little later, the distant noise of drums
from the college band, at practice. Me at my desk,
viewing a snapshot that came from a friend

in yesterday's mail: a group of us, some years ago
in Virginia, standing squint-eyed under strain
of sunlight. On the back she'd scribbled:

> *Found this photo while un-*
> *packing, made copies for all.*
> *I'm sorry, but shots of the*
> *cemetery were badly under-*
> *exposed—it was just too dark*
> *in there.*

"There" was a tangle of blackberry, sweetgum
and sassafras; further in, a space freeing up
beneath limbs of antebellum beech:

in leaf-shadow and tobacco-dark loam, slabs
of knee-high stones upcropped like bad teeth,
like carcass ribs. We had to kneel down

to read the letters and numbers carved there.
I recall the scent of wet stones, the gloss
of moss hiding names and dates we fingered

into legibility. No crosses, no promises—
The Masters' wordy faith too much, perhaps, for hands
that had scratched with nail or knifeblade:

> *william hasson*
> *bon 1819*
> *did 1855*

the letters were a mix of script and print,
some backward, some skewed, some missing altogether.
Still we sensed behind them something more,

a human presence mingled with the dead
leaves, tangled in creepers, echoed in sculpted
silence of afternoon birdsong lull.

In the snapshot, we've just emerged
from the thicket, its swarm of shadows
still behind our backs, but already forced

to the flatness of paper, like this writing
I attempt in order to make sense of what,
for an hour, I could see, and touch, and breathe.

When I look up from the page, my eyes enclose
this rented backyard, its privacy-fenced corners
sliced into a land I've not yet come to

understand. In dry washes breaking away
to the canyon outside of town, sharper eyes,
I'm told, can find the telltale edges

of arrowheads, or, far older, the chipped tools
of earliest hunters. But I've only read
the drive-by history engraved on a steel

plaque in a park named for the Cavalry Colonel
who destroyed the last villages of Comanche, Kiowa,
Southern Cheyenne—its prose, so carefully

subordinated, leading to a final justification:
thereby opening Western Texas to White settlement.
If soil is another history, then the slick

pavements of parking lots unfurled
at the business-edge of town, the clean slates
of lawns are a cultivated emptiness,

an amnesia… All morning,
the nagging brass of the college band rehearsal
has risen from their practice lot, marched

across the path I'd hoped to remember,
negotiating through bramble of my own sentences,
back to a place where illiterate stones

allowed me a glimpse of what always lies
unsaid, unsettling, unspeakable, beneath
our feet. Starting and stopping,

the band's been playing strains
of the national anthem, over and over,
trying to get the ending just right.

    —1999

JAMES CODY
The Heart of Texas

Texas, unlike the rest of the West
has a hole in its heart
Texas has no Indians
The heart of Texas
cut off its own blood stream and
sent it to Oklahoma
but there are signs
where the artery was ripped out
an arrowhead on the Colorado
petroglyphs on the Pecos
a few torn strands of
ancient camping spots on the coast
along the Brazos, the Colorado
Comanche Peak is still there
No red-skins in Palo Duro Canyon
driven out in '39 by Mirabeau B. Lamar
in 1874 by Co. Nelson A. Miles
That is better than in the East, they say
There is not even a heart,
not a single trace.

—1981

* * * * * * * * * * * * *

CHRIS WILLERTON
Battle of Adobe Walls

Headlong down the red dawn galloped
Lone Wolf, Quanah Parker, Stone Calf, White Shield,
three hundred Kiowa, Cheyenne, Comanche
flinging up dust and thunder, riding
red-eyed for scalps of buffalo hunters.
But the white men, warned early, fumbled for guns

in the gray light, yelled between buildings, above the boom
of a thousand hooves, black racket of war whoops,
gun butts battering the trading post doors.

Yet noon came, and nightfall, and corpse
after corpse. Ishatai's charm,
warpaint he said would turn bullets,
was a bad joke: the buffalo guns
spat death a half mile. Lone Wolf,
hair still docked to mourn his son,
watched other men's sons slung down to death.

The third day, squinting through the heat,
Billy Dixon even made sport. "A scratch shot, boys!
Them Indians are most of a mile away!"
Dixon's Sharps 50 flung slugs in a flat arc,
killed two hundred buffalo a week
but not at this range. Still,
when the rifle roared and they waited open-mouthed,
the bullet hit: a warrior jerked backward,
rolled off his horse, falling from the world.
He sopped the dirt red, his ears buzzing with death
and the white men's faint whoops and hurrahs.

The warriors who lived to be penned on the reservation
could tell their children, "The buffalo
would stretch to the edge of sky. Such a herd
took all day to run past." The buffalo were gone
in four years. Even the white men had to turn
barkeeps, marshals, ranchers,
staking the plains down with towns and fences.
Billy Dixon's widow last gazed at the land
from a motorcar.

—1986

VAIDA STEWART MONTGOMERY
Cattle Brands

The pioneer artists had a canvas as wide
As the hairy surface of a steer's hide.

They worked with a red-hot saddle-ring,
An end-gate rod, or any old thing,

But they drew their lines and they curved them well,
From the *Tumbling Crutch* to the *Dinner Bell.*

. . . . .

The Old Timer fumbled and muttered a damn
When they handed him an iron with a monogram.

"Just give me a gaucho, every time—
Them new-fangled curlicues ain't worth a dime."

The Old Timer's Brand was *I C U;*
The rustler changed it to *I C U 2.*

. . . . .

The hard-riding cowhands played just as hard,
Nor batted an eye at the turn of a card.

There was a cowboy, Burk Burnett by name,
Who held four sixes in a poker game.

"I wager my ranch," the ranchman bawled—
He had three aces—and Burk said, "Called!"

So Burk won the ranch on a poker hand,
And henceforth used the *Four Six (6666)* brand.

. . . . .

The pioneer women liked to see
The *Laurel* Leaf and the *Fleur de Lis.*

The pioneer men liked *Spade,* and *Star,*
Pig Pen, Pitchfork, and *Bar V Bar;*

Hog Eye, Mule Shoe, Lazy J,
Buzzard on a Rail, and *Anchor K;*

Buckle, Broad Axe, Straddlebug,
Bow and Arrow, and *Little Brown Jug.*

. . . . .

The pioneer artists had a canvas as wide
As the hairy surface of a steer's hide;

And they drew their lines and they curved them true,
From the *Turkey Track* to the *Flying U.*

 —1946

  ★   ★   ★   ★   ★   ★   ★   ★   ★   ★   ★   ★

GENE SHUFORD
Sam Bass

A man earns greatness.
After I held up four trains,
The rangers broke up my famous gang,
And Jim Murphy betrayed me at Round Rock
On our way to Old Mexico.
        I suffered horribly
While Frank Jackson and I were escaping,
And knowing I was dying, I made him go on.
There under the trees a woman sent me a drink
While I lay tearing up my undershirt
To wipe the blood away.

I could no longer see the sky—
Earth, trees, grass, and unending road
Were rocking together—the blood came too fast;

I felt it fill my throat
As pain drove spike-hard into my bowels
The unendurable agony. That was death.
Soon after,
Someone wrote a song about me.

    —1967

✳   ✳   ✳   ✳   ✳   ✳   ✳   ✳   ✳   ✳   ✳   ✳   ✳

Steven Tye Culbert
Hoodoo Scott Cooley Scalps John Wohrle

Horseback he saw
the unscalped sympathizer
hauling a man from a well,
approached unpoetic
and shot the rope-handler
in plain sight of Mason.
The man in the well fell broken.
Dismounting, Cooley drew his knife
cut along the hair
no one knows where,
across the forehead
around the ear at the bulge,
dug under
clawed fingers fire-hard,
trail-hard, grease-black
the fat flap
and ripped off the skull cap,
waved his coup,
friend's death 'venged,
the spell-sufferer

from snake bite
warrior whooped,
cussed the sympathy
and all alike,
and blood-hot gushing
blank inside
rode from Mason
back to Johnny Ringo.

—2002

* * * * * * * * * * * *

JAS. D. THORN
The Sigh of the Old Cattleman

Oh, to close my desk, lay by my pen
And ride away to the range again;
The broad expanse where cattle roam
Where the great out-doors is home, sweet home.
The city's dust, the city's lust
That fills my soul with sheer disgust;
The lust for power, the lust for gold,
The lust for which our manhood's sold.
Oh, let me leave this hateful grind
And all for which it stands, behind;
The wicked city and its mart,
The seared of soul, the flinty heart.
to hear my pony's hoof-beats fall,
In answer to the wild bird's call—
The Texas plains once more to view
Where flowers flame—red, white and blue;
To lie at night, beneath the skies
That watch me with a million eyes;
To sleep, to dream and sweetly rest
Upon the friendly prairie's breast.

—1931

* * * * * * * * * * * *

The Last Running

That day the plains of Texas tilted north
upon an earth spinning autumn through
careless weed spiraled to drying seed.
The men moved, four and four, thin clad
and pony mounted, dusting hopper-laden grass.

Colonel Goodnight's foreman watched them turn
from dust spots east into the shapes
of mounted men with lances and rawhide clothes.
"From the reservation," he said, spitting
his distaste beside the ranch house porch,
hands flickering across the rifle at his knee.

Within the house, the Colonel watched them come.
He sat, computing an empire of acres and cattle
with black marks in a ledger book, aware
of the seven mounted men and the one
speaking to the foreman on the porch.
Colonel Goodnight listened: voices, silence,
a knock, some words with a servant, another knock,
his own voice allowing entry to his study.

"They's crazy," the foreman said, looking
at the floor. "They heard you got
buffalo, so I guess they want some food.
They ain't got nothing to trade—they want it free."
The Colonel nodded. "Give them a buffalo."
"But they got nothing." The foreman folded his arms.
Goodnight arose and thrust him aside.
He strode outdoors to stand before mounted
hunters from the past, to meet their eyes.
"Give them a buffalo," Colonel Goodnight said.
They cried a single cheerless cheer
and watch cowboys drive a beast before them.

313

They prodded it with lances
and the shouts of hunters,
moving the buffalo
among prairie horsemen to run
the last running.
Surrounded by hoofbeats,
pierced with lances,
it fell
to final dust
and autumn prairie.

"They's crazy," The foreman said, laughing.
The hunters, silent again, dismounted to sit
beside their buffalo, solemn, dreaming,
caught in the shadow of time spinning earth
into the red glow of evening far
far from the time and land summer.

—2002

★　★　★　★　★　★　★　★　★　★　★　★　★

CLAIRE OTTENSTEIN ROSS
The Judge

A lot of Texas tales are told
About old Judge Roy Bean,
Who was "Law West of the Pecos"—
A tough cowboy, lean and mean.

They say he came from San Antone
Where his customers got bilked.
He caused an awful lot of grief
Cause his cows gave funny milk.

The milk had minnows swimmin' in it,
So they ran him out that day.
He claimed the creek they drank from did it,
Then he made his get-a-way.

That's how he got to Langtry,
And with help from Texas Rangers,
He got elected as the judge
Even though he was a stranger.

Folks say he made up his own laws
And some were just for fun,
Like the time he fined one hundred bucks
To a corpse who had a gun.

He had a sense of humor
From the stories I hear told,
Like when he married folks he'd say,
"God have mercy on your soul."

Nobody ever questioned him
Cause they knew he wasn't foolin',
He'd shout them down and yell real loud,
"By gobs, that is my rulin'!"

So please don't doubt this Texas tale,
Or you'll give his corpse a nudge.
His voice will shout out from the grave,
"Don't argue with the Judge!"

—1995

★　★　★　★　★　★　★　★　★　★　★　★　★

CAROL COFFEE REPOSA
Hill Country Rest Home

At the fort the flag flies all night long.
Inside the cold stone rooms
Are broken lanterns
Gusts of wind, Comanche arrows
Memories of spurs and flint
Dingy photographs of Johnston, Thomas, Lee
Behind cracked glass.

From this rise a visitor sees everything:
The tired kaleidoscope
Of storefronts faced in river rock
Tile rooftops, stunted trees
And lines of slowly moving cars.

Beyond the hills
I hear the muffled roar of cannon,
Underbrush snapped
By rag-wrapped, bleeding feet
In quick retreat
A tattered blanket thrown across the back,
Dead dreams ripping at the brain.

Below are rusty pickups,
Tidy hospitals
Retirement homes to house the ghosts
Of other wars
While somewhere
Just before the morning medication
After all the doors are locked
The General surrenders
To the yuccas and bluebonnets,
While scores of wrinkled soldiers
Hobble on to Appomattox.

—1983

VASSAR MILLER
On a Weekend in September

Come God
be man woman child old one
bread breast of the world and water
for that matter
lamb stretched down and down down to the meanest grub
struggling to swim on concrete

merge into mortal stuff
Ancient of Days of Seas
mirroring
hauled to your hard wood
Creator brought to creature

here where I remember Lee Palmer
who 80-odd-years ago
prayed to no book but that terrible book of the deeps
on a weekend in September
I quickly skimmed

> *Dear Jesus*
> *make the waters recede*
> *and give us a pleasant day tomorrow to play*
> *and save my little dog Youno*

nobody remembers Lee Palmer now
why would they
he would be an old man now
dying maybe senile maybe
nobody would like him and would wish to hell he'd hurry

still I hope
Lee Palmer
swept out from Galveston in 1900
was swept up to you on the Gulf's gray tongue

because were one lapped
and lulled in the very body of the beloved
that were not bedding deep enough for one to know
and be known back

when each should tremble
cradling in the other's memory
shifting
such risky ocean

Open Sea
whose sides
eye cannot touch

   —1984

 ✦ ✦ ✦ ✦ ✦ ✦ ✦ ✦ ✦ ✦ ✦ ✦

LARRY D. THOMAS
The Great Storm
(multi-image documentary produced by C. Grant Mitchell)

The quavering words of those who survived
are voiced by sixteen actors
and overlaid with loud sound effects

and a stunning musical score
appropriate to the turn of the century culture.
Their sight barraged for a half hour

·with brittle, Gulf-stained sepia photographs
and renderings of carnage
well beyond the feeble lens of a camera,

the visitors take deep breaths,
ease from the benches of the Pier 21 Theater,
file slowly out into the same

early September sun which finally
broke through the black-green storm clouds
one hundred years to the day before,

and head in their cars for the causeway
linking Galveston Island to the mainland
by the twisting, fraying skin of its teeth.

   —2002

* * * * * * * * * * * *

ROGER JONES
Photo of a Rotary Crew, Sour Lake Oilfield, 1904

Fresh from the earth's insides,
they moon the camera's puff and shudder.
Slickly begrimed, hatted, they lean on
handles of tools, mouths taut, feet
spread on the wealth-granting ground.
They sleep in tents or shacks, eat

gruel scorched over campfires and drink
hot whiskey in shanty bars flung up
in the pines faster than circus tops,
each with its whore and pool of mirrors.
Some have come down for the work only,
others hoping to tap a draft of the wealth.

They stand with scuffed knuckles
poking big as rock bits that gnaw deep
in Texas earth. Distracted, they gaze on
as the photographer leans, draws his head
beneath the blackest cloak, as if to hear
the rich confessions of the ground below.

—1993

★ ★ ★ ★ ★ ★ ★ ★ ★ ★ ★ ★

THOMAS WHITBREAD
The Alcohol Question

Whether to drink or not to drink: that was
The fiery issue in Texas in 1912.
Did individuals have a sacred right
Or even a secular right to ruin lives?
To live in a state of liberty allowed
Or patriotically required a man
To be free to do almost anything he wanted.
But did murders and rapes—bad things—increase because
Of gin? rum? whiskey? —even beer and wine?
Hard question. Commissions studied it. Why not
Allow a man, after a hard day's work,
To seek stimulus, followed by anesthesia.
Many were happy drunks. But the blind rage
In some between first shot and sodden sleep
Was bothersome: the deaths; the broken homes…
Perhaps an amendment to the Constitution?
Texans continued to think, and drink. The end
Of Governor O.B. Colquitt's four-year term
Saw alcohol cussed, discussed, and swallowed down,
And the question of prohibition unresolved.

—1985

★ ★ ★ ★ ★ ★ ★ ★ ★ ★ ★ ★

EDWARD HIRSCH

Evening Star

(Georgia O'Keeffe in Canyon, Texas, 1917)

She was just a schoolteacher then
Walking away from the town
                              in the late-afternoon sunset,
A young woman in love
                    with a treeless place,
The scattered windmills and pounding winds
Of the whole prairie sliding toward dusk,
Something unfenced and wild
                              about the world without roads,
Miles and miles of land
                    rolling like waves into nowhere,
The light settling down in the open country.

She had nothing to do but walk away
From the churches and banks, the college buildings
Of knowledge, the filling stations
                              of the habitable world,
And then she was alone
                    with what she believed—
The shuddering iridescence of heat lightning,
Cattle moving like black lace in the distance,
Wildflowers growing out of bleached skulls,
The searing oranges and yellows of the evening star
Rising in daylight,
              commanding the empty spaces.

—1989

HILTON ROSS GREER
To General Pershing

(On the occasion of his visit to Dallas, Feb. 6, 1920)

Wrested long since from tyranny's black heel
By swords and sons whose shining deeds are fame's,
Mother of men and soldiers, Texas claims
Kinship with hearts of valor, souls of steel.
So ardors old rekindle, pulses peal
Acclaiming trumpets, and her high heart flames,
Greeting the man and soldier whom she names
Kinsman, and servant of a whole world's weal.

"Welcome, great leader! Stern and sure and wise!"
Her cities shout, and their one voice is hers.
But more than living speak! Above them stirs
A hero-host—her younger sons. Their cries
Break like a chorused thunder from the skies:
"Pershing, lead on! New tasks the hour confers!
Fight! And make sure to us, your followers,
That priceless thing we died for never dies!"

—1935

W. E. BARD
The Seventh Seal

Scene: A Farm Yard in South Texas

No, stranger, the cotton was mighty sorry again this
    year, mighty sorry.
I'll not be wantin' to buy a cyar, no siree.
That old hack over yonder'll be good enough, I
    reckon.
You an' me won't be hyar much longer, nohow.

(He paused to wipe the buttermilk from his mouth;
His eyes were kindled with a burning message.)

Stranger, did you know a great calamity air so nigh
That hits black wings air now a-flappin' us in the
        face?
The prophet Daniel an' the Revelations both hev
        spoke of hit
As bein' when the seventh seal air opened.
The ones that hev been opened hed horses fer to go
        with them,
But there are no horses with the ones to come.
The first, hit was a white horse, white fer Holiness.

(His prophetic eyes burned into the soul
Of his visitor as twin balls of fire.)

The second was a red horse,
Just like as though he tramped in blood, ya see.
That was the War that drug so many of our boys
Away from home to die in Europe.

(His hot breath fanned the visitor's cheek.
The man upon the doorstep moved uneasily.)

Then lo, a black horse!
That was the Judgment on the nations,
As though God's finger wrote upon the wall,
*Thou art weighed in the balances and art found
        wanting.*

(With outstretched finger he traced the dread words
        in the air,
Then pointed up as though he were pronouncing
        doom.)

Then last there was a pale horse,
The color of a corpse that hed begun to mortify.
That was the Pestilence that caused more men to bite
        the dust
Than all the shot an'poison gas in Europe.
We called hit floo—*the in-floo-enzy.*

D'ye see them cyars a-passin' to an' fro
Like chaparral birds a-runnin' on the road?
Now look hyar—See those airyplanes
Like lizards flyin' through the air?
Can ye wonder that God has lost his patience
With us with goin'-ons like that?

(He pointed, leveling a lean, prophetic finger.
His visitor felt a queer sensation creeping down his
        spine.)

Now this here cotton, hit's the staple of the world.
The world must hev our cotton or hits mills will
        stop.
So God, he taken the failure of our cotton crop
To point us to the calamity that our sins hev brung
        upon us.

First off, there was the boll weevil.
Then came the boll-worm burrowin' in to kill the
        boll.
Then the leaf-worm stripped the foli'ge off.
An' the root rot hit us—Look at that field over
        yonder.

Stranger, the time air most hyar fer the seventh seal
        to be opened.
A greater calamity than the world has ever seed air
        comin',
An' hits black wings air flappin' us in the face.

(He paused to wipe the buttermilk from his mouth.
The automobile salesman did not wait to mutter a
         farewell,
But passing through the gate, he heard the quavering
         old voice following him:
I'll not be wantin' to buy a cyar.
That old hack air good enough fer me,
An' you an' me won't be hyar much longer, nohow.)

         —1934

★   ★   ★   ★   ★   ★   ★   ★   ★   ★   ★   ★

STANLEY E. BABB
Galveston
Beach-Front

Along this spot where Jean Lafitte once paced
In somber grandeur, snuff-box in his hand,
Watching cloud-rags flapping about the moon,
Above the windy vagueness of the sea,
His heart a turbulence of wanderlust,
Wild jazz-bands at the dance-halls gut the night
With raucous syncopations—
                    (. . . bronze men sneak
through jungles startling monstrous living things
that dart in fright across the glittering stars
while all the air is trembling to the long
gaunt monotone of tom-toms. . . .)
                         —painted girls
Parade the Boulevard with patient smiles
And grey eyes bright with hopeful weariness,
And in the brilliant Arcade with its booths
And "Games of Chance" thin, smiling women shout:
"Come on, boys! . . . Try your luck! . . . Three balls
         for a dime!"

—While overhead the unregarded stars
Weave silver nets to snare the golden mouse
That is the young moon creeping up the sky,
And down the dim grey loneliness of beach
Rings loud the reckless laughter of old waves
Whose eyes have seen strong men go down to death
With gibbering protests on their writhing lips.

—1923

* * * * * * * * * * * * *

LEXIE DEAN ROBERTSON
Pioneer: The Vignette of an Oil-Field

I

All day the wagons have gone by
In a great cloud of dust on the highway,
The horses plodding with down-hung heads,
The harness clanking dully,
Or sometimes jingling with little bells.
The drivers sit immobile on the great iron pipes
Like stolid images dressed in coarse cottons
With dusty hats pulled low, shading dull unseeing
        eyes.
A wheel jolts cruelly in a deep rut,
The dust swirls in a choking fog,
But the driver sits unmoved, staring ahead.
All day the wagons pass in a long dust-enveloped line.

II

Sunset with the derricks standing stark
Against the skyline.
Grim sentinels, black and cruel,
Against the golden splendor of the west.

Row upon row they stand,
Scarring the soft bosom of the prairie,
Silhouettes of wealth and toil and service,
Stark against the scarlet glory of the skyline.

III

At night the rough unpainted shacks are crowded
With a pushing, jostling, coarse humanity,
Eager to spend.
The gambling hall is brilliant with mirrored lights.
The plank floors creak beneath the muddy-booted
        feet;
An officer of the law leans against the door
And hears the click of the dice, the whir of the wheel,
Unheeding.
Painted women, nakedly dressed, eye every man
From under half-closed purple-tinted lids.
In a drug store a reeling loafer drinks raw gin
Handed boldly across the counter.
The blare of a saxophone
Syncopates through the open window of a dance hall.
The people surge through the streets pushing each
        other,
Hurrying from one plank shack to another,
Eager to spend.

    —*1928*

* * * * * * * * * * * * *

WILLIAM D. BARNEY
Wide-Eyed

We all wanted to see it when it came
to Old John, the indisputable proof
of riches.

327

Not so much that we had no shame
as simply, we were curious sons
of bitches.

What would he do with one hundred thousand
of what he'd been used to having at most
by tens?
He, with one Sunday pair of trousers,
a two-room box, a row of collards,
and nine hens?

Oil in Kilgore, all we slaved to squeeze,
flowed no more steady than the sense
in Old John's head.
What should he know of royalties?
Well, first he'd have a gentleman's talk
with Mistah Ledd.

If the signs was right, then he proposed
going over to Shreesport and buy the biggest
old shiny
second-hand Pierce Arrow in the house.
Ne' mind it might be too soft for his
pine hiny.

And he did, too. Went and came back blowing
a-ooga and jerking between gears like a blue
wheelbarrow.
We couldn't tell, for weeks, where he was going.
He had a look wider between the eyes than
the Pierce Arrow.

—1969

GRACE ROSS
Oil Well Fire

Far off it is a rainy smudge against the sky;
Nearer, a storm-cloud in a fear-locked dream;
A mile away it is a volcano, savage and satanic.

The old woman on the hill says, "See,
The Devil has poked a hole through the ground—
Look at his black arm waving in the flame!"

—1936

☆　☆　☆　☆　☆　☆　☆　☆　☆　☆　☆　☆

BOYCE HOUSE
Justice in Old Ranger
(Being an incident during the Boom of 1920)

In rich old Ranger, a synonym for danger,
There was many a stranger who lost his life
When mighty wells became flaming hells,
And there were tolling bells at the end of strife.
But the six-gun's roar o'er barroom floor
Brought far, far more to an early doom—
Graves on the hillside, peaceful as eventide
Mark those who died during the boom.

Now Lon Flewellen was city judge,
And he was irked full sore,
That so many died in their strength and pride,
But no killer paid the score.
For few were found, and fewer tried,
And none were stuck at all
In the dull old room in Eastland-town,
The Criminal District Hall.

A fellow one night provoked a fight,
And was his light put out real quick!
The knifer, one Pace, was—after a race—
Overhauled by a city dick.
But the State delayed and no charge was made;
His lawyer did rant and rail
As this godly man lay languishing
Three days in the Ranger jail.

"He's willing, Judge, to pay a fine
If the city will turn him out" —
And so Flew probed until he knowed
How the matter come about.
The deceased, he found, was mainly to blame
By being slow on the draw.
"However's this feller's been wearing out
Our jail," said the limb o' the law.

In the courtroom dim, the judge was grim
As he pondered the prisoner's fate.
At last the jurist, who at heart was a purist,
Began to expatiate:
"Light as a ditty, you entered our peaceful city" —
(Some thirty thousand in a flock
With a killing each day ere the sun's last ray,
As steady as granddad's clock) —

"And a man of worth, the salt of the earth,
You sent to the grave so dank" —
(A third-class cook but a first-rate crook,
In truth, was the victim's rank).
"For this crime so cold, this slaying bold,
You're fined dollars seventy-five,
And you ought to be chuckful of glee
That you're getting out alive.

"Yes, this should be a lesson—if ye
Kill another in this place,
You'll get the limit of the law,
Two hundred dollars, Pace.
So fare-thee-well and get to hell
Out of Ranger on the fly:
There's a train that's due at 6:02,
Let your first stop be Shanghai!"

In rare old Ranger, that once spelt danger,
Where full many a stranger paid with his life,
No mighty wells become flaming hells,
And tolling bells are no longer rife;
The six-gun's roar is heard no more
O'er saloon-floor or bad poolroom;
But the fame of Flew and the prisoner too
Keeps ever new the grand days of the boom.

—1949

*　*　*　*　*　*　*　*　*　*　*　*

Chuck Taylor
Poem to Ma Ferguson

I've been sleeping out, Miriam,
sleeping out on county land,
working at getting the bucks together
to rent a place, and so public places
like our state capitol are good
for hanging out, passing time like
these old coots in Stetsons outside
on park benches, cracker barreling
wisdom even this late in the century—

So now I sit on a wooden chair
in the capitol rotunda, tourists
all around craning necks up,
up into blue dome—here I sit,
staring at your pleasant face,
Ma Ferguson, first oil portrait
to the right of south entrance.
Although your dress leaves shoulders
bare half covered by a shawl,
the artist hasn't painted you
Hollywood pretty. The chin is
solid, marked with a cleft; your
eyes are set in a serious thinking
frown; your cheeks, though rouged,
are firm. Miriam—Ma Ferguson—
Texas' first woman governor—
two terms yet. Two more
paintings down and there
you are again, older now, plumper,
flecks of gray in your hair,
grandmotherly, no shoulders bare.

Ma, you caught a lot of flak,
a lot of anti-feminist flak,
during both your terms of office;
some just didn't like it when
you said, "many women will be
invited to take an active part
in this administration." First
woman governor of Texas, from
a family with flash and flamboyance,
you passed a law that made it
a crime to wear the Klan's white
hood in public. Your daughter
says you were tough minded
—tough enough not to fear

advice from your husband
Governor Jim. A woman—you
know how they say—needs must
be twice as good as a man.

Ma Ferguson, Texas' first woman
governor, for a man like me, sleeping
out in my car in a camp like the
Hoovervilles of the Depression,
you mean something. A symbol. Right
or wrong, you and your husband gave
the impression of caring for
the little man. I remember you saved
a young Chicano from the electric
chair because it was his first offense.
You symbolized something here
in Texas, something we need to
keep in this greedy time when a
B-movie man strides this land
playing rhinestone cowboy, yes
you symbolized—shall I call it
the maternal? —love for the
family human, progressive populism.

   —1986

   ★   ★   ★   ★   ★   ★   ★   ★   ★   ★

CAROL COFFEE REPOSA
Hempstead, 1923
for My Grandparents

The main street flanked by shabby storefronts, dust
Motes slowly floating in the heat, the hours
Expand to memory. The farmers drive
To town each Saturday. Their faces scan
The sky before they talk about their maize

And cotton, watermelons cracking in
The sun, the campaign of Ma Ferguson,
The cotton gins are running now. Their fierce
Teeth grind out perfect bales from August to
October, giant seeds enclosed in steel,
While linseed oil drips through the years. Across
The street the house still stands, the picket fence
Implied, the swing and pomegranate trees
Almost restored. The silent rooms, the steep
White gables hidden in the trees suggest
The possibility of sound: a sharp
Swift clattering of feet along the stairs,
A spate of scales extracted from the old
Belligerent piano after school,
The lazy whine of ceiling fans, the blades
Describing sleepy circles on the walls.
Above all else, the yearly music of
The tree, a Brazos cedar twelve feet tall,
Unwilling to be dragged along the porch
And crowded through the door, the sullen swish
Of sodden, rainsoaked branches in the hall,
The scent of dark green needles covering
The floor. Those sounds continue somewhere, in
Some other rooms and isolated thoughts.
Around the graves there's just the distant barking
Of a dog, the crawling of two ants
Across the stone, the sprouting of a black
Eyed Susan in the soft red clay, their small
Acts muffled in the fog that rolls in off
The Gulf. Remote events enclosed by time,
They still suggest the possibility of sound.

—1985

William D. Barney
A Ballad for Bill Pickett

Willie got born somewhere near Austin,
        a Texan as all agree.
He was some Black and some Creole
        and part of him Cherokee.

He learned to ride before he could walk
        leastways, that's as they say.
He'd stay in a saddle on a bucking bronc
        or out on the range all day.

He saw some cowboys branding calves;
        they couldn't catch the brutes.
Willie, he said, "I'll catch you a few,
        as sure as my feet is in boots."

They laughed at the skinny kid as he rode
        for a calf that was on the run;
he slid from his horse, grabbed the head,
        and down in the dirt they spun.

And the calf held taut. They still tell
        how Willie got him a grip,
for he held on to that yearling's head
        with his teeth in its upper lip.

"I seen a bulldog do that once,"
        said Willie when he was through.
"I says to myself, if a dog can do that,
        no reason I can't too."

His fame went through the cities around,
        how he could take down a steer,
grabbing its head and chawing its lip—
        he was a man without fear.

He even went down to Mexico City
     to work a wild bull in the ring.
If the crowd hadn't tossed brickbats,
     he'd have bulldogged the damn thing.

The Miller Brothers of 101 Ranch
     got word of Willie's fame.
Zack Miller, he came down to Cowtown
     to see him play his game.

There on the banks of Marine Creek
     Pickett bulldogged with a will.
Said Zack, "Join us, you're our man,
     and your name is henceforth Bill."

They held a big fair near Guthrie Town,
     the biggest ever seen
in the Territory, complete with horses,
     stagecoaches, a beauty queen,

Two hundred Indians from a dozen tribes,
     at their head Old Geronimo.
And cowboys by dozens and dignitaries—
     oh, it was a marvelous show!

But the biggest event of the whole day
     was bulldogging by our Bill.
He did himself proud, he showed them how
     and gave that crowd a true thrill.

He was with Millers the rest of his days,
     a showman they counted a friend.
When a wild horse kicked him in the head,
     Bill came to an untimely end.

And Old Zack Miller wrote a poem to say
       how "Old Bill is Dead" but still
would live on in the hearts of men.
       There's never be any like Bill.

On Exchange Avenue, North Fort Worth,
       there's a sculpture of a brave man,
of a struggling steer got by the horns—
       it's all to an artful plan.

Friends, honor the cowboy. Bill Pickett.
       He was tough. He was good. He was game.
He fought with his hands, his heart, his teeth,
       and he won himself a proud name.

    —1999

★ ★ ★ ★ ★ ★ ★ ★ ★ ★ ★ ★

WHITNEY MONTGOMERY
Outlaws

Billy rode on a pinto horse—
       Billy The Kid, I mean—
And he met Clyde Barrow riding
       In a little gray machine.

Billy drew his bridle rein
       And Barrow stopped his car,
And the dead man talked to the living man
       Under the morning star.

Billy said to the Barrow boy,
       "Is this the way you ride,
In a car that does its ninety per,
       Machine guns at each side?"

"I only had my pinto horse
  And my six-gun tried and true,
And I could shoot, but they got me at last,
  And some day they'll get you!"

"For the men who live like you and me
  Are playing a losing game,
And the way we shoot, or the way we ride
  Is all about the same."

"And the like of us may never hope
  For death to set us free,
For the living are always after you
  And the dead are after me!"

Then out of the East arose the sound
  Of hoof-beats with the dawn,
And Billy pulled his rein, and said,
  "I must be moving on."

And out of the West came the glare of a light
  And the drone of a motor's song,
And Barrow set his foot on the gas
  And shouted back, "So long!"

So into the East Clyde Barrow rode,
  And Billy, into the West;
The living man who can know no peace,
  And the dead who can know no rest.

—1934

*　*　*　*　*　*　*　*　*　*　*　*　*

BONNIE PARKER
The Story of Bonnie and Clyde

You have heard the story of Jesse James,
Of how he lived and died.
If you still are in need of something to read,
Here is the story of Bonnie and Clyde.

Now Bonnie and Clyde are the Barrow gang,
I'm sure you all have read
How they rob and steal
And how those who squeal,
Are usually found dying or dead.

There are lots of untruths to their write-ups,
They are not so merciless as that—
They hate all the laws,
The stool-pigeons, spotters and rats.

If a policeman is killed in Dallas
And they have no clues to guide—
If they can't find a fiend,
They just wipe the slate clean,
And hang it on Bonnie and Clyde.

If they try to act like citizens,
And rent them a nice little flat,
About a third night they are invited to fight,
by a submachine gun rat-tat-tat.

A newsboy once said to his buddy;
"I wish old Clyde would get jumped—
In these awful hard times,
We'd make a few dimes
If five or six cops would get bumped."

They class them as cold-blooded killers,
They say they are heartless and mean,
But I say this with pride,
That once I knew Clyde
When he was honest and upright and clean.

But the law fooled around,
Kept tracking him down,
And locking him up in a cell,
Til he said to me,
"I will never be free,
So I will meet a few of them in hell."

This road was so dimly lighted.
There were no highway signs to guide,
But they made up their minds
If the roads were all blind
They wouldn't give up till they died.

The road gets dimmer and dimmer,
Sometimes you can hardly see,
Still it's fight man to man,
And do all you can,
For they know they can never be free.

They don't think they are too tough or desperate.
They know the law always wins.
They have been shot at before
But they do not ignore
That death is the wages of sin.

For heartbreaks some people have suffered,
From weariness some people have died,
But take it all and all,
Our troubles are small,
Till we get like Bonnie and Clyde.

Some day they will go down together;
And they will bury them side by side.
To a few it means grief,
To the law it's relief,
But it's death to Bonnie and Clyde.

—*1934*

* * * * * * * * * * * * *

Paul Foreman
Huddie Ledbetter

Whip it on down,
                Huddie!
Ten thick fingers
      Whanging a twelve-stringer.

Where we had two chords
           in our voice-box,
You had twelve;
Where we had one heart
        You had ten
Throbbing and bursting
        Inside your chest,
Where Pity and Passion
            played with a guitar pick.

Whang it on down, Huddie!
           Lord, the air's so
thick with your music,
The good ache of it
        forgets me all my blues.

Sing to me of Sugarland
           and cotton pickin'
      On the Brazos.

A thousand pounds a day!
        Lord, sing that again!
A thousand pounds a day!

       "You got to jump around
a bit to pick that much."

What the dude in Houston
        didn't know, Huddie,
Was this: your belly's made
        Of iron, not lead,
And when he had his knife
        In your belly,
And you had your knife
        in his belly,
                your belly
Was made of iron, and
        His was not, no,
His belly was not made of
        Iron.
The saying ain't so, that
          what you don't know
won't hurt you. It's good to know
        That Leadbelly
Was made of iron.
What songs did you sing
        For the old governor,
           Pat Neff,

That day to make him
        Set you free.
Huddie, what songs did you sing?
        Did you sing, "I got stripes,"
Or "Yaller Gal," or
        "Like a turkey through the corn

With his long johns on."
No matter,
you set

Yourself free,
Bunching your hands
And whanging
On your guitar,
Your big flat-bottomed
12-string Blues guitar.

Let me chip this in stone
For you, Huddie,
You still be
the top bottle
On the blue-bottle tree.

*"Yes, they whipped him
Up the hill for me!"*

—1977

✳ ✳ ✳ ✳ ✳ ✳ ✳ ✳ ✳ ✳ ✳ ✳ ✳

Naomi Stroud Simmons
Black Sunday, April 14, 1935

*("Dust Bowl Invades Texas"
Amarillo Globe News)*

April wind travels the snow geese route
south, south, south,
crossing borders, picking up cargo to be
delivered dark before dark.

April wind pushes prayers past store fronts
down side streets through church doors
where banked vigil lights bow in incensed
greeting as warm life invades cool pews.

We eat Mama's Sunday dinner with all the relish
of combines in summer fields while
April wind blows my empty swing
beckoning me for a free ride
winding, twisting, winding
as north horizons dull our sunny Sunday.

Soon Father calls me to the porch to face
the unknown rushing, roiling, rumbling,
swallowing the trees, the windmill, the barn.

We retreat, close the door, fall to our knees
and we are swallowed in darkness.

A drowning black sifts through our walls.

Fumbling for a small light that gives
candle power, Father casts us in sepia.
Wading through grit we seek dampened washcloths,
cover our faces, soothe our eyes,
breath dampness

while silent prayers have question marks.

> —1996

GRACE NOLL CROWELL
A Prayer for Texas
(In Her Centennial Year)

Lord God of every race and every land,
In this great year of Texas' Jubilee,
We come, its people, reaching for Thy hand,
Acknowledging our constant need of Thee.
Look down upon us with approving eyes,
In all we do and say may we be wise.

Because of Thy great bounty we are blessed
Beyond all dreaming! Lord God may we see
Thy hand within the finest and the best
Flowering of a gracious century.
We bring Thee as our offerings of praise
The bright fruits of our past and present days.

Accept them, Lord, and may new beauty rise
Like smoking incense from our gathered store;
May Texas write her name against the skies
As splendidly as she has done before;
Her lone star burning—her six flags unfurled,
Her voice, a call of welcome to the world.

　　　　—1936

✴ 　 ✴ 　 ✴ 　 ✴ 　 ✴ 　 ✴ 　 ✴ 　 ✴ 　 ✴ 　 ✴ 　 ✴ 　 ✴

R. S. GWYNN
Randolph Field, 1938

Hands of men blasted the world asunder;
How they lived God only knew!
If you'd live to be a gray haired wonder,
Keep the nose out of the blue!

Framed by the open window, a lone Stearman
Wobbles, dips right, dips left, then dives and banks
For touch-and-go, seeming barely to miss
The sunlit "Taj Mahal" and a stray egret
That has mistaken grass and shimmering concrete
For salt marsh. Two flies on the windowsill
Wait for their chance. The wind-sock hangs limply
In the thick heat, and lunch is still uncleared.

Indeed, the mess tray resting on the nightstand
Has not been touched, or hardly—half a weiner,

Succotash and boiled carrots stirred around,
Even the tea and gingerbread just tasted,
And the young man there who has no appetite
Has raised himself up from the sweaty pillow
To watch some fledgling's first attempt, as stirring
As a scene from *The West Point of the Air*.

It slips from sight. He leans his head back, dizzy
From the slight effort, shuddering against
The squeal of tires, the buzz-saw radial engine
Over-throttled, straining up to a stall,
And then, a day's sole miracle, the steady
Hum of the prop—somebody else's luck.
For now the chills have come to spike his fever,
Everything holding true to course but him.

The skinny nurse who takes his temperature
Charts the latest, 102.8,
And then connects the dots with a red line
That climbs and plummets like a rookie's struggle
To keep the nose cowl flush with the horizon.
It would be funny, but it simply isn't,
Even when Szulic and Rosenthal, his buddies,
Saunter in after class with Cokes and Luckies.

He'll envy them that night when, after supper,
He lies in bed and smokes. It isn't easy
To think of them with girls along the River—
Dancehalls, music, beer, all with such sweetness
In the mild evening air he'd like to cry.
He has missed the chance, like Aaron Rosenthal,
To burn above Berlin; like Thomas Szulic,
To spin in wingless somewhere over France.

A decade and a war still to be crossed
Before he is my father, he is only
One of the Dodos, barely voting age,
Washed out a week before he gets his wings.
A radio is playing now. Kay Kyser.
. . . *To be in Carolina in the mornin'* . . . .
It's hard to think of what he must go back to.
He banked on everything but going back.

Off to the southeast, thunderheads are building—
Heat lightning flashing like imagined guns,
Faint thunder and a breeze that brings the Gulf
Into this place of starched white sheets and Lysol
Where he lies watching three red points of light,
A late flight coming for night approach.
He shuts his eyes and tries to think of nothing
Before he sideslips into dreams of fire.

> —*1988*

  ✶   ✶   ✶   ✶   ✶   ✶   ✶   ✶   ✶   ✶   ✶   ✶

GOLDIE CAPERS SMITH
Ballad of a Bombardier from Texas

Travis Brown saw the light of day
In a weathered cottage down Texas way;

His father chuckled and swelled with pride,
The happiest man on the prairie-side.

"Doc," he grinned, "here's my last red cent
Says you fetched us a future President."

Travis grew up astride of a pony,
Free as a norther, hating a phony,

As clean a guy as you'd ever meet,
Six-foot-three in his stocking feet.

Before he could blink he was overseas,
Wading in history up to his knees.

He wrote home, "Me and a guy from Dallas
Just went to tea at Buckingham Palace".

"The Queen, she passed us bread and jam;
I remembered my 'Please' and 'Thank-you-ma'am.'"

Then over the channel quick as a rocket
To drop a bomb in Hitler's pocket.

He pulled the lever for "Bombs away,"
Spit through his teeth and crooned this lay:

We're over the top—so let 'em drop:
One for Mother and one for Pop;

One for the Army, one for the Navy,
One for pork-chops, cornbread and gravy;

One for the day when the war is over
And I'm back in Texas living in clover,

Where a spade's a spade, and a man's a man,
And the prairie spreads like a palm-leaf fan.

I'll marry a gal with a freckled face
And raise little dogies all over the place.

We'll teach 'em to cuss and rope and ride,
to skin a steer and stretch its hide,

To pass a football over the goal
For A. & M. in the Cotton Bowl."

"The world's too small—as you've got to know—
Hitler, for you and the *Alamo*.

So junk your medals, and hold your hats:
The name of this ship is "*Rough-on-Rats*."

—1944

* * * * * * * * * * * *

DAVID WESTHEIMER
At the Movies

A Bob Wills LP is on the turntable
And I am reading to the strains of kicker music.
Flowing past almost unheard
Then "La Golondrina" spills out.
The Goodbye Song.
And I am back in a flickering courtyard
In the Italian prison camp
On the wooden stool I have carried from my barracks.
Crowded among other prisoners
Watching a movie about Joaquin Murietta.
The Mexican hero-bandit,
On a hung sheet,
Dubbed in Italian
And the background music is "La Golondrina."
A vivid memory.
But I do not wish I was back there.

—1945, 1999

* * * * * * * * * * * *

8

Things About to Disappear

The body's lips moved, made a soft smile and the eyes narrowed with laughter, breathless, darting laughter moving and echoing like the cries of night birds outside. Emery heard the laughter, listened to the birds, and cradled his arms against his chest. Long after darkness, Emery sat, hugging himself, crying himself to sleep, savoring his sadness, reliving his memories, contained in his deep grief.

⋆ *Alan Wier*

351

Larry McMurtry
For Erwin Smith, Cowboy Photographer

Lead me along the hills,
where naked young mesquites
Shiver in the twelve-day wind
          by stumps of burned ancestors;

Where the last badgers denned
          and yucca bloomed white
Among weed and thorn
          to the weedringed rocks
Where the bones are strown,
          white and dry on the dry ground—

Ribs, skulls, jaws
          with rotting teeth;
Bones of red heifers
          dead of a first bringing;
Bones of the early wounded
          Herd.

And here, the last cracked bones
          of my grandfather's horse,
The gray one who stood in grave
          infirmity under
Horsepasture elms through
          my boyhood.

An old horse, youth
          and the cantering after cattle
Lost, and lost calves,
          and myself, lost
To the white bones and the hills—

Busy with dove and rabbit,
        and the coyote tracks
Fresh every day in the creekbed
        mud—turning finally

Through your book
        and finding those grey doves
And tracks set back,
        the old bones sprung
Together and the unremembered
        hills drawn into line.

You were, at the last,
        as an old horse under elm,
Bending in pain to flavorless
        grass, the dust taste
In your mouth—

You who in your youth
        ranged the browning summertime
Canadian with a Kodak
        and one pair of boots,

You and the onetime three-year-old
        of the blurring dun
Legs, wonderers toward the end:

Was tobacco worth the walk
        to store:
Could another winter
        be endured?

Wondering, at the last,
        if sinew had ever been strong,

If flesh and swift blood
       had been real

If the wildtide Canadian
       ever ran through such green range.

O pards, I hear the whistle,
       but the train has gone.

     —1960

* * * * * * * * * * * * * *

Dave Oliphant
Eugene Wukasch, Texas Architect

Seton Hospital coming down:
photos he took tell the story
of steel girders & cement walls
crumbled, doubled, pounded to dust—
collapsed windows, where twilight rays
floated motes over janitored floors,
his mother rolled from delivery
to a maternity ward
& the further relief of sleep.
Knows the blueprints, the materials,

how substantial they were,
in their way strong as the memory.
Why were they not reused, remembered?
Speaking with quiet rage
of the waste, of energy expended,
of the halls held those hours
where & when he entered the State,
a tear forms in his foreign eye,
streams down his Austin cheek:
"Damn it, I was born there!"

Texas, yes, as any,
though by name & blood a Wend,
his Black Forest, his Slavic race
poling their boats like gondoliers,
laden with cabbage and engravings of
the very scene he paints.
His tale, mortar to our luncheon talk,
glides us through those shadowy waters,
disappears us down basement plumbing,
into her screams at his coming

on a table splintered to smithereens,
the vacant block for sale,
its sidewalks still intact
outlining the emptiness of weeds,
the trees, spreading elms, rooted yet,
though reaching about as exiles
missing landmarks on childhood maps,
the pale smear down to his mouth
seeking a forgotten Sorbian word
would house the lumber of loss.

—1980

☆   ☆   ☆   ☆   ☆   ☆   ☆   ☆   ☆   ☆   ☆   ☆

PAT LITTLEDOG
cowgirl

yes I was a cowgirl
living outside san antonio
on a military reservation
the year began with chinese fire
in korean skies
and you can bet I saw 7000
recruited young men
who moved into tents down the street

from my daddy-the-captain's quarters
january cold front and not enough supplies
my daddy said for so many men
not enough fuel for their tent fires and
from the school bus windows I watched them
swinging arms and legs together
calling out their rhymes
breath cold white

but fire of palominos
in the springtime
fiesta de los caballos
and you better believe I was a cowgirl
got the plastic yellow fringe
on snazzy vest and short-pants
my mama sewed for me
pre-pubescent vamp-of-texas style
(boots next year my daddy promised)
palominos lead all parades in san antonio
city of horses prancing
past ten-year-old cowgirls
lining the sidewalks
while someone is dreaming
of fire soon-to-be
in palomino stables
soon-to-consume palominos
too frenzied to gallop through flames
gala parade palominos

yes wasn't it only a dream
that fire would eat horses and men
up so soon?
burned horseflesh singed hair blowing
already through Gateway of Air
and all of its Forces

but I was only a cowgirl
yearning for boots next year
dreaming of creamy gold horses.

     —1985

*   *   *   *   *   *   *   *   *   *   *   *

Rolando Hinojosa
The Eighth Army at the Chongchon

Creating history (their very words)
by protecting the world from Communism. I suppose
One needs a pep talk now and then, but what
Gen. Walton H. (Johnny) Walker said
Was something else.

Those were darker days, of course,
And the blinding march South
Cannot be believed
Unless you were there. But the point is
That the Chinese
Were stoppable, so Gen. Walker believed.

And he was right; later on he was killed
At one of the fronts, standing up
On a jeep. We understood.

This wasn't Ketch Ridge or Rumbough Hill
Or the Frisco-Rock Island RR Junction at Sill,
But then, it wasn't the Alamo either.

And those who survived
Remember what he said:
     "We should not assume that (the)
     Chinese Communists are committed in force.
     After all, a lot of Mexicans live in Texas."

And that from the Eighth Army Commanding
Himself. It was touching.
And yet, the 219th
Creating history by protecting the world from Communism,
Brought up the rear, protected the guns, continued the mission,
And many of us there
Were again reminded who we were
Thousands of miles from home.

—*1978*

* * * * * * * * * * * * *

ROLANDO HINOJOSA
Rest Due and Taken

General Walker is dead; killed in a road accident.
What a way to go.
No grudges about the Mexican crack;
We don't have to prove anything to anyone here.

I've not seen either Charlie or Joey since the Chongchon,
But we're all coming off the line soon.

—*1978*

* * * * * * * * * * * * *

ROLANDO HINOJOSA
Vale

It's over. Or it is for me, anyway;
I'm leaving; through, finished and done with:
I've hit retirement age, give me my watch…
For the last four months I have forced myself
To think not to think about this day,
And God knows I've thought of little else.

No more deaths and no more killing; not by these hands,
At any rate. That's for those who stay.
          No need to thermite my one one four model
Of my one five five gun;
Just remove the blocks and sights.
          "Leave artillerymen alone, they're an obstinate lot."
But I'm through here, and I'm through with skull in place.
In time, the U.S. Army will tell us how many men
It lost here; for now
I'll tell you how many friends I lost:
Chale Villalón and Pepe Vielma,
Cayo Diaz and a kid named Balderas;
Frank Hatalski and Hook Frazier
Boston John McCreedy from Quincy, Mass.,
(As fine a chaplain as ever punched a can)
And, Phil Brodkey…
Oh, and there was Louie Dodge,
Who though not really a member of the chorus,
We later learned that another outfit
Had sent him to us: Knowing full well he was mad to the core.

Others died as well, strangers when they came
And strangers when they left;
A field full of men mowed down who were later stuffed and crammed
Into trucks by other men who committed Army sins
And thus paid dearly for them. Not quite dearly enough,
Of course, having gotten away with their lives,
Which is more, to be sure, than can be said for the sad-faced Company Clerk
Who finally found a loaded carbine.

And there were others: Not friends, no, but just as dead.
And now, for a good while at least,
It's back to Klail,
And home. Home to Texas, our Texas.

That slice of hell, heaven
Purgatory and land of our Fathers.

—1978

* * * * * * * * * * * *

ROBERT A. FINK
The Certified Public Accountant Recalls the Early 1950s

We wouldn't have a T.V. set for years
and the picture show shut down on Sunday
in a town too private for a population sign.
Everybody went to church or sent regrets,
so after clearing off the table
and the regulation nap,
what was there to do but load the Ford
for a drive in the country?

Every road wore a number
Father, the mathematician, knew by heart
and recited like language
one enjoys against his teeth.
Mother sang the names of towns
(Smyrna, East Point, New Hope)
we could turn to in a jiffy.
Someone there was always distant kin.

Black Gum   Red Oak   Maple
Dogwood   Magnolia   Pine.
Father's pointing finger named each tree,
recounted the legend of its leaves
as if he hadn't changed the ending
so they all lived happily ever after
like the crows laughing
from the new-strung power lines;

the girl sitting on her Shetland pony,
not even casually interested in our passing;
and the pair of Snowy Egrets
lifting from a lily pond,
wings heavy as angels
charged with annunciation.

—1989

* * * * * * * * * * * *

BETTY ADCOCK
Photograph of the Courthouse Square, 1950s

Here is the town with its spine broken,
a cough in the dust just risen
behind that Buick's disappearing tail fins.
Dust smears the plate-glass reflections
of farmers on their way to insurance.
Beyond the white borders of this picture,
thick cotton fields are unraveling fast.

You can see it's a Saturday, spit-shiny
sidewalks are crowded. Barge-bosomed women
are taking on cargo, gossip, the strategy
for a new onslaught of gentility.
Only July or August could make the light
this mean. The camera has caught the heat,
how it can shut like a box,
like the click of a dull knife,
holding everything still.

My two children have climbed to the stone knee
of James Pinckney Henderson,
who sits in his stone lawyer's chair on a rock
left rough as Houston's Texas Republic.

Under the pecan tree by the statue,
the men stall in a knot, a quarrel,
a guffaw, a lie. They are forgiving
the wrong politicians again.

There is still one pair of mules hitched
to a wagon in this picture.

In their beaten hats, old men are leaning
toward just this stopped grainy air,
this fading of detail on a piece of paper:
the handwritten deed naming a *pin oak tree*
as permanent west corner of a farm in 1840,
county tax records that disappeared,
bad debts set afire, the birth date changed,
bogus land certificates, crooked leases,
court records vanished after a murder,
indictments misplaced, feuds unreported in print—
paper and its untrustworthy statements.

And most of those in this photograph dead
who knew the world a condition of memory
tenacious as spidersilk, sticky as fear,
its breath the intractable word
I have come for.

   —1988

* * * * * * * * * * * *

CYD ADAMS
Longview, Texas

When peace brought the men back,
and Ike's moon face still beamed at us
on snowy little T.V.'s,
Letourneau bought Longview

for something to do
and built himself fortunes more
while Eastman and Resistol Hat
fouled the air too rank to breathe,
and Pullman Corp.'s Trailmobile
pumped out the tractor rigs
like mirrored-skinned dominoes,
the gangs of hard-hatted men
flooding past the guard gate
in endless-seeming timeclock shifts,
swinging their lunch pails
to the tune of paychecks,
their fleets of eclectic cars,
like termite armies swarming,
streaming down Estes Parkway
past the river's honkytonks
to feed the crowded, curving lanes
of 149.

And Longview grew on green blood,
a gray-skinned dogtick town,
industry and liquor drunk,
fed on steel and Kilgore crude,
its bars and whores and grocery stores
behind never-closing doors,
its drive-ins teeming with
their worker-ant hungry hordes,
its billboards demanding that
Earl Warren be impeached,
its city limits swelling while,
spooked on Sputnik and
reeling from the Bay of Pigs
and flashing many perfect teeth,
Kennedy demanded the moon.

—1997

* * * * * * * * * * *

THOMAS WHITBREAD
November 25, 1963

The assassination of the President,
Among its many effects, confers upon
The slightest act a clarity of precision.
The sharpening of a pencil with a knife,
My old Scout knife, twenty years old, today
Sharply reseen as its invented self.
The cutting of my nails with old small scissors,
Trying, as always, not to hurt the quick.
Then encountering, taking up the pencil,
Tooth marks, not mine, and breaking it in half
In the frustration of rage, despair, and grief
At life not being as it ought to be.
She bit it. Our love should be alive, as he
Much more should be, and stupidly is not.

—1964

GENE SHUFORD
The Visit
(from The Death in Our Family)

One can never tell what November will be in Texas:
it has that delusive warmth of the blood and love,
promising tenderness forever as though death
will never come: it will let lilacs bloom
in the autumn and the great sun shine with a burning
that invites the ultimate passion for living even
while the frost waits in tonight's sleep.
The rain can fall in the night and the sky will wash blue
as a baby's eyes in the morning and the puddles will dry
and the big jet will slip down out of cottony clouds
and the prince and the princess descend and all the banners

will wave above the spirit's shining armor.
Already this is a legend, a myth we only half believe,
saying, surely it must not have happened; surely, it must
have been a dream; surely, it was long ago,
but now is already encrusted with myth and the passion
for forgetting, strong as the passion for remembering,
so that both have woven a golden cloth for the years
of Camelot that were ours, for the greener fields that were ours,
for the tall castle we saw in the clouds, for the knight
and his lady dropped down from the sky who were our king
and the fairest queen we had ever seen walk proudly
across the tapestry of our time, which before
this day was done, all bloody on the stones
would lie and trampled with the blackest death
a man would ever see or bear to dream of.

    —1965

WILLIAM BURFORD
The Spell

You can almost see him, looking as if well,
Shedding it, shaking it off,
The least shadow on the shoulders
Marking the hurt—as if absorbed almost;
Then the face turning, alive—

Only hesitating momentarily—

Until you remembered how the head
Was horribly shattered
And fell, with the lifted hair,
As from an ax in back—Oswald
Cutting a path for himself
In the midst of America, a wedge;

But was the thing as it sped,
Coppered, leaden, not stopped
Perhaps there was in the invincible thick hair?
Where the woman with her skill
Could pick it away, in her lap,
Breaking the spell? In the cloth of her dress—

It was deeper than that;
Neither burr nor dune thistle,
Nor like the roses she held
Black as blood in the light, so dark red—
But a kind of blunt bud, splintered
Into flower, that could not be touched,
Having its own final force that spread throughout,
The blind dark overwhelming him.

—1966

*　　*　　*　　*　　*　　*　　*　　*　　*　　*　　*　　*　　*

REBECCA SPEARS
Marina's Daughters, 1964*
for Rachel and June

I watched her
as I passed by
walking toward school.
I watched her that winter.
Marina's daughter
quiet on a tricycle.

They taught us to hate her
at school, hate her
and her kind, Russians,
all of them,
even her sister,
the baby.

But I wouldn't,
could see in those daughters'
smooth ivory faces,
in ocean-deep eyes,
their dead father damned,
and sorrow,

sorrow we poured on
Jackie's children,
not on Marina's damned daughters:
Jackie's young drenched in it,
Marina's babies quiet,
burning.

—*2000*

*Lee Harvey Oswald's widow Marina moved to the poet's neighborhood in early 1964.

 ✶ ✶ ✶ ✶ ✶ ✶ ✶ ✶ ✶ ✶ ✶ ✶

Pat Stodghill
August 1, 1966

(Shortly before noon on Monday, August 1, 1966, Charles Joseph Whitman barricaded himself on the observation deck of the University of Texas tower in Austin and began shooting with his high-powered Remington hunting rifle. The final toll was 14 dead, 31 wounded.)

On August 1st in Texas everybody sweats.
The sun sears like a branding iron at noon;
makes some folks argue, curse, or even fight,
and some folks kill.
The dog star shines.
It is the time they say when strange things come…
a time for death.

Self appointed, the executioner waits,
perched thirty stories high in blazing blue.
Below, the town, the lake, the red rooftiles
all seem a peaceful postcard on a sunny day.

Five victims dead: one kin by birth and one by love,
the woman at the desk;
the visitors who had come to see the view
lie crumpled on the steps with viewless eyes
under the big clock
as time ticks by.

The sun has stopped at center sky.
His brain,
constant carrier of its own pain-weight, is bursting,
yet he checks his food, his guns, his shells and waits.
The carillon chimes.
From the tower drifts a cloud of smoke
which breeds a rain of lead.
He loads and aims and fires again,
again, again, again.

On the cement mall
remain shoes and books and pools of blood.
"Why? Why? Why?" keeps burning through the brain
for there is not an answer left
in all the universe of doubt.
We stare,
mute as the wild-eyed stallions rearing in the fountain.

On August 1st in Texas everybody sweats.
The sun sears like a branding iron at noon;
makes some folks argue, curse, or even fight,
and some folks kill…
and some folks kill.

—1983

MARCELLA SIEGEL
Waiting Wife

She sped the daytime hours
in a coffee shop on Powell Street
where commuters, tourists and shoppers
streamed in from the cable cars
to have her serve their hurry.
Nights in her flat in an old skinny house
she wrote him letters
that smiled at how the flower stalls
splashed spring on the downtown winter;
how a rock out in the bay
blossomed sometimes like an April tree
with the satin bodies of seals;
and how a rat she had christened Ben
was her kitchen companion at night.
And she was careful not to tell him how alone she was
listening to young laughter passing by on the sidewalk
outside her window
in that city so alien to her East Texas town,
that city by the sea
where she had come, to feel closer to him
while she waited for his return.
She read in his letters of the refugees
on the road from An Loc
turning their tired backs on their smoking huts,
of the old young mothers and their wasting children
walking the napalmed fields,
and of his buddy stilled in the mud at Quang Nghai.
And she wondered when he lay in a steaming paddy
waiting for a shadow to move or explode
if her love beside him
would be enough.

—1973

At Our Backs

Births were nothing new in New Hope,
the only surprise being the high school Prom Queen
who *wasn't* pregnant. It was, after all, *birth*,
not its barren opposite swinging from the hip
brass knuckles to connect with precarious jawbones,
delicate facial structures collapsing with windshields,
roofs squashed beneath the eighteen-wheeler milk tanker
backing across the county road at 4:00 a.m.,
the driver and the dairy farmer frozen
in the Chevy's headlights topping the hill at 90,
the three Friday-night football heroes
in the front seat, squeezed together.

It was not the speed boat revved to bursting
like a rodeo bronc in its chute,
the engine slammed into gear, a projectile
screaming from the dock, the daredevil driver
acknowledging only a slight bump, a hesitation
bisecting the Sophomore Class Favorites in their rented rowboat.
And it wasn't the Future Farmer of America
who sold his calf and bought a bus ticket to Dallas
for three nights in a hotel on Deep Ellum
before lying to the Marine recruiter and joining up
to be incinerated on a hill north of Da Nang.
We pass, each day, his blown-up, framed yearbook photo
hanging beside the trophy case.

It was the prayed-for climax of sock hops.
Last night, we squeezed our teen angel tight
and ebbed and flowed like the tide we'd never seen
in North East Texas but felt rising
to crest and crash and tug us back where we started

in our fathers' Fords and Chevys, dying again and again
until we parted.

     —1999

  ✱   ✱   ✱   ✱   ✱   ✱   ✱   ✱   ✱   ✱   ✱

ROBERT PHILLIPS
The Death of Janis Joplin
October 4, 1970

        ("Oh, Lord, won't you buy me a Mercedes-Benz…")

Because she was a white girl
      born black-and-blue,
because she was outsized victim
      of her own insides,
because she was voted
      "Ugliest Man on Campus,"
because she looked for something
      and found nothing—
      she became famous.

"Tell me that you love me!"
      she screamed at audiences.
They told. Fat Janis wouldn't
      believe. Twenty-seven,
a star since twenty-four,
      she tried to suck, lick,
smoke, shoot, drip, drop,
      drink the world.
      Nothing worked.

Bought a house, a place
      to go home to.
Bought a dog, something to give
      love to. Nothing worked.
Jimi Hendrix died, Janis cried:

"Goddamn. He beat me
to it!" Not by much. Three weeks
later she joined him.
Part of something at last.

—*1986*

★　★　★　★　★　★　★　★　★　★　★　★

ALBERT HUFFSTICKLER
Johnson City, Texas

Lyndon lay down among the
            wildfowers
and forgot about Vietnam
and being president and
all the things that
trouble a man and drive
him on past endurance
and drive him to do
things he can never
forgive himself for—
perhaps: I don't know.
I know he came home
and let his hair grow
and lay down among
the wildflowers with
Ladybird sitting beside
him because it's on a
postcard. But I don't
know what he
thought. Maybe he
thought death wasn't
so bad. If he went to
Heaven, there'd be wildflowers

and Hell couldn't be
nearly as hard on a
country boy as
Washington, D.C.

—1991

*   *   *   *   *   *   *   *   *   *   *   *

WILLIAM VIRGIL DAVIS
Texas: Sesquicentennial

The Indians found the best places
first. They had everything
they needed: water, fertile soil,
good hunting. Forget the sun
all summer, forget the white men,
coming from the east,
the dark men coming from the south,
the buffalo moving west.

Before long, all the Indians
were gone: driven off, dead, caught
and kept in designated areas
nobody else needed, just then.
Cattle, cotton, the oil,
were the only money. Everything
went west. When enough wagons
broke down, they founded a town
and started to brag on it.

A century and a half later,
nothing's changed. The movies
have arrived. The latest news gets through,
eventually. But the land hasn't forgotten.

It's taking its revenge,
acre by acre, mile by mile, above
and below. The settlers, though,
continue to circle their wagons,
continue to stand and fight,
against the enormous odds.

—1986

*   *   *   *   *   *   *   *   *   *   *   *   *

9
I'm Going to Leave Old Texas Now

I'm going to leave old Texas now,
For they've got no use for the longhorn cow;
They've plowed and fenced my cattle range,
and the people there are all so strange.

Whoo-a-whoo-a

★ traditional, from "The Texas Song" in *Cowboy Songs and Other Frontier Ballads*
by John A. and Alan Lomax

Anna Word Spragins
Farewell to Texas

Fare thee well! bright land of beauty,
    Emerald land, a long farewell;
Words are faint, too faint to speak the
    Sorrow which my heart would tell.
'Tis a sorrow full of weeping,
    And a parting full of gloom,
As I look farewell and turn me
    From thy face of glorious bloom.

Adieu to shades where I have wandered,
    'Neath the elm trees' greenest blow,
And to places bright to sadness
    With the sunshine's mellow glow.
Adieu to the bright green prairies,
    Wild flowers and the river dell;
Groves and birds—oh, land of beauty,
    'Tis a pang to say farewell.

I shall dream of her at morning
    In another home I seek,
Dream of all the wondrous beauty
    Which a Texan morn can make.
And my heart will stop to listen
    To the tinkle of the bells,
Floating o'er the waving grasses
    Like some happy music swells.

And at evening's hour so stilly
     Will my heart fly home to thee,
Fast and far as doth the sailors
     Home, from o'er the rocking sea.
And a loving heart will linger
     Just beyond yon sloping hill
Listening to the low, sad music
     From the solemn whip-poor-will.

Aye, my spirit will come to thee
     In the witching hour of night
When the live oaks on the prairie
     Are aflood with liquid light.
When the sky wears on its bosom
     All the glory of the moon;
And the South sea-wind is coming
     Laden with the heart of June.

When the mesquite bends and quivers
     To the night-wind sighing low,
And the shading moss is waving
     Gently from the trailing bough.
When upon the sea breeze wakens
     Songs the sweetest ever heard,
Pouring in the poet numbers
     From the wakeful mocking-bird.

Ah, bright land the heart which loves thee,
     Loves thy every changeful charm,
Will come home in dreams full often
     With a love as pure and warm,
As the sun which glows and brightens
     On thy peerless emerald brow—
Warm and fresh—the years can dim not
     The great love I bear thee now.

But farewell, thou home of beauty,
 Parting hath a pang today;
Blessings of my saddened spirit
 I will give thee, and away.
Fare thee well, broad, bright prairies,
 Wild flowers and the mossy dell;
Rivers blue and vale of cashmere,
 Emerald land—a long farewell!

—1885

* * * * * * * * * * * * *

PATTIANN ROGERS
Moving God
(Houston to Denver, 1989)

It wasn't easy. I had to get him
to stand up first. After so many years
of feeding him his favorite food—succulent
crayfish, sweet egrets, cicadas and magnolias,
juicy, creamy moons—he was so fat
I couldn't tell what sex he was
under his shorty silk toga.

I put my shoulder into the cushion
of his back and pushed hard, sinking
into the rolling ocean of his bulk
up to my nose, trying to wedge my fingers
at the same time under the folds
and lappings of his ugly rump
and lift. But he was tight
as an old oak in fertile soil.

I told him it wouldn't hurt. I told him

I wouldn't crack or chip him. I said
his porcelain pig wouldn't fall off;
he wouldn't lose his favorite clay
cup. I said his wooden whistle
would work at any altitude,
but he was screaming and wailing
too loud to listen.

I pulled on his oily arms then, his great
breasts hanging and swinging. I pinched him
on the bulb of his nipples. I bit
his pierced ear, but he wouldn't budge,
shaking all over, screaming with the sound
of a thousand wounded oboes.

I promised him a new canopy, fine
white drapery, a birdbath with a spitting
fish-fountain of marble. I promised him
new smoke, new blood. I promised to slap
and scourge him twice a fortnight.

He stuck his fat, berry-stained
fingers in his ears.

Finally when he tried to kick me, lifting
one knee slightly, I saw my chance, slipped
my head under quickly, struggled to my knees, rose,
faltering back, rose again with his huge
greasy stink on my neck, his slippery
thighs spilling over my shoulders.

Such a headache then with his howling,
his ripe breath, sparks and yellow fumes
issuing around us from the rupture
of his unearthing.
Staggering and swaying, it was slow going,

his feet dragging, bumping my ankles.
We almost went over the edge together
more than once, his sticky fingers gripping
my hair. It was snot and sniveling
all the way as he listed over and over,

alphabetically, everything that he was god to,
acacia, armadillo, azalea …,
left behind.

But here he is, ensconced on his new
throne, musing, as usual, pontificating,
his great reeking body molding, absorbing,
exuding, creating another congregation.
He resides so well, takes me in. He hides me,
enfolds me, counsels me, pays me in return.
He's almost happy now, counting
rock ridges, sucking on sagebrush,
almost his place again,
almost divine.

     —1990

*   *   *   *   *   *   *   *   *   *   *   *

Margaret Bell Houston
Song from the Traffic

The black haw is in flower again,
The red bud's rosy tide
Splashes the wood and stains the shade
Where dog-tooth violets hide.
(Manhattan—Manhattan—I walk your streets today,
But I see the Texas prairies bloom a thousand miles away!)

    Primroses burn their yellow fires

Where grass and roadway meet.
Feathered and tasseled like a queen,
Is every old mesquite
(It's raining in the barren parks, but on the prairie-side,
The road is shining in the sun for him who cares to ride!)

The plum tree's arms are burdened white,
And where the shrubs are few

Blue bonnets fold the windy ways—
Is any blue so blue?
(Clouds of them, crowds of them, shining through the grey
Blue bonnets blossoming a thousand miles away!)

How could I live my life so far
From where March plains are green,
But that my gallivanting heart
Knows all the road between?
(Manhattan—Manhattan—when you jostled me today,
You jostled one a-galloping a thousand miles away!)

—1925

＊　＊　＊　＊　＊　＊　＊　＊　＊　＊　＊　＊　＊

BETTYE HAMMER GIVENS
Lonesome Texas

He lay down his hoe, left his cornfield on the side
of Hammer Mountain. Ira Hammer came to Texas
on the Soash Emigrant train. He built a house,
and he built a school before he sent for Kate
and the children. Kate grew silent when she saw
the prairie free from rivers and trees—free
from a swinging bridge. Ira built her a two-story
house. Not like she left in West Virginia—not ten
rooms but two. Two stories high, one atop the other.

381

Kate doffed her white linen dress and lace gloves,
and removed her black plumed hat to pick up cowchips.
She climbed the windmill to cut meat from a side of beef
hanging there. Lonesome Texas, she named the land.
"An abstract title that promised to pass muster with
a square deal all around." And they had bought the farm.

The wind in West Texas could teach the breeze
in Franklin, W.V., how to do sixty by 8 A.M.
The wind that picked up pieces of dirt that settled
on the white clothes until they were the color
of Mama's gravy. Even the white leghorn hens were
a coal miner's gray. In letters home, she boasted
about the milo maize making forty-five bushels
and kafircorn that made forty. Ira wrote
in his diary, "Next year. Next year, when we
have money. Next year when everything is good."
Two children later (he had stopped counting
how many next years had passed) they sold a farm.
Sold part of the land and rented out the rest.
Sold the car, and boarded the train in Plainview.
Kate in her plumed hat, and he in his best gray suit,
with moustache trimmed went back to tell the folks
about their home in the West. They were elegant
in their good taste. Six months later, back
in Texas in time to start over. To get ready
for next year, picking up cowchips, and watching
wind push tumbleweeds that would never arrive
in West Virginia: Even the wind refused
to blow in that direction.

—1985

*　*　*　*　*　*　*　*　*　*　*　*　*

ROBERT A. FINK
Abilene, TX: We Pull Out For New England

There is a reason why the compass needle
time and again lays its seam due north.
If you believe an icy lodestone peaks atop the globe
then you'll buy desert property in Arizona.
The truth is it points home,
the place we started from so long ago
we've lost the recollection of our skin as smooth,
blood thick enough to flow through winter.

Now we are turning back from this land of sky,
the punctual sun wide as all horizons.
Back from the saucy mockingbird
who owns us all. The shy snake of diamonds
coiling his warning. Back down
the oil smooth highway spilled across forever.
The neighbors seem to understand
shaking their heads at what they know
may one day come for them.

The mesquites are sad. Their leaves point us out
for shame. We could endure. Grow tough
sinking tap roots deep, tributaries wide.
We, too, could learn the signs of spring,
how to judge when winter's really passed.
We, too, could learn to camel out the summer.
I want to shout from the station wagon window:
WE'RE COMING BACK. IT'S JUST FOR JUNE TO AUGUST.
The trees know better. Another squatter gone,
run out of town by bullies.
IT'S NOT LIKE THAT! Surprised
I roll the window up, refuse to speak for miles.

—1984

✶ ✶ ✶ ✶ ✶ ✶ ✶ ✶ ✶ ✶ ✶ ✶

10

A Personal Country

If this is a history, it is an emotional history of a boy and a man in a place, and part of that place in them.

★ *A.C. Greene*

SCOTT CAIRNS
In the General Area of North Texas

Except for what is very old (the failing
mill, most bridges, the houses of the poor),
this town looks almost new, or looks intent
on progress of the sort that buffs into brilliance

the otherwise worn and fallow landscape
—so many expansive yellow fields cropped
and staked, most already tracked by a rigid
grid of asphalt road (some kind of brittle net?),

each intersection (each know) fixed to the map
by a bright green metal pole, crossed at the top
by two bright green metal nameplates with bright green names:
Casa Verde, San Verde, Verde Acres, Verde Way.

    —1991

  ✦   ✦   ✦   ✦   ✦   ✦   ✦   ✦   ✦   ✦   ✦   ✦

ROXY GORDON
West Texas Mid-Century

I spent my mysterious childhood
hunting human sign
over miles and miles
of empty
Texas West.

I hunted rusted tin cups and
broken bottles where adobe houses
melted and where dryland farmers'
deserted shacks moaned low in
summers' winds.

Junked cars were beautiful to me
then,
because they offered proof of
living human flesh.

I spent my lonesome childhood
hunting rusted human sign
over miles and miles
of empty West.

I treasured rusted old tin cans
and purpled broken bottles
where dugouts had collapsed
in drywash creekbeds
and where empty limestone
ranch houses stared out
blindly from broken windows.

Junked cars were beautiful to me
then,
because they once had lived
themselves
of human living beings.

—1988

* * * * * * * * * * * * *

MARY LOVING BLANCHARD
East Texas Blues

Some say the voices here meander
down silent alleys, filter through
screen doors
with hot evening breezes, settle in parlors
on front stoops, travel
on the thin veil of air
that whispers from paper fans

to find you
wrap you in memory

I have not heard those voices
I am not witness to their work

Sheltered as I have been from experience
the voices
exist only along the edge of knowing, washed
away in the cool water of a forbidden fountain
vaguely recalled in footprints traced
on a simple brown bag, framed
in understandings borne of habit and reason

when to hold on to sanity
in East Texas cotton fields
is to give notice
to the voices
that call from beneath red dirt   tinged with hope and blood

to the voices
that call from atop stately pines
shedding deadly fruit in the hazy light of morning
for in every voice, hushed
secretive truth is revealed

And joy, should you find her here
hides from flood and drought
memory and reason
fearful

Still there are some
who swear renewal may be found
in those cotton fields.

Some who claim Here, they scratch rhyme from reason
find here the place

Once scorned for a brother's sake
Is now reclaimed for sweet sanity's sake

Hear now those voices!
O, dreaded horseman in the night! O, dark cry that echoes from each shadow

remind ancient memory of its own sinful dreams
those footprints outlined in red dirt
give weight to the voices
that swallow you, tie your tongue
swell your senses
until you are confused by understanding

the voices
whispering from each pine

the voices
crying from beneath red dirt

not merely forefathers who whisper
wrapping you in the false security
of folktales and myths, lies borne of understanding

Not merely forefathers who scream their warning
too late, too late.

Mock me in prayer, East Texas
whisper your danger to my marrow, call
from cotton fields   tinged in hope and blood
call in metaphor   mistaken for song.

        —1999

*   *   *   *   *   *   *   *   *   *   *   *

Chip Dameron
South Texas Boxcar Blues

Long late train hoots under the freeway,
two blocks over, headed north.

Maybe men in one car rock and hope,
maybe not—coyote knows.

Some days sun bakes out each drop of truth:
mouths all open, no one hears.

—1991

* * * * * * * * * * * * *

Richard Sale
Delayed Love Poem to Odem, Texas

Fifteen times the better jock,
Juan Mancias made the block
That let me cross the goal
That once.
Juan Mancias sang the song
That kept away *cabrones.*
The block broke Juan Mancias' collar-bone.
The song broke hexes and *cojones.*
It takes too long for memory to free us,
But now I guess my debt to Juan Mancias—
  The only touchdown that I ever made,
  The happy chant that snipes away at age:
"No me chingas, Juan Dominguez!"
Please God.

—1978

* * * * * * * * * * * * *

COLLEEN BEESON
Minnie Henderson

Such an unlikely lady to teach Spanish.
Tall and lank with bottle blond hair
and light blue eyes.
Her long, pale face even paler with
lavish application of powder and rouge.
A flower pinned to her handmade dress,
and chalk on her fingers.

Miss Minnie opened a world of new sounds
to my Central Texas ear.
"j's" with the sound of "h,"
"r's" that rolled on the tongue,
punctuation upside down before the sentence.
Classroom decorated with bullfight posters
and crepe paper flowers.
We wrote a Spanish play and even managed
to perform it, accompanied by
barely concealed laughter.
She used every opportunity to practice
her adopted language
and make it live for us.
Only "Espana" spoken when we
crossed her threshold for a second term.
Even though I cannot speak it fluently,
I still enjoy listening in on Spanish conversations
and picking out familiar words.
Then I remember Miss Minnie's favorite word,
"sonrisa," meaning smile, and I smile.

—1985

*   *   *   *   *   *   *   *   *   *   *   *

CARMEN TAFOLLA
At the Very Last Battle

The wooden rocking-horse in Reyes Cardenas' yard
Sinks on bended knee like Chief Joseph
at the very last battle.

Staring into the ground and biting on its bit,
Saying "I am tired. My heart is sad and sick.
I will fight no more."

The only Mexican-American principal in Seguin
Waves a sad beer bottle at my Pacer
as it passes.

I drive up to my assigned parking space
And wonder if my lot is taken by the car next door
Or if I really belong.

I turn the key and walk into the empty house,
Alone, like the rest of la raza,
a stranger in my own home.

—1976

* * * * * * * * * * * * *

TINO VILLANUEVA
The Serving of Water

Tell the portly waitress to stay overtime and
She will do it. Dressed in white, she is a
Version of Sarge…Who follows orders well
…Who may have it in her mind she is "The

Sweetest little rosebud that Texas ever knew."
Her whole embodiment is whatever she is doing—:

392

At a booth, here, on a warm, sketchy plain
Of day, it is water she sets out for the
Benedicts: the measurement of water is a ritual
That isolates a face from the many colors of the

Day, and she does so with her eyes aimed at
Anyone she has given a harsh name to—like Juana,

And her child, half-Anglo, who in Juana's womb
Became all Mexican just the same. The waitress,
Entirely conscious of her act, whose eyes, quick,
Flee back to Sarge and now call out in silence,

Brings this moment to the edge of something tense
That spreads to everything. Her sudden look of

Outward regard—then Sarge, stirring dense cloud
Gathering (*entering left*), standing over everyone
in tallness almighty. Ice-cream is what Rock Hudson
Wishes for his grandson: "Ice-cream it shall be,"

His words a revelation of delight: "Give the
Little fella some ice-cream"…Summer is one long

Afternoon when Sarge, moved by deep familiar
Wrath, talks down: "Ice-cream—thought that kid'd
Want a *tamale*." An angry mass of time travels
Back and forth the distance between Sarge and

Rock Hudson, as I sit, shy of speech, in a stammer
Of light, and breathe a breath not fully breathed…

    —1993

Teresa Palomo Acosta
Apparition (ca. 1896)

In the beginning
It was easy to forget them,
And their hands, clawing at my door, begging to be let in.

—No mas arrimados eran
Because that's what I let them be
In the beginning. They were
Bunches de arrimados
Holding me to the past
Holding me to promises
I could not keep.

But

Now they are real pictures and words
Found in a history book.

Now
They stand in front of their jacales
And confront my timid sidelong glance.

In one picture they lie dead. Ropes are looped
Around their necks. Texas Rangers sit on their
Horses over them, refusing to meet anyone's gaze.

Now

Each day
They talk to me on my walks—
Wondering when I will put them in my poems.
They tell me how things were
On their ranchitos
And
How they lost their land in sales

Of 4,000 acres for 200 dollars
Fair and square under Texas laws.

It is impossible to live
With such holy ghosts
As these.

For I cannot breathe
Or get on with anything else
If I cannot
Keep them permanently beloved

And so I bend in closer
To their faces
And their words jumping out
From history

To say
To them

Stay with me.

For I'm on my way home
Across your plains and unfenced lands
Moving toward you to find

Peace

I shall not lose you again.
We will find some permanent place
To live together.

It will be our finest entrada.

—1992

Teresa Palomo Acosta
Museum Piece (ca. Now)

Bones.
Adobe.
Straw baskets.
Facsimiles of our lives
As reported in the National Geographic.
That's what the curator
Wants in the exhibition.

We nod in agreement.
Let her decide what we were.
Then that night
We dream about
Lace and voile
Bracelets
Old tubes of lipstick
Cotton dresses made from flour sacks
Doilies mamá got for starching and ironing all
Twenty shirts for the men of the Falls' mansion at one try.

We change our minds
But it's too late, the curator
Informs us. They're already building the models,
Sure that they will catch us at the right moment. This time
We cannot nod back. Now we know the difference
Between suggestions and decisions.

On the following Sunday,
We open up the family trunk
And go through our museum.

—1992

✦ ✦ ✦ ✦ ✦ ✦ ✦ ✦ ✦ ✦ ✦ ✦

Edward H. Garcia
Chicana

for M.F.

"I just have a sad look sometimes."
Very large brown eyes,
Brown arms downed with brown hair.
Black hair short.

Once the girls I knew
Powdered themselves *less* brown
Hid from the sun,
Wished to be wives.

Now their grandmothers must wonder
About these nice girls.
And what do their brothers say to them,
Sad-eyed and strong?
Don't you go to Mass anymore?
Don't you want to get married?
Is that why you went to college?

Sad eyes bespeak
New seasons of browner skin
And a girl's breasts
loose against a t-shirt,
And a brother's accusations.

—2000

Benjamin Alire Sáenz
Between Worlds

The players dance on the field. The ball, as white
As a full moon on the clearest night of summer,
Bullets up, noiseless as it flies. Then falls.
It is not yet dark, but no longer day. The sun begins
To falter. Yet, in this momentary light, the grass is
Burning green, haloed, luminous. The shadows
Of men ceaselessly running, reach, touch me
And then again they run. They breathe hard, each intake
Of breath, a serious matter. They yell directions
To teammates in Spanish: *¡Ahora si!*" one yells
Then flips as he kicks the ball through the goal.
He lands on his feet laughing, his teeth whiter
Than the moon. He raises his arms in the air
As if to absorb the rays of a dying sun
And trap them in himself (he will save them in his
Body to light his moments of darkness). A companion
Runs to him, jumps in his arms, yells, "*¡Asi, México, asi!*"
And after the celebration, the play resumes.

Once in a playground
At school, two boys I knew were pulled from our team.
The best players, they could only watch for a week.
Their rough Spanish, an offense. "Foul ball. Play
In English." Like them, I spoke Spanish in my home,
Copied words in English on my page. Quick I learned
And soon my father's accent disappeared. English
Was mine, the language of my thought. But
Even now, the Mexico I never knew visits when I dream.
The top layer of memory's palimpsest washes clean
And what is left are prayers learned in tongues
Never to be banished.

A dark man
Whom someone called "*Bolivia*" juggles a ball
With a tap dance down the field. Like a ghost, a man
Appears, and takes the ball away. "*¡Perú!*" they yell,
"*¡Perú!*" He kicks the ball, effortless aim, to another,
And yells, "*¡Llevátela, Chile!*" They call each other
By native lands. They have come from another America
Distant, but here, tonight, the green grass
Is more theirs than those who planted it.

In El Paso

Caught between two countries, I played soccer on
Sunday afternoons, with men who sought asylum,
Who lived crowded in homes for the poor, restless
With nothing but time for remembering. They fled
The newspaper cities of El Salvador, Guatemala,
Nicaragua, came to live and be at peace. I grew close
To one who came from there: he used to raise his arms
To shield himself when he heard familiar blades
Of helicopters. he would not speak of memories
That covered his face with the whiteness of a
Funeral pall. In those moments, though he remained
Beside me, his heart stole him away and I could not
Cross into his sacred awful country. And then
He would return.

     He said strange things
About this country he adopted (but which never adopted
Him): "Such a rich country, and such bad streets. What
Do you do with your money?" He never understood
This America, was permanently lost. Troubled, he had
No place to go, picked up the ways of the streets, never
Spoke the truth about himself, was difficult to
Trust. He had scars, with and without, and his
Moods were dark as his eyes. He grew angry
When he drank, but I was not afraid. He
Was too hurt to hurt me.

                              At my back
A crowd is gathered. They sit on blankets, feast
On healthy foods: salads and grapes, cheese and bread.
There is a quiet joy, expectant laughter, the waiting
For Shakespeare to come alive again. Tonight
A Midsummer Night's Dream (no better setting than a
Sky soon to be burning with stars). The actors
Will adopt Elizabethan speech. The words, having crossed
Oceans of time, will enter our hearts through accents
Distinctly "American." This will seem to no one out of place.
Our minds will open for the players. We will
Take them in. Theseus and Puck will weave their spells
Upon us. Love will cross and uncross, and all will be
Well in the end. The ball flies out of bounds. It almost
Strikes my face. But quick it is gone, on the field again.
The play that will soon begin behind me, as familiar
As the play before my eyes. Neither play is mine
Yet both beckon, call me from their separate worlds,
Will never let me go. Reluctantly, I turn. The Duke
Begins his speech:
                    Now, fair Hippolata, our nuptial hour
                    Draws apace. Four happy days bring in….
The players in the distant field shout on, run on
Their game continues. Their muted Spanish shouts
Mix with careful iambics. The cacophony disturbs
A man behind me:

        "Their games should cease. We've come to watch a play."

                            But soon enough
Too dark to run. The light shines only on the actors.
On the field, quiet. In peace, the play continues:
As the actors word their perfect lines, I see
Latin men in shorts taking perfect leaps
On perfect blades of grass.

In New Mexico, one summer,
I stood on Anazasi ruins. That day, the sky was so
Deep and so blue I felt I was, at last, out of
This tired century. As I touched a crumbling adobe
It was as if I had dipped my hand in waters of the
Church. This place: more full of God than any chapel
I had ever entered. This place: kinder than the cities
Of the world. I sat in caves the ancient ones
had dug, the walls covered with the film of their
Smoke. But there were no bones here, no broken
Bodies or blood. Some angel or god had rolled back
The stone. These tombs were empty, everywhere
Voices: "I have lived. I have lived.
I am living."

From the opening in the stone
I could see an unpolluted earth, a canyon, more ruins
Near the stream. The sun lit them like candles. The waters
Of the stream: a hand that healed. And everything
Was green, though the air was dryer than the sand.
This was a desert. But this was not a desert. This was
A land that existed between times, between worlds, between
Water and drought. This was an ecotone, a place where
All borders were banished. Ruins from a disappeared
People, tourists with fluorescent T-shirts; desert snakes and
Rats made their nests under flowering shrubs; flies
And insects that flourished only in forests landed on vines
And cacti. There were sterile sands, and there was
Topsoil, dark and rich, where rows of corn had once
Fed hungry farmers. A cholla grew tall
Raising its thousand thorns to the Indian god of light,
And next to it, a ponderosa pine forever shed its
Needles. No voices yelled demanding: "Do not cross
This line that I have drawn." And no one asked,
"Why have you come? Who has brought you here?"

The wind, for reasons of its own, was pleased
To blow these seeds from other places and
Drop them in the soil. It pleased the rain
To make the seedlings grow.

—1993

  ✳   ✳   ✳   ✳   ✳   ✳   ✳   ✳   ✳   ✳   ✳   ✳   ✳

JAN EPTON SEALE
Travel North: The Rules

Mile 49: Ladies and gentlemen,
UnitedStatesImmigrationCheckpoint coming
up! Please have your documentation ready.
¡Damas y caballeros tambien!

Now there must be a neatening—
all things vertical, horizontal, squared:
hats removed, hair smoothed, hats replaced;
pant legs worked back down the thighs;
boot toes polished on backs of opposing calves;
lipstick checked; long hair slung-brushed;
babies taken off breast; blouses closed;
waking of older children, Sit up!

Now the *papeles*, always the *papeles*:
from shirt pockets, billfolds, purses,
bosoms, boot tops, jean pocket.
You unfold your papeles
or take your card from its holder:
Do you look like your picture?
Hold your life steady;
practice holding your future
steady in your hands.

The driver will pull into the port.
Stop talking. Cross yourself.
Immigration Checkpoint! He will climb down.
Look clean; look bright;
look like your picture ID.

La Migra will board.
(*La Migra* is not kidding.)
Have your papeles ready.
¡Buenas tardes! He will speak
kind to the *viejos* on the front seat.

La Migra starts down the aisle.
You citizens?
You?
This your bag?
La Migra looks at each passenger,
takes the *papeles*, studies it,
pats the seatback as he passes.

La Migra checks the bathroom.
(You better not be in it.)
Now he returns, his boots sounding.
He will be looking for telltale signs.
(You better not be handing your papeles
back to your friend just yet.)
It is almost over. Everyone is fine…
—wait! He's asking that gringo hippie,
What you doing down in the Valley?

Nothing, man!
That *bolillo*! He doesn't know the rules!
For that he goes with *La Migra*,
keeps us all here, waiting.

Would he empty, please,
the contents of his purple nylon bag
onto the table? Another guy comes.
They take up a book and shake it
like something might fall out.
They examine another object.
Someone looking safely out the window:
Eh, *estúpidos*! That's a *capo* for a guitar,
not a roach clip! The bus laughs.

The gringo hippie is allowed back.

When the bus is under way again,
food will break out all over:
empanadas, gorditas, fruta,
Cocas, Topo Chico.

¡Gracias a Dios! a viejita
will breathe it.

An old cowboy will hear.
¡Palabra! No kidding!

—1999

* * * * * * * * * * * * *

ROSEMARY CATACALOS
La Casa

The house by the *acequia*,
its front porch dark and
cool with begonias,
an old house, always there,
always of the same adobe,
always full of the same lessons.
We would like to stop.

We know we belonged there once.
Our mothers are inside,
lighting candles, swaying
back and forth on their knees,
begging the Virgin's forgiveness
for having reeled us out
on such very weak string.
They are afraid for us.
They know we will not stop.
We will only wave as we pass by.
They will go on praying
that we might be simple again.

    —1972

  ⋆   ⋆   ⋆   ⋆   ⋆   ⋆   ⋆   ⋆   ⋆   ⋆   ⋆   ⋆

RAY GONZÁLEZ
Roberto Meets Cabeza de Vaca in the Desert

Cabeza, where are your clothes?
The actual earth does not allow this.

I have to wear my clothes to survive,
hide my body from the magnet of the desert.

Cabeza, who is your god?
Your bare feet have not been kissed by anyone.

When you cross *La Jornada del Muerto*
tell the dead man you are alive

and have found me walking,
avoiding the river to wait for you.

Cabeza, what are you searching for?
Your cities of gold were destroyed

by your sons long ago, those
who never crossed the sea to explore

because they had no reason to discover
the place to end their walk.

      —1995

*   *   *   *   *   *   *   *   *   *   *   *

Tino Villanueva
Day-Long Day

> "Again the drag of pisca, pis-
> ca, pisca… Daydreams border
> on sunfed hallucinations, eyes
> and hands automatically discri-
> minate whiteness of cotton from
> field of vision. Pisca, pisca."
>
> "Un hijo del sol," Genaro Gonzales

Third generation timetable.
Sweat day-long dripping into open space;
sun blocks out the sky, suffocates the only breeze.
From *el amo desgraciado*, a sentence:

<<I wanna a bale a day, and the boy here
don't haf'ta go to school.>>

In time binding motion—
a family of sinews and backs,
row-trapped,
zig-zagging through Summer-long rows
of cotton: Lubbock by way of Wharton.
<<*Está como si escupieran fuego,*>> a mother moans
in sweat-patched jeans,
stooping
with unbending dreams.
<<*Estudia para que no seas burro como nosotros"*>>

our elders warn, their gloves and cuffs
leaf-stained by seasons.

Bronzed and blurry-eyed by
the blast of degrees,
we blend into earth's rotation.
And sweltering toward saturday, the
day-long day is sunstruck by 6:00 P.M.
One last chug-a-lug from a water jug
old as granddad.
Day-long sweat dripping into open space:
Wharton by way of Lubbock.

    —1979

✶ ✶ ✶ ✶ ✶ ✶ ✶ ✶ ✶ ✶ ✶ ✶ ✶

MARY LOVING BLANCHARD
Picking Cotton

With hands grown learned as cotton stalks have grown fibrous
the women work in perfect meter without stop
                    to quicken the chore: their relief
taken in measured seconds
stolen when the Santa Fe enters from the left—
its bellow reviving overseers who count hours
in wait under trees heavy with heat.
Retrieving chalk-like pieces of sandy loam
from apron pockets, the women press the cool balm
into minute cuts earned
harvesting silken thread from armored bolls.

As the Santa Fe bisects the landscape
it erases their bowed figures from sight of Mr. Charlie's crew
(who wave red bandanas in the noon sun, cheering the train
on its conquest through dense pine and oak)
and the blood-letting goddesses

turn from bent positions, lift heavy spines
from the loam-covered clay
and offer silken thread to Neith.

Such a conscientious lot!
Each woman
picks in time
to the other women about her
row upon row of colored women
bent in attention to manicured rows
as their fingers grow purple and bleed
into the harvest, staining silken threads
with evidence of their mortality,
alerting serpents that escaped Ironosa's swell
that beings other than themselves seek dry land.
Seek sun-warmed soil to rest weary bodies.

Singing out in alarm and admonishment
the women keep watch with their hearts
for skin shed in the path
for fingers cut beyond repair
for a friend fallen beneath the sun's fixed stare.
　　　In prayer more to mother Neith
　　　than to overseer or god, they collect silken thread:
　　　a ransom for the souls of daughters
　　　left waiting at the weigh-in barn.

　　—2002

☆　☆　☆　☆　☆　☆　☆　☆　☆　☆　☆　☆

SUSAN WOOD
Hollow

I never knew, then, why it was named that,
The Hollow, where the Blacks lived—Coloreds,
we called them—where the road from town crested
the hill and wound down past Miller's Gin for a mile

or so, though it seemed like more, open fields
on either side and beyond the field on the left
the town cemetery, Rosemound Cemetery, past their school
with its broken windows, and then the houses began,

shabby and needing paint, the kind of house
Jeanne Crain might have left to pass for white
in *Pinky* if this were the black-and-white past
of the movies and not Commerce, Texas, in 1955. Even

the poorest had a TV and a Cadillac out front. That's what
we said, anyway, and laughed, making ourselves
blameless, an adult's bland dismissal of a foolish child.
I don't know how they lived, the maids and cooks,

the yardmen, who got their whiskey and fruitcakes,
their ten-dollar bills at Christmas, who had their own
plates and cups and silver in the houses
where they worked for years. Even their names weren't ours:

Ruby and Opal and Pearl rolling like jewels
off the tongue, or the ludicrous nicknames, Butter
and Sambo—Sambo, who always had a smile and a kind word,
who, proud of his position, dressed in a white coat

to open doors at parties. Their lives were an infinite
mystery to me, the way everything Other is mysterious,
the subject of curiosity, even a little feared. It's all
confused with smells: the musky odor of bodies, the char

of bacon grease and greens, water standing too long
in a ditch, even the clean scent of sprinkled clothes
and starch when Bessie came to iron on Thursdays. I rode
with my mother to take her home, thrilled and scared to be

going there, doors locked and windows shut, and once,
when I started to climb in the backseat, taught

that's where children sat, she almost pushed me down
insisting I get up front with my mother. Today

a woman in a shop where the rich sell their cast-off
clothes for charity told me her cat had disappeared,
stolen, she was sure, by Mexicans. They drive
through the neighborhood, she said, and when they see

a beautiful cat they come back at night and take it.
And I remembered the telephone jokes we played
as children, how we liked especially to call those names
that seemed so funny to us and say something silly—

"Is your refrigerator running" Well, stop it before it gets
away" —and how we once called Bessie at the number
in my mother's book. A neighbor went next door to get her.
I think she must have hurried from her house, surprised

and expectant, her tiny, bird-like legs moving as fast
as seventy years allowed. I don't remember what we said,
but I'm sure we laughed, afterwards, at her confusion,
at the way she talked "like she has a mouthful of marbles."

I didn't know anything, really, about her life, nor
would I, if I could, have willingly entered it, and so
my pity, after all this time, for what she suffered, my shame
for all our ignorance seem somehow like that name, hollow.

—1991

H. Palmer Hall
Requiem for James Byrd, Jr.

Blacktop yellow stripe down the middle
They dragged a living man down
Down until they dragged a dead man
      Broken into pieces

on either side, tall pines, planted
every ten years pulped after growth
tall enough to mill the paper
      to publish the obituary

these woods have a dead man in them
broken shredded into black asphalt
head legs torso scattered like needles
      deep woods whisper here

a thousand people drive over red specks
spread droplets of raging tears but
a dead man's dying cannot roll dark
      thicket into shinning light.

—1998

James Hoggard
Eye of the Tornado
from Two Gulls One Hawk

We moved to Greenville
when my father was named
District Superintendent

   I later found out
   too late to strut about it

411

he was youngest in the history
of the North Texas Conference

THE BLACKEST LAND
THE WHITEST PEOPLE
the hanging sign on the main street said

one day it fell
on the hood of a car
outside Earnie's
sawdust-floored barbecue place
near the depot
where Thursday nights
the cook for the train
leaned out the window and dropped us
warm sacks of cinnamon rolls

I learned to swim
by refusing to sink
and began going off the highboard,
did a dive I called a gainer
and convinced some kids
it was fun, but one
had to be rescued,
and I had severe pains, too
after bellybusting three times
from a mile in the air

Exploring the town at 5 a.m.
on my rocket Flyer bike

and hot to help
and hot to help
the silent sun rise
I talked to it, sang,
and later in the day,

for fifteen years more,
I might hear it
call me by name

A dead perch in the street one morning

white bellied,
a bloody wound
under its lip,
the body beginning
to pull away
from its scales,
its mouth said O

that fish became
an image I kept
later wondering if
it could have been
Osiris' lost member

—1983

✴ ✴ ✴ ✴ ✴ ✴ ✴ ✴ ✴ ✴ ✴ ✴

ROSEMARY CATACALOS
Swallow Wings

for Maya Angelou, with profound
respect and gratitude

I been to church, folks.
I'm an East Side Meskin Greek and
I been to church. I'm here to say
I grew up hearin' folks sing over hard
time in the key of, *Uh, uh, girl. It ain't nothin'*
'bout lettin' go a this life.
I grew up in a 'hood where every day at noon
black girls at Ralph Waldo Emerson Junior High School

413

made a sacred drum of the corner mailbox, beatin'
on it to raise the dead. And make them dance.
I grew up readin' in the George Washington Carver
Library, and marvelin' at the white
lightnin' gloves that Top Ladies of Distinction
use for church. I grew up where grits is *indeed*
groceries, and a huge mountain of a woman passed
my house daily, always sayin' the same thing:
Your name Rosemary? My name Rosemary, too.
I grew up, folks, and I been down 'til I couldn't
get no more down in me. And now a preacher lady
comes to town and caused me to paint my face and
put on some good clothes and go to church.
And I'm here to say I have a right
to take this tone, 'cause it ain't nothin'
'bout lettin' go a this life.
Swallows keep makin' their wings
out to be commas on the sky.
The world keep sayin' and, and, and, and
and.

—1984

* * * * * * * * * * * *

HARRYETTE MULLEN
Viejas Locas
for Angélica y Cristina

 Oh, you crazy girls from Laredo
I'll always remember you

heating tortillas on an ironingboard
in the freshman dorm

dyeing your straight shiny black hair
even blacker and shinier

telephone black
mystery black of ladies
with unlisted numbers

going to dances in gold and silver puta shoes

and getting me so drunk on tequila
I slid down the stairs
at a party fundraiser

You crazy giggling girls
calling yourselves Chiche y Chona

From you I learned to eat refried beans
for breakfast,
beans you cooked with beer and cilantro
instead of fatback

You gave me la llorona and the evil eye
and abrazoed me into your raza

You girls, you viejas locas
spoke Spanish to me whether I could comprende or not
and if I didn't know all the words
I understood your voices

> *—1981*

* * * * * * * * * * * * *

JANET LOWERY
Texas Splendor

Here in Houston there's no stomach for misery.
That brilliant sun, that curtain of heat indexes
and barometric sweat, those glistening ladies,
those cowboy hats and silver belts and studded spurs

decorating very young old men, those long days
in which the light goes on forever, the hills
flattened, the sky perpetually bright,
and the homeless, the street people panhandling
like smiling buffoons at traffic stop circuses,
like artifacts of wisdom, like pointillist dots
of brown and grey in a landscape of blue glass
and bougainvillea. Here in Houston we remember
there will be poor always and guys who work downtown
tell you bitterly those bums in front of the courthouse
pull in two hundred a day, but anyway, not everyone
can be rich and those who are not live some place
farther north or turn against themselves
in selfish anorexic fits or bouts of cocaine use.
Help is cheap. The barrios sleep, quaint and
dark in distant neighborhoods and even I can not
sustain a complaint, so determined are those around me,
so confident are they of standing ground in the nation
of Texas and besides, who can resist the profusion
of spangled palms at Christmastide, the valet-parking
shopping marts, the rhinestone vests and sequin dresses
suggesting we sparkle our glittered way across
the two-step double-turn neon-lit western-swing
dance floor into a heaven where Stevie Ray
and Reba's band and Daniel Boone and Davy Crockett
and all the other heroes of the country western rock-n-roll
Alamo wait for us in radiant Texas splendor.

    —1994

SUNSHINE DICKINSON RYMAN
from Street Scenes: Houston

"Matthew, Mark, Luke and John,"
She chanted,
Sitting against the sunny wall of Kress.
"Matthew, Mark, Luke and John,"
Shuffling her little paper books
With hands as lovely as white pigeons,
Hands so poignantly like my mother's
That I gasped, and stopped.

"Matthew, Mark, Luke and John!
Buy one, leddy, for the love o' mercy!"
And turned to me a face
Where on all the devils fought and never died,
Fought, but kept themselves clear
Of the ghastly mouth that twisted out:
"Matthew, Mark, Luke and John."

I bought and fled.

—1936

* * * * * * * * * * * * * * *

CYNTHIA MACDONALD
The Kilgore Rangerette Whose
Life Was Ruined

There we were that beautiful line, synchronized as
A row of pistons in an Eldorado, except
There were only eight of them and there were a hundred of us
(Flowers weeded out of flowers, the cream of the crop).
There we were in the Cotton Bowl, the world-famous
Kilgore Rangerettes, kicking to "The Eyes of Texas Are Upon You"
And they were. In our white cowhide skirts and white felt hats

And red satin shirts and vests with silver stars and
I kicked with the wrong leg and the heel of
My white patent boot got caught in Marybelle's heel on the right
And we both fell and knocked into
The girls on either side of us who sprawled into
Others and half the line went down
Like a keyboard in a demo derby whacked by an axe.

Maybe I should have known—there had been
Problems of appearances before:

Hugging Grandma too tight after she'd had her surgery.
She held the empty place and cried.
Grandpa said she loves you; be more careful.
He bought me a grey suede bag to keep things in.

Giggling in my Hark the Herald Angels Sing duet,
Infecting my partner, too.
The principal said we ruined the Christmas Concert.
My father gave me a garnet and emerald
Synthastone pin in the shape of a clef.

Having a nosebleed when I was shaking hands with
The head of Pan American who came for dinner.
A drop fell on his tan pants.
My father didn't get promoted
But he said that wasn't why.
My mother gave me a box of linen handkerchiefs
Embroidered Monday, Tuesday, Wednesday . . . .

Not only did I have to leave the Rangerettes
I left Kilgore, too, even though my roommate,
Who'd been the Maid of Cotton, told me she still loved me.
My intended said the same and gave me
A satin slip, but I don't know. . . .
I felt he shouldn't have a ruined wife.

It was that way with any good job, too.
How could I work in the fine crystal section at Neiman's?
All those long-stemmed goblets. Cascades of glass chimes
Woke me every night. I asked to be transferred to
Sterling and Gems. But the tines, the blades, the facets
Menaced me. I learned you break or are broken.
And then a Texaco receptionist, Jack-In-The-Box waitress…
no need to spell the perils out.

They know me in Dallas—the only bag lady—lots in NYC—
But all of them are old and I am not. I saw them
On a Kilgore trip to catch the Rockettes and the Balanchine
Swan Lake. (We all agreed those swans would be
Hissed off the field at any Southwest half-time show.)
It's not a bad life. No one expects grace or precision.

Outdoors scavenging the city's trash—presents for yourself—
You can collect what you can, what you want, what you need.
Last night I found a Lilly Daché hat and three foam mats.
Street life has it dangers: cold, jail, insults.
But no humiliation. A year ago I got knocked up.
Rape, yes, but no mutilation.
It wasn't bad. I don't feel much these days.
I keep the baby, Billielou, in my bag, snug
In a nest of rags, a Dallas kangaroo.
If Beebeelou—that's what I call her—wants
To be a Rangerette. . . .Well, I don't know…
Her fingers curl around my thumb like little tongues.
She'll have her chance to kick her boots to the sky,
To slice it with her legs, the perfect blue
Deep in the heart of Texas.

—*1980*

FRANCES NEIDHARDT
Street Flower in Big D

By day she spreads her broomstick
skirt around hips cushioning on
concrete, leaning a beanpole back
against the glass-walled public
library, carefree as a grackle
snatching breakfast from the open
trashcan. A human hollyhock
uncombed and smiling vaguely
at familial feet, shoes scuffing
clopping by and blurring when the
detour rounds her without breaking
pace. Diversion endless in the
constant faces rippling, floating
from windowed capsules rolling
glistening on the street. Herself
the watcher of all people, all
components bound to chaos by
the mystery of movement flowing
whocareswhere beyond her ebbing
garden, sliding away like ice cream.
Instant erasures from her tiny
elemental world where in the
moment glass suns mother her with
multiple reflections, and neon stars
hang high above by night when
now she lays her down to sleep.

—2002

ROSEMARY CATACALOS
Letter to a Brother in Exile

Good news from the town of our birth!
The Boxer remains faithful.
Every evening he gets drunk
and makes his way along the curve
of St. Mary's Street just south
of Our Lady of Sorrows,
between there and the triangle
of the Chinaman's, the J & A Ice House
and Salinas' Bonanza Club.
The stations vary.
Sometimes he stands under awnings,
sometimes beside a telephone pole
or somebody's parked car.
There, just at dusk, he begins to punch at shadows
until they regain their voices
and take up the shoes of the night with him.
That's when we can all rest easy.
When the Boxer has stopped fighting
and begun to sing.

But some evenings, like this one,
he stays furious. It has rained
for seven days straight
and Señora Degollado complains
that her tomatoes will rot
if one more drop of rain falls.
The once simple green of the trees
has turned menacing.
So the Boxer stands directly across
the street from the Greek church
and shakes his fists and rants
at Byzantium's double-headed eagle.

He knows that the gods always sleep in the east
and that to face them is to pray,
even if in anger.

—*1984*

✳ ✳ ✳ ✳ ✳ ✳ ✳ ✳ ✳ ✳ ✳ ✳ ✳

Edyth Renshaw
Pantoum
In a Texas Farm-House Kitchen

It's dinner time once more
The men will soon be in,
They'll dirty up the floor.
This batter is too thin.
The men will soon be in.
The meat is almost done.
This batter is too thin,
And cooking is no fun.

The meat is almost done.
I'm almost cooked myself,
And cooking is no fun!
The pitcher's on the shelf.

I'm almost cooked myself.
Oh why are stoves so hot?
The pitcher's on the shelf.
Oh where's that little pot?

Oh why are stoves so hot?
My fingers are all burned.
(Oh where's that little pot?)
These pancakes must be turned.

My fingers are all burned.
I get so tired of this—
(Those pancakes must be turned)
To rest would be such bliss.

I get so tired of this
I'd like to run away—
To rest would be such bliss
If only for a day.

I'd like to run away
Back east to old Lagore
If only for a day—
It's dinner time once more.

The city knew that spring had come
With its rains and growing things,
The new leaves hid some of the ugly buildings,
But where was the spring of the prairie—
The broad, sweeping Texas prairie
With its cover of young green grass?
This is not Texas—
Not the home of the Longhorn
And the cowboys with chaps and sombreros.
This is only a town,
A dull, conventional city,
Not Eastern, not Western,
Not Northern, not Southern,
Only a town in the springtime,
Just like ten thousand others.

   —1924

CYNTHIA MACDONALD
And Cause His Countenance
to Shine Upon You
(Corpus Christi, Texas)

The rabbi and his wife live in the body of Christ.
They break bread in it and drink dark, red Mogen David
To break the Yom Kippur fast. The ribs of the city
Rise around them, and its long watery arms and legs
Embrace them as the belt of the causeway lights up at dusk,
Securing the sky's dark fabric around the heart of the town,
Covering its pubis, South Bluff Park, which shelters
The strolling Rabbi and his wife from the Gulf Coast's sexual heat.
The city's beard, seaweed studded with shrimp, oysters and crayfish,
Hangs from the face of the sea with its changeable weathers—
Tense as religion or grammar, calm as beatitude or the full moon,
Joyous as a dance in the shtetl or on Fat Tuesday, as the mouth's
First savour of Aunt Martha's matzoh balls, swimming
In a richer salty broth. The eyes of Christ span the gulf of
Time looking back at himself, just after B.C., when he sat
At the long table, dividing the Passover matzoh. There was no
Poland yet so the matzoh was still a wafer, flat as the world.

The Rabbi prepares for Yom Kippur. His best friend is
The Methodist minister. Perhaps here in Corpus Christi—the body
Of Christ—there will be no pogroms. My Great-grandfather Kiam—
Loch Chaim— kissed the ground when he landed in New Orleans,
Kissed the body of American earth, thanked God, and set off
For the middle of Texas where a town which no longer exists
Was named after him. He celebrated Passover
Outside in the American desert of Amarillo, eating fried
Pinto beans, chili peppers and a boiled egg, which was
What there was. My mother showed me Kiam, Texas
In the 1934 Rand McNally Atlas while my sister tried
To straighten her crossed eyes by exercising them with
The stereopticon. Then we had Sunday breakfast, always

424

Bacon, eggs and popovers. My grandfather's wife, Fanny Tim,

A New Yorker, a German Jew, stuck a hat pin in her
Fine straw hat or her winter felt with its grosgrain ribbon
And rosette or flowers or cherries, and left to hear
John Haynes Holmes preach at the Congregational Church.

At night, the rigs burn their anointing oils to provide a halo of light
For the head of Christ. The rabbi dives into the black water,
With its rainbow patina, swimming laps after the Day of Atonement,
Struggling, like all Jews, to know the place where he lives.

—1991

*   *   *   *   *   *   *   *   *   *   *   *

Pat LittleDog
in austin reigns a bald-headed queen

when the door opened
a bald-headed woman came into the room
she was taller than everyone
in her white baggy pants
and her head gleamed
with a rubbed spitshine

women stood around her when she stood up
and when she sat down
they all sat as close as they could

they touched her hems and sleeves
they ran their fingers on her shirttails

they laughed when she laughed
and swayed toward her like flowers
on weak stems

oh bald-headed woman
I whispered from my own place at the crowd's edge
when I go home tonight
I will look for you in my mirror

since then
I have seen only glimpses of her
several times

—1982

* * * * * * * * * * * *

R.S. GYWNN
At Rose's Range

Old Gladys, in lime polyester slacks,
Might rate a laugh until she puts her weight
Squarely behind the snubnosed .38,
Draws down and pulls. The bulldog muzzle cracks
And barks six times, and six black daisies flower
Dead in the heart of Saddam's silhouette.
She turns aside, empties, reloads, gets set
And fires again. This goes on for an hour.

Later, we pass the time at the front door
Where she sits smoking, waiting for the friend
Who drives her places after dark: *You know,*
Earl's free next month. He says he wants some more
Of what she's got, and she's my daughter so
I reckon there's just one way this can end.

—2002

* * * * * * * * * * * *

426

BETSY BERRY
Afternoon in Austin

She has been shown fear more than once
      and her only thirtyish or so
She has vague aches and can remember a car
      which she filled with scent
The feeling of knowing what the gaze
      upon her would bring
Doesn't come anymore, maybe that's a good thing

Whish goes the spray on thinning hair
Spritz goes cologne on the sluggish pulse
Down goes the drink to set things right
Loose in the limbs, but the mind is tight
She frequents pool halls at the odd hours
      And sees there men with amber liquids
Who drop their dreams in pockets on the side
      They ignore her, for she has traded her cue
For a pen to scribble on napkins and such
      (Trouble there, they can see that plain enough)

Plunk, a ball drops in its pocket
Ching, an ice cube rattles against a piece of glass
Silence, a woman in a short skirt stalks by
They are desperate sounds
Suspended like dust motes in the air around

She watches the TV above for an excuse to be
      And freezes at the sight
Of an exercise device which promises time
      (They all do, you know)
Like a fixed broken fender, never the same

Crackle goes the glass in a windshield outside
A scrap yard sound, the hood wrinkles up

Ring goes the phone at 911
They are tinny sounds
Which summon help—always a wrong number

In "The Rack" they play on
            Clacking balls on the green
Here the game's neverending
            A freeze-frame scene

So her afternoon begins
And in keeping with the sport
Hears the squad car slip away
Sees the nine ball spin short

            —1991

* * * * * * * * * * * *

TERESA PALOMO ACOSTA
Dangereux avril

Tonight
In my neighborhood HEB where español is le langue
De muchos de nosotros consumidores
I review my French lessons,
Making up a little something—
Dangereux avril—
to entertain myself as I look for cheap food to buy
With my tiny paycheck.

At the bread bin, I consider the bagels
But mainly I talk myself
About where I am heading en los abriles
Que vienen aunque no se con cual dinero.

Dangereux avril.
I repeat it
As I peer into the bread bins

For bagels:
Four on sale for $1.19. I settle on two.
Yes, avril is coming
And in February I am
Already preparing for it:
Sewing spring prints into dresses
And donning them in late winter
To urge on avril's arrival.
To keep appointments with myself.

My corazon turns somersaults
Over decisions I have already made
To walk into el abril donde quiero caminar.
Head out one door.
Into another.
Go from one road
To the next
Au naturel.

In my neighborhood HEB at night
When I wander entre nous, gente cosmica,
I am finding the syllables of my dangereux avril: one at a time.

In the intricately woven strands
Of the raza surround me.
In their knotty threads:
Le dangereux avril
Awaits me.

—1992

DAVE OLIPHANT
from Beaumont: Class Reunion

too talented to give a hot damn
it all came
too easy to care

the beauty queens who called
or hung about as the tennis king
reigned on clay or asphalt court

the nonchalance of his passing shot
or at marching practice on the field
where he hurled his horn in the air

could play it better crumpled up
than those with dentless trumpets
giving it all they had

dressed like the rebel James Dean
with his ducktail & pants pulled low
cigarettes hidden from parents

a meek mother worshipped the earth
where he stepped danced outdid the rest
then gave it all up

took a refinery job like his dad's
the same father whose effusive love
shamed him in front of his friends

married a nobody plain & poor
rented a house happy as hell two blocks
from the home his genius had mocked

—1978

* * * * * * * * * * * * *

Dorys Crow Grover

The Ranch on the Limpia

for John Graves

As I was passing by the ruins
Of an old ranch house,
I chanced upon a letter, torn
But legible, and dated 1889.
It read, in part, "He said today
We had been here Twenty years,
and I began to cry, Dear Mother,
Because I do not believe that we
Are like to see Each Other any more. . . ."

I tell this story years hence.
Of how he built the ranch house
In a canyon along Limpia Creek
In the Trans-Pecos,
Where the dark green cedars grow on
Clay-loam hills and rugged bluffs.
The stage road passes nearby,
Fleeing daily toward Fort Davis
From the rolling staked plains.
Mountains rise with every dawn,
But she never sees the sky,
Nor the water-rushing creek,
Nor the wind-tossed trees,
For she waits day and night—
Watches even while she works—
Waits to have the first sight
Of a traveler passing by.
The hypocritic days linger,
And the long nights—
Fill her world with silence
Or the wild coyote's song,

She leans on the window sill,
Passing the hours.

One day, when pounding hoofs rang
Against her swirling thoughts,
She never gave a sign.
The winters were always the worst.
Snow keeps everything distant,
And he found her drifting
Farther and farther away.

—1990

* * * * * * * * * * * * *

DARYL E. JONES
Triangulation

The Lubbock night is glittering, the shake roofs
glazed with starlight, and low in the west,
past the pale orange glow of the city,
a green pinpoint of light is blinking

on the wing outside the window from a stewardess
gathering trays. Her feet still sore from dancing
all night the night before, she now leans
back in the arms of nothing, making way
for the balding school-supply salesman from Dallas,
who grasping each seatback moves along the aisle
to the restroom in the stern. There he will sit
cramped and self-conscious on the vibrating stainless steel seat,
cursing his migraine, while the whole of space
drones in his ears and shrinks
to a small white pulsing point that

blips on the black grid of a radar screen
scanning the night sky over El Paso,
a city in a desert, a star on the Texas map.

　　　—1990

*　*　*　*　*　*　*　*　*　*　*　*　*

CHRIS WILLERTON
Our Speaker This Morning

If you come early to one of these little churches,
there's nobody but you and the midmorning
summerlight, thunk of your car door,
crunch of gravel as you walk watching
strands of yellow grass tap the wooden porch.
The door is never locked, the bathroom
never has towels.

You may or may not find a map
of The Divided Kingdom, among dusty
Vacation Bible School projects.
Since the placid class may or may not remember what
the regular man said last week about Solomon,
prepare an extra scripture, an extra illustration
about dictators. You may need it to even up
the portion of wisdom.

Whenever they come, family at a time,
in pickups or five-year-old sedans,
you clutch for names, remark
the need for rain, squint
past at the sidewalk and hope for fifteen
or twenty. Mount to the speaker's stand
and the banks of the Jordan,
painted above the dry baptistery.

Someone leads a hymn, then you just
teach. Fifteen faces among fifty seats
in a forty-year-old frame building
aren't a threat. They've seen better teachers
and much worse. At the worship service
don't worry either. Sufficient unto the day
is the guest preacher thereof. They've
put up with nineteen-year-old preaching-students,
yammering missionaries, mumbling profs
who haven't preached fulltime in years.
These folk know charity. There isn't much
you could tell them anyway.

Don't go out to preach unless you want to.
On the hour's drive out, your only companions are
fenceline hawks and Herefords, dead armadillos, and
(angels in dark glasses)
the Texas Department of Public Safety.
The radio has only county/ western whining
or gospel bellowing. And whoever's turn it is
may take you home to fried chicken and okra
or tough leftover pork roast and shrunken peas.

I'll tell you really why you go:
gradually the people turn into brethren.
Old Bennie Sanders hates the liberals;
get him to talk instead
about his fifty-four gray Studebaker truck
or his grandson playing basketball in college
or his leading songs, before his emphysema came.
Get Maude to show you butterbeans she put up.
Sympathize on the cost of her eight medicines
and the red tape with Medicare.
While she puts ice cream on the peaches,
look out the window at the grain elevator

and neighbor's brick house that weren't there
when Bennie set the window in.

After the evening service you won't have
any trouble thanking them.
They used to have sixty members,
now have twenty. And the kids
keep growing up and moving away.

—1983

PAUL CHRISTENSEN
What the Citizens of Corpus,
Rockport, Palacios, or Bryan Need

What the citizens of Corpus, Rockport,
Palacios, or Bryan need is
        not a new tiller, or a pair of radials, a
goose-neck trailer to pull
        the yearlings into market, or tubs of loam to
green up the bushes
        along the drive. What they need least is that
dish revolving in the yard, up on its white leg with a
face as lonely as abandoned children,
        looking for some satellite to hug, to suck up
love beams in its empty
        bowl and pipe them to a house of anxious
tempers and fried fish,
        and the wonder bread piled up on a dinner
plate.

        What they need can't be bought or traded for a
pair of Red Wings,
        or settled out of court. It lies there like veil
of ice high in the

winter twilight, the ghostly whisper of a
phantom jet streaking its
     way toward San Antonio. You can almost spell
the letters out of
     sheer and stubborn emptiness as he wings it
over the colors of divorce
     and sickness of heart—the great way stations
of the living.

    —1991

⁂

CYD ADAMS
Pete's Poem

Five miles from Tatum down State 43,
black Pete Clay herds a white El Camino
to the Exxon-guarded grocery where the Justice of the Peace
sells barbecue, minnows, and Skoal.

He pumps leaded regular onto outboard-motor oil,
two gallons mixed in plastic Prestone jugs.
He grazes on Fritos, files a yellow Poulan
to scavenge dead-pine pulpwood to swap for dry-green paper.
He is forty-one years and two lifetimes old.

     (Oh sweet Pete, how all the girls loved him,
     how they'd dampen and drool for his Ali body,
     his Marvin Gaye tenor, his James Brown cool.)

For over ten years now he is lost in the jungle.
Shellfire, sporadic, flares the thick, humid night
in his delta-muddied eyes;
his body, *Semper fi*, blindly jerks to
static-slurred commands, but
his wire-capped skull is a camouflaged Claymore,

for Pete is yet in Asia, missing on patrol,
stealthy still and bush-wise,
loathe to show a target to all he can't control.

—1984

*   *   *   *   *   *   *   *   *   *   *   *   *

WALTER MCDONALD
After the Rains of Saigon

I put back the rifle on a steel rack
stuck in adobe and dump a split log
on the fire. Nothing to do daily
but ride eighty acres of mesquite

and cactus, count cattle and goats
and keep the windmills turning. Nights,
I lie in the shack with windows wide,
my wife and daughters asleep

in cotton sheaths. My daughters sigh
and kick the sheets. Tonight
in the east, I hear thunder,
the rumble of bombs. Propped up,

I try to piece together why I'm here. Nothing
about this flat dry land is like Vietnam
but my own damned eyes and ears.
I walk on cool linoleum outside to smoke.

Lightning flashes in the east like flares.
Running, I shove the shack's back windows tight.
Crouched on the damp porch, smoking,
digging at splinters, I watch hard rain

and wonder how many calves will die tonight
by drowning, how many angels dance
in a flash flood, how many years
we'll live out here in a desert.

—1989

H. Palmer Hall
Ghost Lights

A still breath on the summer breeze
and high hills in Dak To loom
over us. No quick answers ever
spring to mind, no drops of peace,
not even less than slow, perhaps,
now, inertia, a gradual "settling in."

We no longer even move our lips to ask
or, if we do, old slogans drop from voices
that always have an answer and never find
a truth, just wriggling obfuscations and
something like the Marfa lights dancing
at the dark ends of ancient tunnels.

—1998

Chris Willerton
Campsite

Army-surplus tents baked
browner in the afternoon glare.
Merit-badge cards went to sweaty pulp in hip pockets.
We aimed our compasses at windmills and pump jacks.
Only senior patrol leaders had cigarettes,

only a Tenderfoot put cow chips on the fire.
Grinning with his cigarette Mick chalked
HALE'S RANCH THIS IS A HOLE
on the canvas. Our puptent centered
the dry riverbed sand,
yucca, mesquite, dead grass above gullies,
tadpole pools where kid brothers went.

Did Mick remember me, Hale's Ranch,
Dinty Moore stew, star-swollen night sky
on any damp afternoon in Vietnam
before he died?
I still have the tent
and children who play in it.

    —1984

*   *   *   *   *   *   *   *   *   *   *   *

WALTER McDONALD
The Flying Dutchman

Someone I flew with
has gone to the moon and back.
I haven't touched a rudder in ten years,
my only cockpit the family wagon
with a cracked windshield. Still,
I'm up there in famous make-believe,

but I'm dreaming of Stuart,
straight-in from 20,000', Dave
who scooped a sand crane in the engine
but steered away from Waco
where he crashed, Keith
vaporized when a bomb
exploded in midair near Hanoi.

I might have died like Karnes
in Georgia, his first night solo.
He pitched too steep,
and the wings kept rolling.
When the controller called *Pull up*
Karnes jerked the stick back
tight to his groin, trying to obey
at two hundred knots, a thousand feet,
wings level by now, but inverted,
nose coming down, diving, someone
screaming *Pull up* in his headset.

Chandelles and loops, snap rolls,
tight Immelmanns
with a twist on top—
each turn was to get behind
somebody else, nothing beat
being second, a touch, a touch

on the button to bring him down.
The fun meant war.
The last aerobatic trick we were taught
was the victory roll.

Sometimes, squirting a thin jet
to water Texas grass trying to survive
another drought, I feel flames
in my fingertips and squeeze
to strafe begonias like a practice run.
At dawn, driving to work, I keep feeling
a tingling in my hands
and the weight on my backbone in a turn.

—1985

* * * * * * * * * * * * * *

440

BOBBY BYRD
On Karma at 9.11.85

Pete Rose hit number
four thousand one hundred and ninety-two tonight
exactly
fifty-seven years to the day
after Ty Cobb hung up his spikes.
Charlie Hustle and the Georgia Peach.
Ahh, baseball.
The holy mathematics.
NBC loves the symmetry.
Also on this day my son Andy
checked into the Shriners' Burns Hospital
in Galveston, Texas.
Four and a half years ago he and his brother Johnny were burned.
Bad. Real bad.
A kid's play fort
—cardboard boxes, palm leaves, a Christmas tree—
exploded into flames.
I still remember the stink of burnt hair and flesh,
the stunned face of my wife,
rocking and moaning in a waiting room chair.
Andy, four years old, almost died,
his little body sixty percent third degree burn,
and Johnny, his older brother, half that much,
but the doctors grafted skin
from one place to another.
They lived.
They come back here maybe once a year.
Reconstruction.
Everybody says they are doing wonderfully well.
They are.
We walk the beaches. We swim.
We watch the gulls, the fishes.

We are the random thoughts of God.
All of us.
Even the bum who sleeps out on the beach,
Pete Rose,
and my little sister Patty who died last month.
Our business is the breathing of air,
living and dying,
a prayer,
X plus Y, squared and cubed,
the miraculous axis of our presence
on the round globe of the earth,
September 11, 1985,
sprung from the sun
and somehow
the calculation becomes
the love of God.
Nothing more or less.

Okay.

—1987

*   *   *   *   *   *   *   *   *   *   *   *

BETSY FEAGAN COLQUITT
the man in the VA hospital

mornings he hobbles around
checking Waco's second-hand shops
that sell him prints, old photos,
a scrapbook of somebody's life.

by noon he's ready for the p.o.,
his weekday trade in catalogs,
postage for packages he sends
every week—to a sister a long way away,
to her children so scattered
they never can find his address.

afternoons back home at the hospital,
he "cheers up the boys" saying
God knows what. it doesn't matter.
they only half listen, better half
turned to TV, but they know
how he is, how they are, how it is
when no prosthesis ever fits right.
nights if he sleeps,
in-heat mares buck him awake.
good nights he lies abed trying
to string together thoughts
about legs, how two help arrest falling,
about how words turn into poems,
lines on canvas limn a world.

nights his chart labels "bad,"
he balances at a make-shift easel
jabbing at dark with layers
of paint hottest July can't dry.
flowers no botanist knows
bloom in vivid colors crippling,
their dyes bleeding before his eyes.

come dawn, the nurse checks,
calls housekeeping as he hides
paints, brushes, washes up,
hopes syringe she brings lets him wake
by ten to begin his day, its regimen
an order against chaos, his victory
in holding on, a sort of sorting out.

—1997

ALBERT HUFFSTICKLER
In the Compound

In the dream, I am Koresh.
I am waiting.
I am not so sure anymore.
If there is certainty,
it is beyond the tightening circle.
It is in the smell of things,
an animal smell like lust
borne on the night air,
the lust for my death
sifting like smoke
through the walls of the compound.
Yes, I know they lust for me
as I in my godliness have lusted
for these sad women
who look at me now with their stricken eyes,
searching for that primal assurance
they felt when I mounted them.
Where is it?
Faded
as the glory has faded.
Now there's only
the interplay of our lust
wafted on the air between
myself and my invisible destroyers—
my lovers.
The hours stretch out.
We will die.
I know I could stop it
but there is no will to.
The lust must be played out.
The devil must have his dance.
In the dark, I lie
touching my wound,

womanless,
wondering. . . .

April 5, 1993
Medical Arts Square #17
Austin Radiology

—*1993*

*   *   *   *   *   *   *   *   *   *   *   *

JACK E. MURPHY
Heave Me a Mountain, Lord!
(Prayer from the Plainview Rest Home)

Heave me a mountain, Lord,
from this plain land;
heave me a mountain frosted
white, for these scarred eyes
to climb.

Let it rise west, in view
of room 102; I'll give my potted plant
away and sit all day and night
before my window.

At night when the moon lights
waterfalls, and aspen leaves
reflect its glow I'll have no need
of sleep, I know.

Lord, heave me a mountain
just like the one I knew. . . .
no timid mountain, Lord, but bold,
with granite temples etched
in canyon walls, reminding me
of You.

When you heave me a mountain, Lord,
there'll be no need to bury me
300 miles away.

Remember, Lord…west of Room 102,
heave my mountain.

—*1982*

* * * * * * * * * * * * *

Charlotte Renk
Past Perm and Glitz

He looked at me and I at him; we did not see the same.
I cannot know what he saw in me beneath his drooping, purpled lids
where eyes, half-hid, studied me, and most that mirrors reflect.
Senior Citizens Day; Choctaw County College of Cosmetology.

Shirley, my operator, recommended sun glitz and perm.
Wanda, pumping his chair, combing his hair, patronized
him with a sweet nasal high-pitched drawl: "Do you want your
hair parted? . . . Okayee, on the left…or on the right?"

(She didn't know, you see, that men once knew…and women too
which side to part or not.) "It won't matter," he muttered.
He felt and fumbled beneath his cape, lifted one hip, then
the other, drew a folded handkerchief where he sneezed

and blew, unabashed by honk or gunk, then swept both away
with a smear of his speckled, blue-veined palsied hand.
Embarrassed by both his blowing and fumbling, Wanda turned
to Shirley, "What you gonna do to her?"

Shirley hurried her reply, "Perm and glitz."
"Good," said Wanda, "glad it ain't a frost; that's so
old fashioned, ain't it! Makes 'em look even older, don't it."
Wanda parted the man's hair on the right. He studied me more

---

on his left. I pretended not to check his part.
He was thin and his skin fell fragile across cheekbones
sculpted so sharp above lips so fully formed that any
woman his age might have felt elegantly defined by such

decline. But narrow shoulders slumped, barely able to hold
the head that held the misty days, framed at last by
ample silver waves. I tried not to see as he stared at me.
His eyes widened and furrowed—some sorting perhaps—
of whether or when I was or wasn't someone he might have
known. Had he seen me move before his eyes before this time?
And were we lovers then? Was my name Eula Pearl, Ruth or Helen?
Was I his timid tenth grade student, fourth hour, third row,

1927, '28 . . . or was it '29? Perhaps, I was Miss Esther Cline
who read with feeling and whom he loved in third grade.
Maybe for a moment, I was his wife who left him six "years ago for
   afterlife." …Whatever. I sat still and saw so terrified

that I too shall sit soon among the seniors; I shall fill
his chair before the mirrors way past the point of perm and
glitz. With eyes like his, I'll stare startled at patterns.
I'll compare mirages, present and past, of someones somewhere.

   —1994

Cyd Adams
Omens

Hearse-dark grackles pockmark
February slate,
scavenging, portentous.
Below their roiling appetites,
an eighty-year-old post oak
labors up beneath its load

of leeching mistletoe.
The sun is a proposal
not carried through
in Henderson, a piss stop,
gas when I need it.

The message on a post-it square
scalds with suggestion:
"Emergency…urgent…"
—pictures the mind keeps
locked in some drawer.

Outside Marshall,
a gold doubloon moon
teeters on the treetops,
a bile engorged inner tube,
Buddha-like, inscrutable,
where beyond the winking lights
Daddy lies beneath the knife.

—1993

* * * * * * * * * * * * *

JERRY CRAVEN
Midsummer Farewell

Golden in July sun, her black hair floating,
she walked the twisted juniper,
the saber lily, mesquite
and grassy paths of Palo Duro Park,
living the canyon night
beneath a jagged cottonwood's thrust into damp
blackness green amid
neon specks and oval moon floating
in leaves, in owl song
low along the palisading echo,

in the splash of desert waters where all
deny the zodiacal crab
within her veins.

Her black hair floating, her skin golden in blue
cotton she walked cement
and pavement to floors squared
in linoleum gray and stairs of false granite
with halls awash in neon
flicker to bring her valediction to us
and summer, her blue eyes
gray for the twisted juniper and cottonwood life,
stars, moon and feathered
lilies left beyond these sheetrock
and painted walls,
beyond blinded eyes
and cancerous claws of darkness.

—1990

* * * * * * * * * * * *

ALBERT HUFFSTICKLER
The Passing of the Old Man

One day he woke up tired, bone-tired
It wasn't the first time. It had been happening for weeks.
But there was a finality about this time that he'd never felt before.
"This is it," he told himself and, climbing out of bed, he washed his
  face and dressed carefully,
then he filled the battered percolator and put it on the stove
and, while the coffee was making, he rummaged through the
  cupboard and found a thermos bottle.
He drank one cup and put the rest in the thermos, he walked out of
  the cottage and down the path to the road.
There, he stood a moment looking back at the little adobe shell
with its sagging porch, the weathered outhouse behind it.

He realized that he had left the door open, started to go back,
then, with a shrug, turned and walked slowly down the road.
It was still early morning. He breathed deeply of the freshness of
  things, nodding with contentment.
Passing through the town, he greeted the few early-risers politely.
They watched him pass. "He's going to the mesa," they told each
  other.
He walked on. Soon the town was behind and the mesa rose before
  him.
There were several levels—as though the flat hills had been terraced
out of consideration for old men. He reached the first level,
looked around him, nodded, then turned, facing outward, looking off
  to the distant mountains.
Seating himself, he poured coffee and opened the pack of cigarettes.
He lit one and sat there, sipping his coffee and smoking, humming to
  himself
a tune by Waylon Jennings, that great comforter of men,
or perhaps it was Willie Nelson, who understood also.
His eyes dropped and he dozed a while, then woke, poured more
  coffee and smoked again.
The day passed slowly.

He felt the wind and breathed it in to him,
dozed again and woke and dozed again. As evening came
he poured the last of the coffee and lit the last cigarette.
The lights were coming on now in the little town. He smiled.
This time when he dozed off he did not awaken but, instead, felt
  himself lifting
and very gently rising above the body that sat nodding off, the smoke
from the last cigarette trailing up between its fingers.
For a moment, he was drawn back and then lifted once more till he
  was far above everything.
Once more he seemed to pause and, as he did, someone joined
  him—
someone golden and beautiful from far back in his youth—

and it seemed to him that the two of them merged into a single
         golden being
that lifted now one final time and sailed upward with absolute
         certainty
toward a distant and remembered light.

—1981

* * * * * * * * * * * * * *

Jan Epton Seale
To a Late Local Environmentalist

You went away to die, like an ailing pet
we search the neighborhood for.
I had a new book for you,
one about our river lands,
the precious ribbon of life
you took so personally,
worked at as an antidote
for the slow poison taking you.
The book was inscribed,
"To ___, friend of all Valley creatures,
with my love and admiration."

Today I take it from its mailer,
cut out its inscription page,
tape on a note: Damaged.
Back on the shelf.
I hate the envelope,
its accusing "Return to Sender" finger,
start to toss it, but
you wouldn't want me wasting a tree.
Remember how we held that funeral
for a cluster of palms uprooted,
replaced by a discount shoe store?

Just now at dawn the red-crowned parrots
make their daily flight over my house,
their sudden hilarious screeching
saying it's *el primer día* of their world,

saying you rest in *el primer día*
of your new habitat, that you smile,
seeing the bobcat hides in his
necessary brush along the Rio Grande.

Note on the origin of poem: With the coming of the North American Free Trade Agreement, the Lower Rio Grande Valley of Texas changed, almost overnight, from agricultural to urban. Now, only about 4% of original habitat remains to support our unique wildlife. I had a friend who worked especially hard to preserve habitat in the years before his death from AIDS. He was passionately opposed to the plan to clear all the brush from the edge of the Rio Grande and install floodlights, to deter illegal immigration from Mexico. Through his work, concessions were made, allowing the animals to pass up and down the river at night in their usual patterns.

—*2002*

★ ★ ★ ★ ★ ★ ★ ★ ★ ★ ★ ★ ★

R. G. VLIET
from Clem Maverick

goodnight sweet prince

Dear Clem,
            we got the word
by phone you've gone away
bound for Home on the Glory Train
to a Brighter Day.

Dallas is pretty far
from Him in His Judgments There.
The Big Boss of the Roundup likely
wanted you near.

Now you're in Hillbilly Heaven.
Oh what a star-studded Land.
You'll write for the greatest singers Clem.
The Angel Band.

You'll broadcast from the Holy Station.
You'll purely pick your guitar.
The Heavenly Music will make us look
to the Western Star.
You'll sing again you see.
They'll do you Up Yonder in style.
Still and all we're glad you sung
our way awhile.

Rest in Peace. May
your songs Clem Maverick
make *His* Top Chart.
                    Sincerely,
                            WE
AT TOPNOTCH MUSIC.

    —1983

  ✶   ✶   ✶   ✶   ✶   ✶   ✶   ✶   ✶   ✶   ✶

Joseph Colin Murphey
The First Birthday After Death

I still would take a day for your demise
or walk beside the sea at Padre Island
to let you know I care that you are gone

The world has seemed less gripping
since your death to hold me here alone
so I would take a day for your demise

Since you're not so exposed across those reefs
I do not have to chart the killer storms
to let you know I care that you are gone

Yet, those you love are grieving still around
that bay, left thinking now of this one day alone
So we would take a day for your demise

A birthday is a birthday still, though one
takes now a graveyard walk to walk with you
to let you know he cares that you are gone
Lip to the wind, I speak to you again
and face the south where by the sea you sleep
I still would take a day for your demise
to let you know I care that you are gone

    —1981

  *   *   *   *   *   *   *   *   *   *   *   *

ISABEL NATHANIEL
Elegy at Mustang Island

The Mayan Princess fronts the Gulf,
crescent of white stucco.
Its surprise, its excess—
for this wind-blown barrier island—
is an extravaganza of pools and gardens,
pinks of perfumed blooms, jungly greens,
all vigilantly tended
to thrive so in the hunkered-down space
between hotel and ridge of dunes.

April weather chancy, the place
is all ours. We're warmed,
lulled in man-made Eden.
The sea we came for is just over there,

surf-sound close, continuous.
On white chaises longues we lie
in an attitude of mild happiness
and find amusement in gulls'
periodic fracas overhead.

For passion we substitute politeness.
Our paradise was more than this,
once, but a swift strike of the gods
has rendered us quiet and untroublesome.
There's a way out: a boardwalk
snakes over sand little-Sierras
and a door alone against the sky
guards the ramp's descent to beach.
Arm in arm, we've been out there

for dutiful strolls, our delicate feet
just managing not to touch
blue-neon *physalia physalis,*
those man-of-war hellions delivered onto shore,
tendrils still armed to sting
into agony. We step right along
taking menace for granted.
For us the tideline's runes
spell out tragedy already happened.

My tragedy that happened
is always there, dark
as the west side of the dunes
in this early-morning, low-angled light.
Sea oats, dove weeds, pennyworts,
goatsfoot morning glory
make the rich mat of vegetation
that traps the sand. These plants,
like a long-there grief,

lie half buried, roots and runners spreading,
sprouting blooms at night
to know full beauty at the dawn.
I make the ascent. Last day, there is some calm
or horror yet to be identified.
Grey veils of air are walls and ceiling
for the boardwalk door which opens
hard against the southeast wind.
From here it is possible to call
long sing-song sounds, the way
kids call—and I send out in graceful glide
my dead son's name in syllables: *Jer-ry* . . .
Jer-ry . . . *Jer-ry* . . . his name offered to him.
And that most important word
skips naturally and unimpeded
across the ghostly beach,
over the silvering water,
past the horizon of oil-rigs

and out there joins him,
my boy, O so wholly himself
this brief morning moment,
because his own name is far sweeter
than silence, his own name
rising and falling in the air,
a music he has missed,
his name *Jer-ry* . . . *J er-ry* . . . *Jer-ry* . . .
coming to him.

    —1996

★   ★   ★   ★   ★   ★   ★   ★   ★   ★   ★   ★   ★

MARTHA E. WHITTEN
Beautiful in Death

(In memory of Miss Bettie Costley and Miss Griffith, who were drowned in the Colorado River while bathing, May, 1867.)

At the river's verge;
    Where the restless surge
Into glistening spray was breaking;
    Its rippling song,
    As it rushed along,
The blushing flowerets waking;
    Their dimpled feet,
    Pressed the mosses sweet,
Bright hopes each breast elating;
    They stepped with prde,
    In the flowing tide;
And knew not that Death was waiting.

    So tempting fair
    Were the bright waves there,
Just stirred by the wind's low sighing,
    They little knew,
    With that passing view,
Of the river onward flying;
    That crouching there,
    In his watery lair
The Death-Angel hovered near;
    That 'neath that wave,
    They should find a grave,
It's foamy crest their bier.

    Oh was there ever
    Thou fatal river!
A lovelier gem on thy bosom worn?
    Than those blooming girls,
    With their dripping curls,
Asleep down thy current borne?

Each gentle face,
In thy chill embrace
Shall kindle with joy no more'
And the dimpled feet,
Thy cold waves greet,
Ne'er again shall press thy shore.

But far away,
In that world of day
Where the pure and happy come;
They joyful wait,
At the Pearly Gate,
For the stricken ones at home.
No grief or care,
Shall enter there,
To mar the soul's deep joy;
And there no death,
With pois'nous breath,
Our treasures shall destroy.

—1886

* * * * * * * * * * * *

NICK NORWOOD
For the Drowned

First, the river unclothes them, washes
Toward the Gulf their t-shirts and tennishoes,
Their torn khakis and simple house dresses,
And even, eventually, the finer points
Of their faces, the identifying features,
So that, often, they seem to arrive incomplete,
Like lumps of clay not yet fully formed,
Flesh unpronounceable. Arturo says it's fish—
Mudcats and alligator gars—that take what's
Missing. They'll eat anything, he says,
And I imagine as much with each rising bubble

In the draft. We find ten or twelve a year,
And all of them aliens, illegals, wetbacks.
Or so it goes in the reports. Who knows?
Who can tell by looking? Here in The Valley,
Our tongues are already swollen with two languages,
The contents of our stomachs is the same,
And most of us are too poor for dentists.
But it makes life less complicated for the coroner.
The county's reserved a special place for them
In the graveyard. He applies the tags. Arturo and I
Backhoe the graves out of dirt too thin for planting,
Inter the bodies, reclothed, faceless in white bags.

—2002

* * * * * * * * * * * *

H. PALMER HALL
A Death on Village Creek

The lightning struck directly in the center
of the creek. We could not escape the glare
of it from our too small house on the slope.
The sound rushed through rain-soaked woods
and we cowered as the shock of noise
rolled over us for much too long.

September tricked us, made the flowers
bloom: azaleas filled with pink blossoms,
giant hydrangeas in both pink and blue
tomatoes fruited out and mulberries and
blackberries. We picked and ate, stopped
and drank. We talked about the lightning.

Village Creek rose high and strong that night.
Dark waters dug away the banks from outer
bends, under-cutting beech and magnolia trees.
When a tree fell, the water washed around,

stripped it of leaves, left branches behind, for those
who thought the creek always slow and placid.

My father said "The creek's too much this time.
You can swim tomorrow. Too much current, too
many snags. See how it surges and then dips down,
beneath the submerged branch." We watched, agreed,
then found a secret place to swim in the creek,
above the bend just off the racing stream. Yet still
Billy died there. He dove into the water and
hit a tree that could not free itself from broken
roots. His head stuck beneath the creek in the fork
of two not-yet-rotted limbs. Three days later,
we followed hearse and grieving family members.
This was the first procession for the dead.

My father drove slowly, watched the lights
of the cars ahead. "It's a shame beer's not right
for this," he said. The cars passed so many bars:
Yvonne's and the Red Lion, LouAnne's and
Thibodeaux's. A drive in the thicket just like
so many others except for the boy five cars ahead

Of all my friends, I think of Billy first and knew
him least of all. I can see still the color of his hair,
his skinny frame, his neck wedged between two limbs,
the odd appearance of his face when we looked
inside the casket. It was not like Billy, rouge reddened
his cheek, he smiled, a boy who would never be a man.

—2002

✳   ✳   ✳   ✳   ✳   ✳   ✳   ✳   ✳   ✳   ✳   ✳

Carol Cullar
he's crossed the river

the local scandal
rag has said
foul play is suspected;
they fetched his body
up from the river
below the black train-bridge
where it had snagged
on pilings half in
half out of water;
he wore his blue jeans
about his ankles;
six stab wounds to the heart,
seven cuts to the liver,
and three throat slashes
where his life ran out;
two roses and a snake,
a girl's name and five
other tattoos on
unnamed body parts
adorn his corpse;
they hauled his puffy
four-day-dead remains
out the texas side
of the *rio grande*—
which must mean
that this is Hell.

—1992

11

No Quittin' Sense

I said, "Marty, you're just as bad as me. You ain't got quittin' sense, either."

Reverend C. C. White

DARYL E. JONES

Going On

"We'll come back from this. We'll go on." Wichita Falls resident,
after April 10, 1979, tornado

Forever witnessing
that moment when the store windows
billowed like sails and burst
in a whirl of glass.
the mannequins at Sykes Center Mall
recoil, as if in a tableau of terror,
their torsos and arms
wrenched into macabre poses.

But the living, trying to forget,
Go on. For years they will wake
Suddenly in the night, the bedclothes
twisted around them. For years
thunderheads will find them
trembling in bathtubs or closets,
their eyes squeezed shut.

But now, sorting through rubble
in the morning light,
they marvel at the random
or miraculous—the cinder block
skewered by a broom straw,
the china closet spared
in a roofless house—
and salvage what they can.

Holding each other, glad to be alive,
they watch the sky, and turn
to what the future holds,

forever changed,
like the cracked cups they will drink from,
gently, with both hands.

—1985

* * * * * * * * * * *

CHARLES BEHLEN
Widow Zebach

Off Interstate 20
she whirls her hoe
the acreage now
a bedroom wall
a six foot
stand of weeds
Husband dead
(a farming mishap)
both sons dead
("Nam" Korea)
the house lost to
a lightning fire in
'68 and she
whirls her hoe
It lifts and
disappears
lifts
disappears
in the sun
in the moon
The relatives pass
at 70 yelling
GIVE IT UP BEATRICE

The weeds keep working
at that one
charred wall
remaining

—1979

* * * * * * * * * * * *

SANDRA CISNEROS
Las Girlfriends

Tip the barmaid in tight jeans.
She's my friend.
Been to hell and back again.
I've been there too.

Girlfriend, I believe in Gandhi.
But some nights nothing says it
quite precise like a Lone Star
cracked on someone's head.

Last week in this same bar,
kicked a cowboy in the butt
who made a grab for Terry's ass.
How do I explain, it was all
of Texas I was kicking,
and all our asses on the line.

At Tacoland, Cat flamencoing crazy
circles round the pool
player with the furry tongue.
A warpath of sorts for every
wrong ever wronged us.

And Terry here has her own history.
A bar down the street she can't
go in, and one downtown. Me,
a French café in Austin
where they don't say—*entrez-vous*.

Little Rose of San Antone
is the queen bee of kick-*nalga*.
When you go out with her,
don't wear your good clothes.

But the best story is la Bárbara
who runs for the biggest kitchen knife
in the house every bad-ass domestic quarrel.
Points it towards her own heart
like some Aztec priestess gone *loca*.
¡ME MATO!

I tell you, nights like these,
something bubbles from
the tips of our pointy boots
to the top of our coyote yowl.

Ya'll wicked mean, a voice at the bar
claims. Naw, not mean. Shit!
Been to hell and back again.
Girl, me too.

—1994

*   *   *   *   *   *   *   *   *   *   *   *   *

CYD ADAMS
Rock Pickers

Yesterday we root-picked up the new ground,
The old man and me, mostly me though, now his
back's no longer what it used to be—
(Hell, whose is? And I'm only forty.)
See, dozers can cause more work than they save, with
their craters and their wallows, their claw marks and
root globs and stump holes and all. You have to finish it.
And so we were at it.
He drug the land plane, paring down the dirt mounds,
filling in the swags; he's hell on a tractor still, can stand
              more than I can;
I helped him make it dump and chopped a jillion root snags
              the dozer'd
haggled off. And so we paced the sun.
But this morning, with his coffee, taking stock, he chose
we'd harvest off the worst of the rock crop,
the sharding shelf of moonstone this sandhill perches on
(Ever grind a bushhog blade when it's whacked iron ore?).
So with the sled behind the 9-N, me humping on, except in
the thick spots where the cat had clawed a tree and
carved down to grapefruit the watermelon stone, we were
reapers of boulder bones, sparrows on the gravel
grain that mountains once glaciered made,
him and me, tenants for a season on this scrub-hickoried
sandhip four acres cheeked.

We drag in three pickup loads, morning and afternoon,
dump them at the stone stack over on the Mays Place
to feed foundation forms, and save on steel, the
littler ones for pullpost holes to stretch the Portland out.
We bar them up like spuds in June, double-team the
big ones, end up chaining one or two down to the fenceline
for someone else to find.

After lunch it's harder, the bending over and all,
and by five-thirty we're pretty well done in.
The sun throws our shadows long over where we've been.
He kills the guttural Ford's spark and hikes up his
pants leg to fish out the snuff lid, leans on the
fender peak, pushes back his Lone Star cap, and nostril
by nostril, snorts out his nose clots.
"You just love this, but you wouldn't say so."
I skid and hump and drop my rock, straighten up
halfway to stars against the sun.
"Oh, yeah, the hell I do!"
He grins then and bumps the coil, spits short across
the hood, but then shuts her off again—
"Son," he says, woodenly, like he gets when talk won't do,
but then, shakes his head, falls silent, stares off
the hillfall into the shadows through his Copenhagen haze.

    —1991

CHUCK TAYLOR
our texas economy

seems like every boy I know
has been cut back or laid off—
or the business they run
ain't got no business

Larry's moved in with his mom
and sold his 'Vet;
Kim is talking about
reconciling with her old man.
they've been separated a year.
"I just can't support these kids
on my own," she says

why, high tech got so high—
eight miles high they say—
that it just rides the jet stream
from California to Boston,
back and forth
                    back and forth,
missing Texas

And crude oil got so plentifully crude
it's almost oozing out of the floorboards.
I heard a chemist talking
of converting the stuff
to synthetic chocolate

But don't despair
with the coming cold of December.
Your lover's eyes
are just as warm as ever
and a kiss is still a kiss,
guaranteeing higher yield
than a jumbo CD

and goodness—oh yes goodness—
it's painted all over the asphalt,
all over homes and buildings
just like it always was.
goodness, your best investment,
that outlasts all greed
and all the pennies of despair

  —1986

* * * * * * * * * * * * *

STEVE HARRIGAN
Pecos Bill in Decline

A disease has attacked
the plumage of his chaps.
He sheds in the parlor
while the ladies feel his muscle.

All that fluff and fur, that dream:
a grizzly cub nuzzling him down
into the secret corners of his crib;
the desert; a sky filled with
ice and minerals;

the cold nose of his coyote mother
and her wide-set eyes
stunned with love.

Before the mirror
he sees his bare legs bowed
like railroad ties.

It has been long time
since he has lassoed a train
or the far bank of a river.
But trust him: he may yet
bury his face in the grasslands.

He may take up the state of Texas
and wear its hide
next to his skin.

—1980

About the Poets

Teresa Palomo Acosta teaches at the University of Texas at Austin. Her prose and poetry have appeared in *The New Handbook of Texas, descant,* and *The United States in Literature*. She has co-written a study of women of Mexican origin in Texas from 1700-2000, forthcoming in 2003 from the University of Texas Press.

Cyd Adams is in the English department at Stephen F. Austin State University. His work has appeared in such publications as *Stone Drum, Borderlands, descant, RE: Artes Liberales,* and *New Texas*. His collection, *Blackjack, Bull Pine, Post Oak Glade*, was published in 1999 by Crazy Creek Press.

Betty Adcock is Kenan Writer-in-Residence at Meredith College in Raleigh, North Carolina. Her books include *Beholdings, Nettles,* and *Walking Out*. In 2001, Louisiana State University Press released Adcock's *Intervale: New and Selected Poems*.

Ai received the Lamont Poetry Award from the Academy of American Poets for *Killing Floor* (1978) and an American Book Award for *Sin* (1987). She earned the 2000 Henry Blakely Poetry Award and a National Book Award for *Vice* (2001). Ai, now the visiting Matte Chair at Oklahoma State University, will return to Texas in 2002 as a member of the creative writing faculty at Southwest Texas State University.

Stanley E. Babb published *Death of a Buccaneer and Other Voices* (1927), a collection about maritime Texas. A native of England, Babb spent much of his life in Galveston, where he was book editor of the *Galveston News*. His poetry appears in such anthologies as *Voices of the Southwest, The Southwest in Literature,* and J. Frank Dobie's *Legends of Texas*.

Karle Wilson Baker, author of nine books, was nominated for the Pulitzer Prize for her 1931 collection, *Dreamers on Horseback*. Ms. Baker was a charter member and one of the first presidents of the Texas Institute of Letters. Her poems appeared in *Yale Review, Scribner's Magazine,* and *Atlantic Monthly*. Her best-known novel is *Family Style*.

W.E. Bard graduated from Southern Methodist University and lived in Dallas. William E. Bard's collection, *A Little Flame Blown*, was awarded the 1934 publication prize from the Poetry Society of Texas.

William D. Barney, a Fort Worth resident for some sixty years, received the Robert Frost Poetry Award in New York City from Frost himself. Barney worked as a postal inspector while writing his often-anthologized poetry. Two of his books, *Kneel for the Stone* and *Permitted Proof*, received Texas Institute of Letters awards. His other titles include *The Killdeer Crying, Words for a Wide Land,* and *A Cowtown Chronicle*.

Colleen Beeson grew up in Belton, Texas. Now a businesswoman in Odessa, she has been included in the yearbooks of the Poetry Society of Texas and *Behold Texas*. "Minnie Henderson" recalls her high school Spanish teacher.

Charles Behlen has published in such anthologies as *Travois, The New Breed, Anthology of Magazine Verse,* and *Yearbook of American Poetry*. His work has appeared in *The Texas Observer, The Pawn Review, New Texas,* and other periodicals. Behlen's books include *Perdition's Keepsake, The Voices Under the Floor,* and *Dreaming at the Wheel*. Charles Behlen, who was recipient of a Dobie Paisano Fellowship, lives in Sulphur Springs, Texas.

Betsy Berry holds a Ph.D. from the University of Texas at Austin. Berry's poetry has appeared in numerous publications, including *descant, New Texas,* and *Texas Observer*. The Austin writer also teaches college English.

Alan Birkelbach has two books of poetry, *Bone Song* and *Weighed in the Balances*. A longtime member of the Poetry Society of Texas, his work has appeared in two editions of the *New Texas* series, in *Suddenly,* and in *Borderlands*.

Mary Loving Blanchard teaches English at New Jersey City University. Her poetry and short fiction, under the nia akimbo pseudonym, has been published in *The African American Review, Texas Short Stories 2,* and *Calyx: A Journal of Art and Literature by Women*.

Robert Bonazzi founded Latitudes Press. His poetry, fiction, and nonfiction have appeared in over three hundred journals. Bonazzi's 1999 *Man in the Mirror* is a critical study of John Howard Griffin's *Black Like Me.* Now living in Florida, Bonazzi has written five books of poetry. A sixth collection, *The Scribbling Cure*, is forthcoming from Wings Press in 2003.

Margie B. Boswell lived most of her life in Tarrant County. She graduated from Texas Christian University and taught in Fort Worth public schools.

Jerry Bradley is the author of four books, including the collection of verse *Simple Versions of Disaster.* His poems and stories have appeared in *New England Review, American Literary Review, New Texas,* and *Poetry Magazine.* A member of the Texas Institute of Letters, Bradley is the poetry editor of *Concho River Review* and was the founder and editor of *New Mexico Humanities Review.* Jerry Bradley is a dean at Lamar University.

Susan Bright is the publisher of Plain View Press. Her poems have been published in *Travois, The Texas Anthology, Southwest,* and *From Hide and Horn.* She is the author of the collections *Atomic Basket, Far Side of the Word,* and *Tirades and Evidence of Grace.*

William Burford, who lives in Fort Worth, has enjoyed the appearance of his poems in *Poetry* and *Partisan Review.* In 1955, his first book of poetry, *Man Now*, received a Texas Institute of Letters award. His other collections are *A World, A Beginning,* and *Faccia Della Terra/Face of the Earth.* His work has been published in *The New Pocket Anthology of American Verse* and *The Poetry Anthology: Sixty-five Years of America's Distinguished Verse* magazine.

Robert Burlingame has resided near El Paso since 1954 and now lives on a ranch near the Guadalupe Mountains. A professor emeritus at the University of Texas at El Paso, Burlingame is widely published and received a Pushcart Prize for his *Eighteen Poems.*

Bobby Byrd, author of ten poetry collections, has received a fellowship from the National Endowment for the Arts and a D.H. Lawrence Fellowship. In 1978, he became publisher of Cinco Puntos Press in El Paso. In 1996, he co-edited the nonfiction book *The Late Great Mexican Border: Reports from a Disappearing Line.*

Scott Cairns, the author of six collections, has been published in a Pushcart anthology, *The Atlantic Monthly,* and *The Paris Review.* Cairns has taught creative writing at Westminster College and the University of North Texas and is now on the faculty of the University of Missouri, Columbia. Recently, Zoo Press released Cairn's *PhiloKalia: New and Selected Poems.*

Rosemary Catacalos was a Dobie Paisano fellow and a Wallace Stegner fellow at Stanford University. Her poems have appeared in *Bloomsbury Review, Southwest Review,* and *Poetry in Review,* and her work has been collected in such anthologies as *Mexican American Literature* and *Best American Poetry 1996.*

William Lawrence Chittenden was once known throughout America as "The Poet Ranchman." Chittenden began writing poetry while cowboying on his uncle's ranch along the Old Mackenzie Trail in Jones County. His *Ranch Verses* became a national bestseller, and by his death in 1934, Putnam and Sons had reprinted *Ranch Verses* fifteen times.

Paul Christensen is a poet, critic, and award-winning short-story writer, as well as a professor at Texas A&M University. His poetry collections include *Old and Lost Rivers, Gulfsongs, The Vectory, Weights & Measures, Signs of the Whelming,* and *Blue Alley.* Christensen has written such books of literary criticism as *Minding the Underworld: Clayton Eshleman and Late Postmodernism* and *West of the American Dream: An Encounter with Texas.*

Sandra Cisneros is author of the award-winning *The House on Mango Street* (1983) and has published the collections *My Wicked Wicked Ways* and *Loose Woman.* In 1991, Random House released *Woman Hollering Creek and Other Stories.* Sandra Cisneros, a recipient of two NEA grants, lives in San Antonio.

Brian Clements is the author of *Essays Against Ruin,* co-editor of *Best Texas Writing 1,* and editor of *Best Texas Writing 2.* Clements currently teaches at the Writer's Garret in Dallas. His poems and essays have appeared in *American Poetry Review* and elsewhere.

James Cody is a publisher, registered nurse, scholar, and writer. He is the author of *Colorado River,* a nonfiction book; *Return,* a collection of poems; *Prayer to Fish,* a long poem; and *A Book of Wonders,* a collection of prose poems. *My Body Is A Flute* is a collection of poems written between 1974 through 1993. Cody's most recent book is *Elvis, Immortality.*

MAUDE E. COLE came of age in Erath County in the last days of the Old West. Her first-hand knowledge of the frontier can be seen in her 1941 novel, *Wind Against Stone*. Maude E. Cole was the head librarian at Abilene's Carnegie Library. Her 1935 book of poetry was *Clay-Bound*.

BETSY FEAGAN COLQUITT lives in Fort Worth. She was, for many years, a member of the English faculty at Texas Christian University and editor of *descant*. She edited several books, among them William D. Barney's *A Cowtown Chronicle* and the anthology *A Part of Space: Ten Texas Writers*. Her poems are collected in *Honor Card* and *Eve—From the Autobiography*.

SARAH CORTEZ won the 1999 PEN Texas Literary Award for Poetry. She teaches at the University of Houston's Center for Mexican American Studies, while working as a police officer. In 2000, Arte Público Press published Cortez's *How to Undress a Cop*.

JERRY CRAVEN'S poetry, fiction, and drama have appeared in *Concho River Review, RE: Arts and Letters, Texas Short Fiction, Isaac Asimov's Analog, The Southwest Review,* and *New Texas*. His books of poetry are *The Last Running, My Own Choric Song,* and *Oleander Wine*. His novel, *Snake Mountain,* appeared in 2000. He teaches at West Texas A&M in Canyon.

SHERRY CRAVEN teaches English at West Texas A & M in Canyon. She has published poetry and fiction in both English and Spanish in such collections as *RiverSedge, Suddenly,* and *New Texas*. Her poetry has been read on National Public Radio. She is currently working on a collection of creative non-fiction.

A. L. CROUCH, a Fort Worth lawyer, was anthologized in *Out West Where the West Begins*. A graduate of Texas Christian University and the University of Texas, Crouch first wrote poetry while fighting in Asia during World War II.

GRACE NOLL CROWELL was a Dallasite. Her first book of poetry, *White Fire* (1925), won awards in both America and England. Crowell, the Centennial Year Texas Poet Laureate (1936), was one of the first Texas poets with a national readership. Crowell's work appeared in such publications as *McCalls, Good Housekeeping, Christian Science Monitor,* and *The New York Times.* and her *Songs of Courage* was reprinted twenty-five times. Grace Noll Crowell wrote thirty books of stories and poems before her death in 1969.

NORMAN H. CROWELL, husband of poet Grace Noll Crowell, had his own literary accomplishments. His poems and articles appeared in *The Country Gentleman, Field and Stream,* and The Saturday Evening Post.

STEVEN TYE CULBERT has had three novels published in hardcover since 1993: *The Beautiful Woman Without Mercy, The King of Scarecrows,* and *Lovesong for the Giant Contessa*. Culbert teaches in the College of Business at The University of Texas at Arlington.

CAROL CULLAR is executive director of the Rio Bravo Nature Center Foundation in Eagle Pass. Cullar has published poetry in *Southwestern American Literature, New Texas 92, New Texas 93, Sulphur River Review,* and *Concho River Review*. Her most recent book is *Maverick in the Chaparral: The Eagle Pass Poems*.

CHIP DAMERON, a native of Dallas, has published four collections of poems, among them, *Hook & Bloodline* (2000) and *Greatest Hits* (2001). His poems, essays, and reviews have appeared in more than sixty literary magazines and journals. Dameron teaches creative writing and literature at the University of Texas at Brownsville.

WILLIAM VIRGIL DAVIS' *One Way to Reconstruct the Scene* won the Yale Series of Younger Poets Award in 1980. *The Dark Hours* won the Calliope Press Chapbook Prize. He is also the author of the collection *Winter Light*. In addition, he has published several books of literary criticism as well as scores of critical essays on American and British literature. Davis is Centennial Professor of English and writer-in-residence at Baylor University.

FRANK DESPREZ, a native of Bristol, England, was a journalist and world traveler who spent three years on a Texas ranch. His poem "Lasca," first published in 1882 in a London magazine, is a tale about a Texas cowboy and his beloved *vaquera*. "Lasca" was a favorite for classroom declamations before World War I.

J. FRANK DOBIE, teacher, folklorist, anthologist, and author, was for many years Texas's best-known writer. He was the main force behind the Texas Folklore Society for many years and was a charter member of the Texas Institute of Letters. He is best known for his collections of folktales and other books about Texas. Among his many volumes are

Apache Gold and Yaqui Silver, Coronado's Children, The Mustangs, and *A Vaquero of the Brush Country.*

MARTHA ELIZABETH, a former Dobie Paisano fellow, has published stories and poems in various periodicals, including *American Literary Review* and *Bloomsbury Review*. Her first chapbook of poetry, *Basics of the Dance*, was published in 1990 and her most recent, *Considering Manon*, was released in 2000.

SYBIL ESTESS teaches at the University of Houston. Her poems have appeared in *The New Republic, Shenandoah, Western Humanities Review,* and *The Paris Review*. Estess co-edited *Elizabeth Bishop and Her Art* (University of Michigan Press) and *Field of Words* (Prentice-Hall). Her book of poetry is *Seeing the Desert Green* (Latitudes Press).

MAYME EVANS was a longtime Corpus Christi resident and a frequent contributor to the yearbooks of the Poetry Society of Texas. Her *Of Me I Sing* was published in 1969.

ROBERT A. FINK is W. D. Bond Professor of English and director of creative writing at Hardin-Simmons University in Abilene, Texas. His first collection of poetry is *The Ghostly Hitchhiker* and his most recent *The Tongues of Men and of Angels*. His poems have been published in *Southwest Review, Harvard Magazine, Iron Horse Literary Review, New Texas, TriQuarterly,* and *Poetry*.

PAUL FOREMAN was the editor of Thorp Springs Press. Foreman was also the founder of *Hyperion Poetry Journal* and co-editor of *Travois: An Anthology of Texas Poetry* (1976). Foreman's books of prose and poetry include *Redwing Blackbird, Sugarland, Quanah, Texas Liveoak, The Unknown Law,* and *Feather River.*

EDWARD H. GARCIA teaches English and creative writing at Brookhaven College in Dallas. Garcia contributes to the book pages of *The Dallas Morning News* and has written for various Texas publications, among them, *Texas Observer, Pawn Review,* and *The Texas Humanist.*

BETTYE HAMMER GIVENS won the 2000 PEN Texas Award and has taught creative writing internationally. Her work has appeared in *The Christian Science Monitor, RiverSedge,* and *Paris Atlantic.*

RAY GONZÁLEZ is author of the memoir *Memory Fever* and the volumes of poetry *Turtle Pictures, The Heat of Arrivals,* and *Hawk Temple at Tierra Grande*. His short story collections are *The Ghost of John Wayne* and *Circling the Tortilla Dragon*. González is author of a collection of essays and several anthologies. He teaches at the University of Minnesota in Minneapolis.

ROXY GORDON, essayist, songwriter, and poet, is author of *Some Things I Did, Breeds, West Texas Mid-Century, Crazy Horse Never Died* and *Smaller Circles.*

A.C. GREENE was the author of more than twenty-seven books, among them a novel and a short story collection, local and regional history, memoirs, and a book of poetry. His histories include the winner of a Fehrenbach Prize, *900 Miles on the Butterfield Trail*, and a Texas Institute of Letters Award winner, *The Last Captive*. His first book, *A Personal Country*, published by Alfred A. Knopf in 1969, is still in print, as is *The Santa Claus Bank Robbery* and an updated version of *The 50+ Best Books on Texas.*

HILTON ROSS GREER was a newspaperman as well as poet. The author of four collections, Greer edited or co-edited the anthologies *Voices from the Southwest, Best Short Stories from the Southwest,* and *New Voices from the Southwest*. In 1921, he co-founded of the Poetry Society of Texas and served as its first president. Hilton Ross Greer also helped found the Texas Institute of Letters and served as that organization's president.

DORYS CROW GROVER was a professor of English at Texas A&M, Commerce, for many years. A former president of the American Studies Association of Texas, Grover received the Fort Concho Centennial Award for "The River Ranch on the Limpia," which was first published in the *Concho River Review* and reprinted in her collection, *The Valley of the Tutuilla and Other Lines* (Pine Hill Press). She now lives in the Pacific Northwest.

R.S. GWYNN's latest book is *No Word of Farewell: Selected Poems 1970-2000*. He was named Distinguished Faculty Lecturer at Lamar University in 2001 and has a number of publications in literary journals. Penguin published the third edition of Gwynn's book, *A Pocket Anthology,* in 2001.

H. PALMER HALL has published prose and poetry in such publications as *Texas Short Stories 2, Florida Review, New Texas,* and *North American Review*. Hall is the co-editor and director of

Pecan Grove Press. He also directs the library and teaches English at St. Mary's University in San Antonio. The Vietnam veteran is the author of the book of poetry, *Deep Thicket and Still Waters,* and edited the anthology, *A Measured Response,* a collection about the Persian Gulf War.

CYNTHIA HARPER lives in San Antonio and also teaches English for Palo Alto College. Her collections include *Ruffled Socks* and *Snow in South Texas.* She is editor and publisher of Chili Verde Press.

STEPHEN HARRIGAN'S novel *Aransas* was listed by *The New York Times* as one of the notable books of 1980. Besides writing screenplays for Hollywood, Harrigan has published three non-fiction books: *Water and Light: A Diver's Journey to a Coral Reef, A Natural State,* and *Comanche Midnight.* His other novels are *Jacob's Well* and *The Gates of the Alamo,* which won the TCU Texas Book Award, the Western Heritage Award, and the Spur Award for the Best Novel of the West.

CLYDE WALTON HILL'S prose and poetry appeared in *The Southwest in Literature, The Literary Digest,* and *The Saturday Evening Post.* Hill's 1926 book of poems, *Shining Trails,* contains his "Little Towns of Texas."

ROLANDO HINOJOSA teaches creative writing at the University of Texas. His *Korean Love Songs* (1978), a book of poetry, is part of Hinojosa's *Klail City Death Trip* series. His novels in this series include *Rites and Witnesses* (1982), *Dear Rafe* (1985), *The Valley* (1981), which won the Casa de las Americas Award, and *The Useless Servants* (1993).

EDWARD HIRSCH received a McArthur Fellowship in 1998 and is winner of the Lyndhurst Prize, the Texas Institute of Letters Award in Poetry, a Guggenheim fellowship, an American Academy of Arts and Letters award in literature, and the National Book Critics Circle Award. His most recent book is the national bestseller *How to Read a Poem and Fall in Love with Poetry.*

JAMES HOGGARD, who served as Poet Laureate of Texas for 2000, is the author of fifteen books, including six collections of poems, six collections of translations, two novels, and a collection of stories. Hoggard was the recipient of the 1990 Texas Institute of Letters Award in the short story category. He teaches at Midwestern State University.

MARY AUSTIN HOLLEY, a first cousin of Stephen F. Austin, was an unofficial ambassador to the United States, raising money and support for the newly established Republic of Texas. Although many modern readers may see her poems as propaganda, her journal of daily events is a valuable cultural document. With poems like "The Plea of Texas," Mary Austin Holley effectively lobbied for Texas statehood.

BOYCE HOUSE is remembered as a staff reporter for the *Fort Worth Star-Telegram.* The historian, newspaperman, radio personality, and poet wrote a syndicated humor column, "I Give You Texas," and his articles also appeared in *The Saturday Evening Post.* He briefly worked in Hollywood as a technical advisor and once unsuccessfully ran for lieutenant governor of Texas. House was a member of the Texas Institute of Letters. His books include *Oil Boom, Roundup of Texas Humor,* and *Cow Town Columnist.* His book of poetry, *Texas Rhythm and Other Poems,* was published in 1950.

MARGARET BELL HOUSTON, poet and novelist, was the daughter of the hero of San Jacinto. Her poetry was anthologized in *Voices of the Southwest, The Southwest in Literature,* and elsewhere, and her work was published in *McCall's, Harper's,* and *Poetry.* Her books of poetry include *Prairie Flowers, Lanterns in the Dusk,* and *The Singing Heart.* Margaret Bell Houston also published thirteen novels and was a member of the Texas Institute of Letters.

MARGARET MOFFETTE LEA HOUSTON married General Sam Houston in Alabama when he was forty-seven years old and she twenty-one. Mrs. Houston died in 1867 about four years after her legendary husband. Her poetry appeared in Samuel Dixon's 1893 anthology, *Poets and Poetry of Texas.*

SAM HOUSTON, first president of the Republic of Texas and a governor of both Tennessee and Texas, is known for many things but not, admittedly, for his poetry. There are two poems credited to Houston: a youthful love poem written in Tennessee and the poem in this book, "Texian Call to Arms," found in *Ever Thine Truly, Love Letters from Sam Houston to Anna Raquet.*

ALBERT HUFFSTICKLER published poems in *Travois, Stone Drum, New Mexico Humanities Review, Concho River Review,* and in many chapbooks. Huffstickler's collection, *Walking Wounded,* received an Austin Book Award.

ROB JOHNSON has published his poetry and short stories in many literary journals. Johnson lives in McAllen and is professor of English at the University of Texas Pan-American. He is currently completing a biography of William S. Burroughs entitled, *Tiger in the Valley: The Adventures of William S. Burroughs on the Texas/Mexico Border 1946-1950.*

DARYL E. JONES taught creative writing at Texas Tech University. His *Someone Going Home Late* was the winner of a Texas Institute of Letters award in poetry. He now is a college dean in Idaho.Roger Jones lives in San Marcos and teaches creative writing at Southwest Texas State University. His writing has appeared in many national journals. His collections are *Remembering New London* and *Strata,* winner of the 1993 Texas Review award. He has been nominated for a Pushcart Prize and has won the Academy of American Poets Prize.

ROGER JONES lives in San Marcos and teaches creative writing at Southwest Texas State University. His writing has appeared in many national journals. His collections are *Remembering New London* and *Strata,* winner of the 1993 Texas Review award. He has been nominated for a Pushcart Prize and has won the Academy of American Poets Prize.

MIRABEAU B. LAMAR was the second president of the Republic of Texas and the enemy of Sam Houston and of the Cherokees in eastern Texas. He made a serious attempt to be a poet and was the "Father of Texas Education" and a U.S. Ambassador to Nicaragua and Costa Rica. His 1857 book of poems, *Verse Memorials,* is of scholarly interest.

MICHAEL LIND, a former Texas resident, has written articles and books on political and cultural topics. *Texas in Poetry 2* contains an excerpt from his book-length poem, *The Alamo: An Epic* published by Houghton Mifflin. Lind's *Bluebonnet Girl* is forthcoming from Henry Holt.

JIM LINEBARGER, emeritus professor of English at the University of North Texas, was poet-in-residence there. His poetry can be found in *The New Breed, descant,* and *Southern Humanities Review.* His collections include *Texas Blues and Other Poems, Anecdotal Evidence, The Worcester Poems,* and *Five Faces.*

PAT LITTLEDOG'S short fiction has appeared in *Common Bonds: Stories By and About Modern Texas Women, New Growth: Contemporary Short Stories by Texas Writers,* and *Her Work: Stories by Texas Women.* LittleDog's collection of stories, *Afoot in a Field of Men,* received an Austin Book Award and was reprinted by *Atlantic Monthly.* She is also an NEA fellowship winner,

JANET LOWERY'S poems have appeared in the *Houston Chronicle, Concho River Review,* and *Poetry East.* Lowery's *Thin Dimes,* published by Wings Press in the New Texas Poetry Sampler Series, was released in a second printing in 1997.

PEGGY ZULEIKA LYNCH'S poetry has appeared in the first edition of *Texas in Poetry, Sulphur River Review, Touchstone,* and elsewhere. Peggy Lynch is the author of eight collections, among them, *Stacks and Files, Ups and Downs,* and *The Gandy Dancers.* She co-edited the anthology, *From Hide and Horn.*

CYNTHIA MACDONALD is founder and first director of the creative writing program at the University of Houston. Her work has appeared in such periodicals as *The Paris Review, TriQuarterly Review,* and *The New Yorker.* Macdonald's awards include three NEA grants, a Guggenheim fellowship and an American Academy and Institute of Arts and Letters award. Her six books are *Amputations, Transplants, (W)holes, Alternate Means of Transport, Living Wills: New and Selected Poems,* and *I Can't Remember.*

WALTER MCDONALD, a former Air Force pilot, was Texas Poet Laureate in 2001. Some of his recent books are *All Occasions, Blessings the Body Gave, The Flying Dutchman, Celebrating West Texas and the Near Southwest, Rafting the Brazos, Where Skies Are Not Cloudy, Night Landings,* and *After the Noise of Saigon.* McDonald has won six Texas Institute of Letters awards, including the Lon Tinkle Award for career excellence and four National Cowboy Hall of Fame Western Heritage Awards.

NJOKI MCELROY, playwright, folklorist, poet, and teacher, is on the English department faculties of Northwestern and Southern Methodist universities. She has had twelve plays produced as well as fiction and other works published in numerous anthologies. She is working on a memoir, *Fruits of the Spirit.*

LARRY MCMURTRY'S most recent novel is *Sin Killers,* the first book in *The Berrybender Narratives.* McMurtry has written twenty-four novels, two collections of essays, three memoirs, more than thirty screenplays, and has edited an anthology of modern western fiction. He is a winner of the Pulitzer Prize and served as president of PEN International.

JAS. MARDIS received the 2000 Pushcart Prize in poetry for his "Invisible Man," published in the anthology *Kente Cloth: Southwest Voices of the African Diaspora,* which he also edited. Mardis has produced three volumes of poetry: *Southern Tongue, Hanging Time,* and *The Ticking and the Time Going Past.*

VASSAR MILLER was a Houston native whose nationally acclaimed books include *Adam's Footprint, Wage War on Silence, My Bones Being Wiser, If I Could Sleep Deep Enough, Onions and Roses,* and *If I Had Wheels Or Love.* A Texas poet laureate, Miller was honored with three Texas Institute of Letters awards and a number of Pulitzer Prize nominations.

BRYCE MILLIGAN, publisher of Wings Press, is author of four collections of poetry; the best-known is *Working the Stone* (1994). He also edited the anthologies *Daughters of the Fifth Sun: Latina Poetry and Fiction* and *¡Floricanto Sí! A Collection of Latina Poetry.* He directs the creative writing program at the North East School of the Arts in San Antonio.

VAIDA STEWART MONTGOMERY was born in the Texas Panhandle in 1888 and as a child lived in a clay dugout. Before becoming a publisher and a writer, she taught business courses in Dallas. In 1948, she won a Texas Institute of Letters poetry award for *Hail for Rain.* Montgomery was co-publisher and co-editor of Kaleidograph Press. Her other poetry collection, *Locoed and Other Poems,* preceded a reference work, *A Century with Texas Poets and Poetry.*

WHITNEY MAXWELL MONTGOMERY began life in Navarro County in 1877 and worked as a farmer and stockman on his family's homestead. Montgomery helped found the Poetry Society of Texas and served as president of the Texas Institute of Letters. Along with his wife, Vaida Stewart Montgomery, he co-published some five hundred books with Kaleidograph Press. His poetry books are *Joseph's Coat, Corn Silks and Cotton Blossoms, Brown Fields and Bright Lights,* and *Hounds in the Hills.*

ERIC MUIRHEAD'S poetry and prose have been included in *Travois, The Fountain, Texas Short Fiction, New Texas,* and *The Texas Humanist.* He teaches creative writing at San Jacinto College in Pasadena, Texas, and is working on a translation of the collected poetry of Friedrich Nietzsche.

HARRYETTE MULLEN was a Dobie Paisano fellow and currently teaches African American literature and creative writing at the University of California at Los Angeles. Her scholarship is widely published and her poetry has been included in such anthologies as *Washing the Cow's Skull, Trouble the Water: 250 Years of African-American Poetry,* and *African American Literature: A Brief Introduction and Anthology.* Mullen's books of poetry include *Three Tall Women, S*PeRM**K*T,* and *Muse & Drudge.* In 2002, she will have two new poetry collections, *Baby Blues: Early Poems* and *Sleeping with the Dictionary.*

JOSEPH COLIN MURPHEY was the editor of the literary journal *Stone Drum.* Murphey has published in *Latitudes* and *The Texas Quarterly* and his work appears in *Washing the Cow's Skull, Three Texas Poets,* and *New Texas 93.* Among his collections are *A Return to the Landscape* and *Waiting for Nightfall.*

JACK E. MURPHY was a poet and a business executive. His education began in a one-room rural school in Grayson County and continued through graduate studies at Harvard University. Murphy served as president of the Poetry Society of Texas and was active in the National Federation of the State Poetry Societies. His books of poetry are *Where Rainbows Wait* and *The West Side of the Mountain.*

JACK MYERS is director of creative writing at Southern Methodist University. Myers is the author of six books of poetry, among them *The Family War, As Long as You're Happy,* and *Blindsided.* He has co-edited and edited a number of anthologies, including *New American Poets of the '90s.* Myers has been awarded two NEA fellowships and two Texas Institute of Letters awards. His latest collection is *The Glowing River.* A nonfiction book, *The Poet's Workshop,* is forthcoming in 2003.

Berta Hart Nance was born near Albany, Texas, in 1883. Nance's father ran a store just outside the walls of old Fort Griffin, and she grew up hearing about the frontier. Nance was anthologized in *A Century with Texas Poets and Poetry* and *Southwest Writers Anthology*. Her Texas classroom favorite, "Cattle," appeared in her 1935 collection *Flute in the Distance*.

Isabel Nathaniel's *Dominion of Lights* received the Texas Institute of Letters Award for Best Book of Poetry. Other honors include a Discovery/The Nations prize and five Poetry Society of America awards. Her work has been published in *Best Texas Writing*, *¡TEX!*, *Texas Observer*, *Ravishing DisUnites*, *Southern Poetry Review*, *Ploughshares*, *Prairie Schooner*, and *The Nation*.

Frances Neidhardt has taught English at Texas A&M University in Commerce, Brookhaven and Austin colleges. Her poetry book, *Things Seen and Seen Again* from Austin's Sulphur River Press (1997), is in its second printing.

Violette Newton wrote *The Proxy* (1973), *Scandal and Other Poems* (1981), and, most recently, *The Shamrock Cross* (1993). Her poetry has appeared in such publications as *Travois*, *Texas Stories and Poems*, and *New Texas 92*, and her short fiction was featured in *Stone Drum* and in *Fiction and Poetry by Texas Women*. A former Poet Laureate of Texas, she lives in Beaumont.

Nick Norwood has poems in *Western Humanities Review*, *Concho River Review*, *Borderlands*, *The Paris Review*, and *Southwest Review*. He was awarded an International Merit Award in Poetry from *Atlantic Review* in 2000. River City Press will publish his first book of poems, *The Soft Blare*, in the Andrew Hudgins Poetry Series in 2003. He has taught creative writing at the University of North Texas and Hardin-Simmons.

Naomi Shihab Nye, anthologist, teacher, and poet, lives in San Antonio. Recently, she published *Space Between Our Footsteps: Poems and Paintings from the Middle East* and an autobiographical novel, *Habibi*, In addition she wrote *Sitti's Secrets*, a book for children, and *Selected Early Poems*. Her other poetry books include *Different Ways to Pray*, a Texas Institute of Letters award winner (1980); *Hugging the Jukebox* (1982), a recipient of both a National Poetry Series and a second Texas Institute of Letters award; and *Yellow Glove* (1986). Nye edited an anthology of poems from around the world, *This Same Sky*, (selected a Notable Book by the American Library Association.)

W. Lee O'Daniel was elected the president of Fort Worth Chamber of Commerce in 1933, five years before he was elected governor of Texas. In 1941, Wilbert Lee O'Daniel defeated Lyndon Baines Johnson to win a United States senatorial seat. But by 1956, his days in politics were over. The fictional politician in the movie, *O Brother, Where Are Thou*, is not unlike the real "Pappy" O'Daniel. He came to poetry and politics by way of music on the radio, leading his hillbilly band, the Light Crust Doughboys. The lyrics of "Beautiful Texas," the best known of his many songs, appeared as a poem in the 1937 *Greater Texas Anthology of Verse*.

Caley O'Dwyer's first collection of poems, *Full Nova*, was published by Orchises Press in 2001. Before that, his poems appeared in *Santa Barbara Review*, *The Texas Review*, and *¡TEX!*. He is a winner of an Academy of American Poets Prize and a recipient of a Helene Wurlitzer grant for poetry.

Dave Oliphant is a Fort Worth native whose prose and poetry have been published in *Southwest*, *Southern Poetry Review*, and *Southwestern Historical Quarterly*. Under his Prickly Pear imprint, Oliphant has edited and published such small press books as *The Killdeer Crying*, *Washing the Cow's Skull*, and *Roundup: An Anthology of Texas Poets, 1973-1998*. His prose works include *On a High Horse* and *Texas Jazz* and his poetry collections include *Maria's Poems* (Austin Book Award) and *Memories of Texas Towns & Cities*. Oliphant's study, *The Early Swing Era*, was released in Spring 2002.

Bonnie Parker was born in Rowena in 1910. After her father died, her family relocated to Dallas. In high school, she was an honor student who wrote poetry. When she was twenty, Bonnie Parker met Clyde Barrow and soon joined him on the run. While in jail, she wrote the 1932 "The Ballad of Bonnie and Clyde." The folkloric outlaws died in an ambush set up by Texas Ranger Frank Hamer. "The Ballad of Bonnie and Clyde" ends with a true prediction: "To few it'll be grief—To the law a relief—But it's death for Bonnie and Clyde."

Robert Phillips has written or edited some thirty volumes of poetry, fiction, criticism, and *belles lettres*. Among his honors are a Pushcart Prize and an American Academy and Institute of Arts and Letters Award in Literature. Phillips is a Moores Professor at the University of Houston. Johns Hopkins released his sixth book of poetry, *Spinach Days*, in 2001. In 2002,

Phillips' edition of the selected poems of Marya Zaturensha was released by Syracuse University.

CHARLOTTE RENK has taught creative writing since receiving her Ph.D. from Louisiana State University. She has been published in *New Texas 93, Southwestern American Literature, RE: Arts and Letters, Concho River Review, Atelier, RiverSedge*, and elsewhere. Renk teaches in Athens in her native East Texas.

EDYTH RENSHAW was a student at Southern Methodist University. In 1922, she was a member of the poetry club at SMU.

CAROL COFFEE REPOSA'S work has appeared in a number of publications, among them *descant, Revista /Review Interamericana, Blue Mesa Review, New Texas,* and *Bloomsbury Review.* Her poetry collections are *At the Border: Winter Lights,* and *The Green Room.* Another book, *Facts in Life,* is forthcoming from Browder Springs Press. Reposa teaches English at San Antonio College.

LEXIE DEAN ROBERTSON, in 1920, moved with her husband to Rising Star in Eastland County, where, for five years, she was a high school principal. "The Poet of Rising Star" served as a Poet Laureate of Texas and president of the Texas Institute of Letters. Robertson's work was featured in national publications such as *Ladies Home Journal, Holland's,* and *New York World.* Her books are *Red Heels* (1928), *I Keep a Rainbow* (1932), *Acorn on the Roof* (1939), and *Answer in the Night* (1948). *Red Heels* was reprinted ten times.

DEL MARIE ROGERS is best known as the author of *Close to Ground.* Other books of poems include *Breaking Free* and the new *She'll Never Want More Than This.* Her poetry has appeared in such magazines as *Texas Observer, Colorado Review,* and *The Nation.* Her work has been included in a number of anthologies, beginning with *The New Breed* (Prickly Pear Press, 1973).

PATTIANN ROGERS' poetry has appeared in *The American Review, The Paris Review,* and in various literary journals. The recipient of two NEA grants, Rogers has been honored with four Pushcart Prizes. Her 1993 collection is *Geocentric,* and her forthcoming book is entitled *Firekeeper: New and Selected Poems.*

CLAIRE OTTENSTEIN ROSS is an editor, publisher, and poet. A longtime member of the Poetry Society of Texas, she has published in various national and regional literary journals and anthologies.

GRACE ROSS was a native Texan. She served as an officer of both the Poetry Society of Texas and the Fort Worth Poetry Club.

PAUL RUFFIN is director of creative writing at Sam Houston State University and the editor of *The Texas Review* and director of Texas Review Press. He is the author of two books of stories *The Man Who Would Be God* and *Islands, Women, and God,* along with a novel, *Pompeii Man* (2002). Ruffin has also published four collections of poetry.

DAVID RUSSELL was a member of the Texas Institute of Letters, former president of the Poetry Society of Texas, and Poet Laureate of Texas from 1945 to 1947. His poetry appeared in *The Christian Science Monitor, The Saturday Evening Post,* and *The New York Times.* His collections are *There Is No Night, Sing With Me Now, The Silver Fawn,* and *The Incredible Flower.*

SUNSHINE DICKINSON RYMAN was born in Rusk and studied at Southwestern University. Her first book of poems was *Moon Conjure* and her second, *Needle and Thread.* Ryman was a longtime resident of Houston and member of the Poetry Society of Texas.

BENJAMIN ALIRE SÁENZ teaches in the bilingual MFA program at the University of Texas at El Paso. The children's author, novelist, and poet received a Stegner fellowship in poetry from Stanford University. His first book, *Calendar of Dust* (poetry, 1991 American Book Award) was followed by *Dark and Perfect Angels* (poetry, 1995 Southwest Book Award.) Sáenz's recent books include his third poetry collection, *Elegies in Blue,* and novels, *Carry Me Like Water* and *House of Forgetting. Grandma Fina's Wonderful Umbrella* was recently named the Best Children's Book by the Texas Institute of Letters.

RICHARD SALE'S poetry has appeared in *Travois, Inheritance of Light, Roundup,* and elsewhere. His collections include *The Return of the Sunrise Kid* (1975), *Dime Western* (1978), *The Tortilla of Heaven* (1990) and *Curing Susto* (1997). Sale is a professor emeritus at the University of North Texas and is editor of Trilobite Press.

481

ARTHUR M. SAMPLEY was Distinguished Professor of English at North Texas State University and was the author of *This is Our Time, Of the Strong and the Fleet, Furrow with Blackbirds*, and *Selected Poems*, the last two winners of Texas Institute of Letters awards. Sampley, president of both the Texas Institute of Letters and the Poetry Society of Texas, was a Poet Laureate of Texas.

JAN EPTON SEALE lives in McAllen, where she writes short fiction, poetry, and essays and teaches creative and autobiographical writing. Her poems are collected in four volumes: *Bonds, Sharing the House, Texas Poets in Concert: A Quartet,* and *The Yin of It.* Her latest prose work is *The Nuts-&-Bolts Guide to Writing Your Life Story.*

TIM SEIBLES attended Southern Methodist University and taught high school English in Dallas for a decade. He now teaches creative writing at Old Dominion. His collections include his 1988 *Body Moves* and the 1992 *Hurdy-Gurdy.*

MARTIN S. SHOCKLEY'S prose and poetry has appeared widely in journals. For decades, Shockley was a professor at North Texas State University. He was the editor of the collection *Southwest Writers Anthology* as well as the author of a number of books, among them *The Richmond State Theatre: 1984-1812* and *Last Roundup* (1994). Shockley lives in Denton and Allenspark, Colorado.

GENE SHUFORD was a member of the Poetry Society of Texas and the Poetry Society of America and served for many years as the chairman of the department of journalism at North Texas State University. His poetry won some fifty regional and national awards and appeared in such publications as *Saturday Evening Post, Southwest Review, Southwest Writers Anthology,* and *Scribner's.* Among Shuford's collections are *The Red Bull and Other Poems, The Flowering Noose, 1300 Main Street,* and *Selected Poems: 1933-1971,* the latter a recipient of a Texas Institute of Letters award.

MARCELLA SIEGAL served as president of Southwest Writers and of the Poetry Society of Texas. Siegal's prose and poetry have been published in *The Christian Science Monitor, Saturday Evening Post, The Dallas Morning News,* and in the yearbooks of the Poetry Society of Texas. Siegal's book-length poetry collection is *Swift Season.*

NAOMI STROUD SIMMONS teaches poetry in Fort Worth area schools. She has published six books of poetry , and her work has appeared in *Grasslands, Suddenly,* and in the yearbooks of the Poetry Society of Texas, as well as in the *New Texas* series.

JOHN PETER SJOLANDER, years after leaving his native Sweden, became known as the "Dean of Texas Poets." Before becoming a Texas farmer, he had been a sailor like his father. Individual pieces from his 1928 *Salt of the Earth and Sea* were included in *Legends of Texas, The Southwest in Literature,* and *Voices of the Southwest.*

GOLDIE CAPERS SMITH was a Dallas journalist and poet. *Swords in the Dawn* (1932) and *Deep in the Furrow* (1950) are two of six books of poetry. Smith is also remembered for her 1926 annotated bibliography, *Creative Arts in Texas.*

JAMES GREGORY SMITH was born in Canyon, Texas, and has taught English at Lamar University, Pan American University, and the University of North Texas. He lives in Houston and is honors program director at San Jacinto College South. Smith's poetry has appeared in such publications as *Concho River Review, New Texas 92,* and *Texas Review.*

REBECCA SPEARS is an MFA student in poetry at Bennington College in Vermont. She is also the writer-in-residence at Houston's High School for the Performing and Visual Arts. "Marina's Daughters, 1964" is based on personal experience.

CHERIE FOREMAN SPENCER, who lived in El Paso and Oklahoma City, was a contributor to the early yearbooks of the Poetry Society of Texas.

ANNA WORD SPRAGINS was frequently published in southern periodicals in the second half of the nineteenth century. Her once famous "Farewell to Texas" was published in the 1888 anthology, *Poets and Poetry of Texas.*

PAT STODGHILL has been a Texas Poet Laureate and a five-time president of the Poetry Society of Texas as well as a former president of the National Federation of State Poetry Societies. Stodghill has taught at Southern Methodist University and lives in Dallas. Her books of poems include *Mirrored Images* and *Kaleidoscope Pieces.*

CARMEN TAFOLLA is author of the nonfiction work, *To Split a Human: Mitos, Machos, y la*

Mujer Chicana. Her collection of new and selected prose and poetry, *Sonnets to Human Beings* (1992), won first place in the UCI National Chicano Literary Competition and was published in Germany in a bilingual edition. A native of the west side of San Antonio, Tafolla is the author of the 2001 collection of poetry, *Sonnets and Salsa*, published by Wings Press.

CHUCK TAYLOR edited Cedar Rock and Slough presses and has published in such periodicals as *Travois, Texas Review, Concho River Review*, and Texas *Quarterly*. His poetry collection, *What Do You Want, Blood?* received an Austin Book Award. He teaches creative writing at Texas A&M at College Station.

LARRY D. THOMAS has three books of poems, *The Lighthouse Keeper, Amazing Grace*, and *The Woodlanders*. His work has appeared in magazines, including *The Journal of the American Medical Association, descant,* and *Southwest Review.*

LORENZO THOMAS was born in the Republic of Panama, lived in New York City, and served in Vietnam. He has published his poetry in *Kente Cloth, Liquid City*, and *New Black Voices*. Thomas is a member of the Texas Institute of Letters. His award-winning books of poems are *A Visible Island, Fit Music, Dracula, Framing the Sunrise, Chances are Few*, and *The Bathers*. Two of his recent books are *Extraordinary Measures: Afrocentric Modernism and 20th-Century American Poetry* and *Sing the Sun Up*. Thomas is professor of creative writing at the University of Houston, Downtown.

JAS. D. THORN was a member of the Barrington Fiction Club, a Dallas critique group. "The Sigh of the Old Cattlemen" appeared in a 1931 anthology.

ROBERT TRAMMELL'S work has been published a variety of literary magazines, including *Salt Lick, Southwest Review*, and *Alternative Poetry and Fiction*. Among his fifteen books of poetry are *Evidence* and *Jack Ruby and the Origins of the Avant-Garde in Dallas*. Trammell is the director of the literary organization, WordSpace

FREDERICK TURNER is a poet, critic, and former editor of *The Kenyon Review*, Turner has published the books *Genesis: an Epic Poem, Natural Classicism, Foamy Sky, The Major Poems of Miklos Radnoti* (translation, with Zsuzanna Ozvath), *The Culture of Hope, April Wind, Hadean Eclogues*, and *Shakespeare's Twenty-first Century Economics: The Morality of Love and Money*. Turner is presently on the faculty of the University of Texas at Dallas.

LESLIE ULLMAN is the author of three poetry collections: *Natural Histories* (Yale Series of Younger Poets Award, 1979), *Dreams by No One's Daughter*, and *Slow Work Through Sand*, (co-winner of the 1997 Iowa Poetry Prize). She has been awarded two NEA fellowships, and her poems have appeared in magazines such as *Poetry, The Kenyon Review*, and *The New Yorke*r. She teaches in the MFA Program at the University of Texas at El Paso.

ALICE EWING VAIL was featured in such publications as *The New York Times Magazine* and *American Bard*. Her 1952 narrative poem is *The Big Thicket*.

MARY VANEK, who lives in Amarillo, is a recipient of grants from the MacDowell Artists' Colony and the Ulcross Foundation. Vanek's poetry has appeared in the *Bloomsbury Review, American Literary Review,* and other journals.

TINO VILLANUEVA, a San Marcos native, now teaches creative writing at Boston University. He is the author of several collections of poetry, including *Scene from the Movie GIANT* (1993), *Shaking Off the Dark* (reissued in 1998), *Chronicle of My Worst Years* (1994, translated by James Hoggard), and *Primera Causa: First Cause* (1999, translated by Lisa Horowitz).

R.G. VLIET was a poet, playwright, and novelist. He is the only writer to receive Texas Institute of Letters awards for both a novel (*Solitudes,* 1977), and poetry (for *Events and Celebrations,* 1966, and *The Man With the Black Mouth,* 1977). Vliet was honored with Dobie Paisano, Ford Foundation, and Rockefeller Foundation fellowships. Vliet's other publications include the novel, *Scorpio Rising,* and the play, *The Regions of Noon*.

ROBERT JAMES WALLER is better known for his novels. His recently released book is *A Thousand Country Roads: An Epilogue to Bridges of Madison County*. Waller lives on a ranch in the Big Bend of Texas and writes occasional poetry.

WILLIAM ALLEN WARD lived in Corsicana, El Paso, Fort Worth, and Dallas. He held various jobs in journalism, including serving as a war correspondent for the *El Paso Times*.

WILLIAM WENTHE has two books of poems, *Birds of Hoboken* (Orchises, 1995) and *Not Till We Are Lost* (LSU Press, forthcoming 2003). A creative writing teacher at Texas Tech University, Wenthe has received fellowships from the National Endowment for the Arts. His poems have appeared in numerous journals including *Poetry, TriQuarterly, The Texas Review, Tar River Poetry,* and *Pushcart Prize XXV.*

DAVID WESTHEIMER, a Houston native, was the author of fifteen novels, including *Von Ryan's Express, My Sweet Charlie,* and *Lighter Than a Feather.* He also published *Sitting It Out,* a World War II POW memoir, and a book of poetry, *The Great Wounded Bird.*

THOMAS WHITBREAD has had poetry published in such literary journals as *Atlantic Monthly, Harper's, The Kenyon Review,* and *The New Yorker.* His first book of poems, *Four Infinitives,* won and his second, *Whomp and Moonshiver,* co-won the poetry award from the Texas Institute of Letters.

BRENDA BLACK WHITE'S poetry has been published in *Sulphur River Review, Texas Review,* and *McCall's.* Her 1988 poetry collection, *Callahan County,* was published by Plain View Press.

MARTHA E. WHITTEN was born in Travis County in1842. Her occasional pieces, published in nineteenth-century newspapers, are collected in Whitten's 1886 book of poetry, *Texas Garlands.*

CHRIS WILLERTON has directed the Texas Reading Circuit and worked with the Texas Commission on the Arts. His poetry has appeared in *Southern Poetry Review, descant, Windhover,* and *Tar River.*

SUSAN WOOD was awarded a Guggenheim fellowship in 1998. The Commerce, Texas, native is a professor of English at Rice University. Her book of poetry, *Campo Santo,* was the Lamont Poetry selection for 1991. Her other collections include *Bazaar, Counting the Losses,* and *Asunder.*

LILLIAN WRIGHT was a native of Childress and a longtime Dallas resident. Her poem "West Texas Suicide" appeared in the 1936 anthology, *Moon in the Steeple.*

DAVID C. YATES founded *Cedar Rock Literary Magazine* and Cedar Rock Press. His poetry can be found in a number of anthologies and journals. Yates' books are *Making Bread, Motion,* and *Riding for the Dome.*

FAY M. YAUGER is known for her 1935 collection, *Planter's Charm.* In the 1952 bibliography, *Life and Literature of the Southwest,* J. Frank Dobie proclaimed one of her pieces to be the best poem by a southwestern writer: "At the top of all I should place Fay Yauger's 'Planter's Charm,' published in a volume of the same title."

Credits

ACOSTA, TERESA PALOMO. "For Maximino Palomo," *Passing Time*; "Fragile soy," *Nile and Other Poems*; "Dangereux avril," *Texas in Poetry*, (Center for Texas Studies); "Apparition (ca. 1896)," *New Texas 92,* (Center for Texas Studies); "Museum Piece (ca. Now)," *descant*.

ADAMS, CYD. "Pete's Poem," *RE Arts & Letters*; "Azaleas and Dogwoods," *RE Arts & Letters;* "Rock Pickers," *New Texas 91,* (University of North Texas Press); "Omens," *Borderlands*; "River Road," *New Texas 93,* (Center for Texas Studies); "Longview, Texas," *RE Arts and Letters* and *Blackjack, Bull Pine, Post Oak Glade,* (Crazy Creek Press).

ADCOCK, BETTY. "Kaiser's Burnout" and "Photograph of the Courthouse Square, 1950s," *Beholdings,* (Louisiana State University Press). Reprinted courtesy Louisiana State University Press.

BABB, STANLEY E. "Galveston," *Voices of the Southwest,* (Macmillan); "Portrait of a Pirate," *Death of a Buccaneer and Other Poems,* (P.L. Turner Co.).

BAKER, KARLE WILSON. "Texas Cowboy," excerpt from "Some Towns of Texas," and "Nacogdoches Speaks," *Dreamers on Horseback,* (Southwest Press).

BARD, W.E. "The Seventh Seal," *A Little Flame Blown,* (Southwest Press).

BARNEY, WILLIAM D. "Long Gone To Texas," *Long Gone To Texas,* (Nortex Press); "Mr. Bloomer's Birds," "A Rufous-Crowned Sparrow Seen Loitering below Possum Kingdom Dam," and "Wide-Eyed," *A Part of Space: Ten Texas Writers,* (TCU Press) and *The Killdeer Crying,* (Prickly Pear Press); "Mr. Watts and the Whirlwind," *A Cowtown Chronicle,* (Browder Springs Press); "A Ballad for Bill Pickett," *A Cowtown Chronicle*.

BEESON, COLLEEN. "Minnie Henderson," *A Book of the Year, 1985,* (Poetry Society of Texas).

BEHLEN, CHARLES. "Two Ice Storms," *From Hide and Horn: A Sesquicentennial Anthology of Texas Poets,* (Eakin Press), *Uirsche's First Three Decades,* (Firewheel Press) and *Dreaming at the Wheel,* (Corona Press); "Widow Zebach," *Images from the High Plains,* (Staked Plains Press) and *Three Texas Poets,* (Prickly Pear Press) and *Dreaming at the Wheel*; "Windy Day/Slayton, Texas," *Bitterroot, The New Breed: An Anthology of Texas Poets,* (Prickly Pear Press) and *Perdition's Keepsake,* (Prickly Pear Press); "My Grandfather's Hammer," Mesilla Pamphlet Series, *I Am of All That I Have Met,* (Chawed Rawzin), *Three Texas Poets,* and *Dreaming at the Wheel*.

BERRY, BETSY. "Afternoon in Austin," *New Texas 91*.

BIRKELBACH, ALAN. "Coronado Points," *Weighed in the Balances,* (Plain View Press).

BLANCHARD, MARY LOVING. "East Texas Blues," *African American Review*.

BONAZZI, ROBERT. "Houston's Adolescence," *Southwest: A Contemporary Anthology,* (Red Earth Press); "Changing Borders," *There Must Be A Way,* (Latitudes Press).

BOSWELL, MARGIE B. "Girls of the Rodeo," *Out Where the West Begins,* (Kaleidograph Press).

BRADLEY, JERRY. "How the Big Thicket Got Smaller," *Newsletter Inago* and *Simple Versions of Disaster,* (University of North Texas Press); "For a Texas Beauty," *Simple Versions of Disaster*. Reprinted courtesy the University of North Texas Press.

BRIGHT, SUSAN. "Makes Them Wild," *Behold Texas: The Poet's View,* (Eakin Press); "Riding the Currents," *Breathing Under Water,* (Plain View Press).

BURFORD, WILLIAM. "South, Southwest" and "The Spell," *A Beginning,* (W. W. Norton) and *Washing the Cow's Skull,* (Prickly Pear Press).

BURLINGAME, ROBERT. "Desert, Not Wasteland," *Washing the Cow's Skull*; "After Bird Watching near the Mexican Border," *Blue Mesa Review*; "Late Winter in West Texas," *The Ohio Review*.

BYRD, BOBBY. "On Karma at 9.11.85," *Get Some Fuses For The House: Householder Poems,* (Texas North Atlantic Books); "Things You Can't Do in Albuquerque or Santa Fe, # 11" and "The Good Life," *On the Transmigration of Souls in El Paso,* (Cinco Puntos Press).

CAIRNS, SCOTT. "In the General Area of North Texas," *The Texas Review* and *Texas College English*.

CATACALOS, ROSEMARY. "Homesteaders," *Again for the First Time,* (Tooth of Time Books); "Katakalos," *Washing the Cow's Skull, Mexican American Literature,* (Harcourt Brace Jovanovich), *Literature and Language,* (McDougal, Littell), *English and World Literature,* (McDougal, Littell), and *Again for the First Time*; "La Casa," *Washing the Cow's Skull, Mexican American Literature,* and *Latino Poetry,* (Simon & Schuster), *inheritance of light,* (University of North Texas Press), and *Again for the First Time*; "Letter to a Brother in Exile" and "Swallow Wings," *Again for the First Time.*

CHITTENDEN, LAWRENCE. "The Old Mackenzie Trail," "Old Fort Phantom Hill," "The Cowboys' Christmas Ball," and "Ennui," *Ranch Verses,* (G.P. Putnam's Sons).

CHRISTENSEN, PAUL. "Summer Nights," excerpt from "Houston: An Ode," *Signs of the Whelming,* (Latitudes Press); "Driving Toward Houston," *Southwestern American Literature* and *Ecotropic Works,* (Ecotropic Books); "What the Citizens of Corpus, Rockport, Palacios, or Bryan Need," *New Texas 91.*

CISNEROS, SANDRA. "Black Lace Bra Kind of Woman," "Las Girlfriends," *"Bienvenido* Poem for Sophie," and "I Am on My Way to Oklahoma to Bury the Man I Nearly Left My Husband For," *Loose Woman,* (Alfred A. Knopf). These poems reprinted by permission of Susan Bergholz Literary Services.

CLEMENTS, BRIAN. "Historia," *Essays Against Ruin,* (Texas Review Press).

CODY, JAMES. "Whooping Crane," *My Body Is a Flute,* (Place of Herons Press) and *Return,* (Place of Herons Press); "Big Thicket Words" and "The Heart of Texas," *Return.*

COLE, MAUDE E. "Prairie Friend," *A Book of the Year 1948,* (Poetry Society of Texas) and *Clay-Bound,* (Kaleidograph Press); "Over Texas Hills," *Clay-Bound.*

COLQUITT, BETSY FEAGAN. "Honor Card," *Southwest, Honor Card,* (Saurian Press) and *Eve— from the Autobiography and Other Poems,* (TCU Press); "Poetry and Post, Texas," *English in Texas, The Texas Anthology,* (Sam Houston State University Press), and *Eve*; "the man in the VA hospital" and "Duet," *Eve.*

CORTEZ, SARAH. "Reunion," "Interlude," and "Attempt to Locate," *How to Undress a Cop,* (Arte Público Press).

CRAVEN, JERRY. "Spring in Palo Duro Canyon," *The Texas Anthology* and *My Own Choric Song,* (Jelm Mountain Press); "Midsummer Farewell," *Oleander Wine,* (Jelm Mountain Press).

CROUCH, A.L. "Mirabeau B. Lamar," *Out Where the West Begins,* (Kaleidograph Press).

CROWELL, GRACE NOLL. "Texas Autumn," *New Voices of the Southwest,* (Tardy Publishing Co.) and *Bright Destiny,* (Centennial Edition, Tardy Publishing Co.); "Summer Nights in Texas," *Flame in the Wind,* (Southwest Press) and *Bright Destiny*; "A Prayer for Texas," *The Dallas Morning News* and *Bright Destiny.*

CROWELL, NORMAN H. "Texas Trails," *Moon in the Steeple,* (Kaleidograph Press).

CULLAR, CAROL. "he's crossed the river," *Borderlands, Life & Death, Mostly,* (Maverick Press), and *Maverick in the Chaparral—The Eagle Pass Poems,* (Maverick Press); "12,000 Years Is Not Too Long," *Inexplicable Burnings,* (Press of the Guadalupe).

DAMERON, CHIP. "South Texas Boxcar Blues," *Tar River Poetry*; "Banding near the South Texas Coast, Late April," *Borders Review* and *Hook & Bloodline,* (Wings Press).

DAVIS, WILLIAM VIRGIL. "Texas: Sesquicentennial," and "Overnight Winter: Texas," *New Texas 92*; "On Lookout: Guadalupe River Ranch," *Southwest Review*; "I-35, South of Waco," *Light Year '87.*

DESPREZ, FRANK. "Lasca," *London Society Magazine* and *The Southwest in Literature,* (Macmillan).

DOBIE, J. FRANK. "Vanitas," *Greater Texas Anthology of Verse,* (Naylor Co.) and *Tales of Old-Time Texas,* (Little, Brown and Co.).

ELIZABETH, MARTHA. "The Way of Words," *cold-drill*; "On the Porch—Denton, Texas," *Texas in Poetry.*

ESTESS, SYBIL. "Mastodon Teeth" and "Sunset on the Bayou," *Seeing the Desert Green,* (Latitudes Press).

EVANS, MAYME. "Whiskey-Bomb Battle," *A Book of the Year 1957,* (Poetry Society of Texas) and *This Friendly Shore* (Naylor Co.); "Song for a Baby on Padre Island," *This Friendly Shore.*

FINK, ROBERT A. "Abilene, TX: We Pull Out For New England," and "At Our Backs," *Gulf Coast*; "Aunt May," *Iron Horse Literary Review*; "Drought: Sure Signs in Merkle, Texas," *Country Journal* and *The Ghostly Hitchhiker*, (Corona Press); "Mesquite," *Poetry* and *The Ghostly Hitchhiker*; "The Certified Public Accountant Recalls the Early 1950s," *The Ghostly Hitchhiker*.

FOREMAN, PAUL. "Impressionist," *Texas Liveoak*, (Thorp Springs Press); "Pecans," *Travois: An Anthology of Texas Poetry*, (Contemporary Arts Museum of Houston and Thorp Springs Press) and *Red Wing Blackbird*, (Headstone Press); "Huddie Ledbetter," *Texas Liveoak*; "Brazos de Dios," *Travois* and *Texas Liveoak*.

GARCIA, EDWARD H. "Chicana," *New Texas 2000*, (University of Mary Hardin-Baylor).

GIVENS, BETTYE HAMMER. "West Texas," *The Texas Anthology* and *Red Headed Tree*, (Plain View Press); "Lonesome, Texas," *From Hide and Horn* and *Red Headed Tree*, (Plain View Press).

GONZÁLEZ, RAY. "Roberto Meets Cabeza de Vaca in the Desert," *Railroad Face*, (Chili Verde Press); "The Prison, San Elizario, Texas," *Southwest* and *Washing the Cow's Skull*; "Paso del Norte," *Washing the Cow's Skull*; "The Angels of Juárez, Mexico" and "The Head of Pancho Villa," *Cabarto Sentora*, (BOA Editions).

GORDON, ROXY. "West Texas Mid-Century," *West Texas Mid-Century*, (Wowapi Press); "Living Life as a Living Target," *Living Life as a Living Target*, (Paperbacks Plus Press).

GOYEN, WILLIAM. Excerpt from *Faces of Blood Kindred*, (Random House).

GREENE, A.C. "A Hawk Over Inwood Road," *Memory of Snow*, (Browder Springs Press); excerpt from *A Personal Country*, (Knopf).

GREER, HILTON ROSS. "To General Pershing," *Ten and Twenty Aprils*, (Tardy Publishing Co.).

GROVER, DORYS CROW. "The Ranch on the Limpia," *Concho River Review*.

GWYNN, R.S. "Randolph Field, 1938," *Articles of War*, (University of Arkansas Press), *Tar River*, and *A Quartet: Texas Poets in Concert*, (University of North Texas Press).

HALL, H. PALMER. "Requiem for James Byrd, Jr.," *Palo Alto Review* and *Deep Thicket & Still Waters*, (Chili Verde Press); "Ghost Lights" and "A Death on Village Creek," *Deep Thicket & Still Waters*.

HARPER, CYNTHIA. "Día de Los Muertos," *Snow in South Texas*, (Pecan Grove Press); "Water Birds," *Concho River Review*.

HARRIGAN, STEPHEN. "A Poem of Adulthood," *Sleepyhead*, (Calliope Press) and *Washing the Cow's Skull*; "Pecos Bill in Decline," *Sleepyhead* and *Washing the Cow's Skull*; "Papalote Creek," *Travois* and *Sleepyhead*.

HILL, CLYDE WALTON. "The Little Towns of Texas," *The Buccaneer, A Book of the Year 1924*, (Poetry Society of Texas), and *Shining Trails*, (Kaleidograph Press).

HINOJOSA, ROLANDO. "The Eighth Army at the Chongchon," "Rest Due and Taken," and "Vale," *Korean Love Songs*, (Justa Editorial).

HIRSCH, EDWARD. "Evening Star, *The Nation* and *The Night Parade*, (Knopf).

HOGGARD, JAMES. "Oil Field Road off Clyte Escarpment," *Texas Observer* and *Medea in Taos*, (Pecan Grove Press); "November," *Texas Observer*; "Eye of the Tornado," *Two Gulls, One Hawk*, (Prickly Pear Press); "Anniversary Trip" and "Dove Hunting Each Labor Day," *Medea in Taos*.

HOLLEY, MARY AUSTIN. "The Plea of Texas," *The Red-Lander and Early Texas Verse: Collected from the Original Newspapers of Texas before 1850*, (The Steck Co.).

HOUSE, BOYCE. "Justice in Old Ranger," *Texas Rhythm and Other Poems*, (Naylor Co.); "Beauty is Elsewhere," *Texas Rhythm and Other Poems* and *Out Where the West Begins*; "A Mocking-bird," *Texas Rhythm and Other Poems*.

HOUSTON, MARGARET BELL. "The Old Oak Speaks," *Treaty Oaks Poems*, (The Scroll Press); "Song from the Traffic," *The Singing Heart and Other Poems*, (Cokesbury Press).

HOUSTON, MARGARET LEA. "To My Husband—December 1844," *Poets and Poetry of Texas*, (Dixon Publishing Co.).

HOUSTON, SAM. "Texian Call to Arms," *Ever Thine Truly: Love Letters from Sam Houston to Anna Raque*, (Jenkins Garrett Press).

HUFFSTICKLER, ALBERT. "Johnson City, Texas," *Concho River Review*; "October 31, 1981," *Texas Observer* and *her*, (Aileron Press); "In the Compound," *The Smell of Things*, (Press of

Circumstance); "The Passing of the Old Man," *River Rat Review* and *Working on My Death Chant,* (Backyard Press); "Travel Note," *Texas in Poetry.*

JONES, DARYL E. "Going On," *From Hide and Horn* and *Someone Going Home Late,* (Texas Tech University Press); "Triangulation," *Someone Going Home Late.*

JONES, ROGER. "Photo of a Rotary Crew, Sour Lake Oilfield, 1904," "Strata," and "Uncle Fenster's Grave," *Strata,* (Texas Review Press).

KIRKLAND, ELITHE HAMILTON. Excerpt from *Love is a Wild Assault,* (Doubleday & Co.).

LAMAR, MIRABEAU B. "Carmelita," *Verse Memorial, The Austin Tri-Weekly Intelligencer, The Southwest in Literature,* (Macmillan) and *The Life and Poems of Mirabeau B. Lamar,* (University of North Carolina Press); "San Jacinto," *Educational Free Press* and *The Life and Poems of Mirabeau B. Lamar.*

LASSWELL, MARY. *I'll Take Texas,* (Houghton Mifflin.)

LIND, MICHAEL. Excerpt from *The Alamo: An Epic,* (Houghton Mifflin)

LINEBARGER, JIM. "Oppa," *Southwest Review* and *The New Breed,* (Prickly Pear Press), *Five Faces,* (Trilobite Press), and *The Texas Anthology;* "Coyote," *descant* and *Texas Blues,* (Point Rider Press).

LITTLEDOG, PAT. "crossing the river to juárez," *The Texas Anthology;* "cowgirl," *From Hide and Horn;* "in austin reigns a bald-headed queen," *Tonics, Teas, Roots, and Remedies,* (Slough Press).

LOMAX, JOHN A. Excerpt from "Blessing of the Animals," *Southwest Review;* "I'm Going to Leave Old Texas Now," *Cowboy Songs and Other Frontier Ballads,* (Macmillan).

LOWERY, JANET. "Texas Splendor" and "Houston Heights," *Texas in Poetry* .

LYNCH, PEGGY ZULEIKA. "A True Texan," *Stacks and Files,* (Keyhole Press) and *Behold Texas.*

MACDONALD, CYNTHIA. "The Kilgore Rangerette Whose Life Was Ruined," *W(Holes),* (Knopf) and *Living Wills,* (Knopf); "And Cause His Countenance to Shine Upon You," *Living Wills.*

McDONALD, WALTER. "Starting a Pasture," *American Poetry Review, The Made Thing,* (University of Arkansas Press), *Rafting the Brazos,* (University of North Texas Press); "Losing a Boat on the Brazos," *Poetry* and *Night Landings,* (Harper and Row); "Hawks in a Bitter Blizzard," *The Atlantic*; "Wind and Hardscrabble," *TriQuarterly* and *The Flying Dutchman,* (Ohio State University Press); "The Flying Dutchman," *TriQuarterly* and *The Flying Dutchman;* "After the Rains of Saigon," *Pequod* and *Night Landings*; "After the Random Tornado," *All Occasions,* (University of Notre Dame Press); "All the Old Songs," *Roundup,* (Prickly Pear Press) and *Where Skies Are Not Cloudy,* (University of North Texas Press); "In Fields of Buffalo," *Where Skies Are Not Cloudy.* "All the Old Songs" and "In Fields of Buffalo" are reprinted by permission of the University of Notre Dame Press.

McMURTRY, LARRY. "For Erwin Smith, Cowboy Photographer," *Southwest Review.*

MARDIS, JAS. "Good-bye Summer," *Southern Tongue,* (B-Fest Publishing).

MILLER, VASSAR. "On a Weekend in September," *Poetry* and *From Hide and Horn;* "Whitewash of Houston," *Roundup* and *Struggling to Swim on Concrete,* (The New Orleans Poetry Journal Press) and *Liquid City,* (Corona Press). "Whitewash of Houston" is reprinted by permission of *Poetry.*

MILLIGAN, BRYCE. "trusting steel," *New Texas 91* and *Working the Stone,* (Wings Press); "San Antonio Nights," *Working the Stone;* "Copano, 1834," *Daysleepers,* (Corona Press).

MONTGOMERY, VAIDA STEWART. "Cattle Brands," *Year Book 1946,* (Poetry Society of Texas) and *Hail for Rain,* (Kaleidograph Press); "Funeral" and "To the Rattlesnake," *Locoed* (Kaleidograph Press).

MONTGOMERY, WHITNEY. "Death Rode a Pinto Pony" and "Outlaws," *Hounds in the Hills,* (Kaleidograph Press).

MUIRHEAD, ERIC. "Closing Time" and "A Reflection on the Paintings of Mark Rothko's Chapel," *Travois.*

MULLEN, HARRYETTE. "Momma Sayings," *Tree Tall Women,* (Energy Earth Communications) and *Washing the Cow's Skull;* "Viejas Locas" and "Father," *Tree Tall Women.*

MURPHEY, JOSEPH COLIN. "Re-stringing 100 Year Old Wire," *Three Texas Poets;* "The First Birthday After Death," *Washing the Cow's Skull;* "Texas Boomer," *A Return to the Landscape,*

(Prickly Pear Press), *Southwest: A Contemporary Anthology;* "Lake Austin Diorama," *Waiting for Nightfall,* (Prickly Pear Press).

MURPHY, JACK E. "I Dreamt of Lasca," *Book of the Year 1983,* (Poetry Society of Texas); "Heave Me a Mountain, Lord! (Prayer from the Plainview Rest Home)," *Book of the Year 1982,* (Poetry Society of Texas) and *The West Side of the Mountain,* (Nortex Press).

MYERS, JACK. "We Go Away at Home," *Sou'wester, The Texas Anthology,* and *Texas Stories & Poems,* (Texas Center for Writers Press); "The Gift," *As Long As You're Happy,* (Graywolf Press) and *The Glowing River: New and Selected Poems,* (Invisible Cities Press); "The Experts," *The American Poetry Review* and *Blindsided,* (Godine Publishers) and *The Glowing River.*

NANCE, BERTA HART. "Cattle," "Old Fort Griffin," "Frontier Mystery," and "Rio Grande Hills (A Pioneer Speaks)," *Flute in the Distance,* (Kaleidograph Press); "State Song," *Texas Legacy,* (The Naylor Co.); "Moonlight," *Flute in the Distance.*

NATHANIEL, ISABEL. "The Weepers," *Field* and *The Dominion of Lights: Poems by Isabel Nathaniel,* (Copper Beach Press); "Elegy at Mustang Island," *The Nation* and *The Dominion of Lights;* "The Coast of Texas," *Ploughshares* and *The Dominion of Lights;* "Galveston," *The Nation* and *Dominion of Lights.*

NEWTON, VIOLETTE. "Going Back to Ireland," *The Shamrock Cross,* (Harp & Quill Press); "Texas Poetry," *The Scandal and Other Poems,* (Nortex Press); "A Mythology of Snow," *The Scandal;* "The Caddo Mounds," *A Book of the Year 1982,* (Poetry Society of Texas); "The Witness, Susanna Dickinson," *This Is A House To Stand,* (Newton Notebook).

NORWOOD, NICK. "For the Drowned," *Borderlands.*

NYE, NAOMI SHIHAB. "Thinking About Cows at Ten O'Clock in the Morning, Abilene," *The New Breed: An Anthology of Texas Poets,* (Prickly Pear Press) and *Southwest: A Contemporary Anthology;* "Site of the Indian Fights of 1871, Abilene," *Southwest: A Contemporary Anthology;* "The Little Brother Poem," *Different Ways to Pray,* (Breitenbush Books) and *Words Under the Words: Selected Poems,* (Far Corner Books); "The Lost Parrot," *Hugging the Jukebox,* (E.P. Dutton) and *Words Under the Words;* "The Endurance of Poth, Texas," *Mint,* (State Street Press).

O'DANIEL, W. LEE. "Beautiful Texas," *Greater Texas Anthology of Verse,* (The Naylor Co.). Reprinted by permission of Hal Leonard Corporation.

O'DWYER, CALEY. "Texas," *Full Nova,* (Orchises Press).

OLIPHANT, DAVE. "Eugene Wukasch, Texas Architect," *Footprints: Poems 1961-1978,* (Thorp Springs Press) and *Washing the Cow's Skull;* Excerpt from "Beaumont: Class Reunion," *Footprints, Texas Stories and Poems,* (Texas Center for Writers Press) and *Memories of Texas Towns & Cities,* (Host Publishing, Inc.); "Dallas," *Lines and Mounds,* (Thorp Springs Press) and *Memories of Texas Towns & Cities;* "Denton," *New Texas 95,* (University of Mary-Hardin Baylor) and *Memories of Texas Towns & Cities.*

OWENS, WILLIAM A. Excerpt from *This Stubborn Soil,* (Charles Scribner's Sons).

PERRY, GEORGE SESSIONS. Excerpt from *Texas: A World in Itself,* (McGraw-Hill).

PHILLIPS, ROBERT. "Drive Friendly," *Borderlands;* "The Death of Janis Joplin," *Personal Accounts: New and Selected Poems: 1966-1986,* (Ontario Review Press).

RENK, CHARLOTTE. "Mistletoe Kills" and "Past Perm and Glitz," *Texas in Poetry.*

RENSHAW, EDYTH. "Pantoum," *Prairie Pegasus,* (Southwest Printing).

REPOSA, CAROL COFFEE. "At Fort Clark," *Concho River Review;* "Hill Country Rest Home," *At the Border: Winter Lights,* (Pecan Grove Press); "Hempstead, 1923," *From Hide and Horn, Concho River Review,* and *At the Border: Winter Lights;* "Alamo Plaza at Night" *Acequia;* "Dawn in El Paso," *New Texas 98.*

ROBERTSON, LEXIE DEAN. "Texas Memoranda,*" New Declamations for Seniors, Juniors, and Sub-Juniors,* (Banks Upshaw and Co.) and *Texas Poems;* "Pioneer: The Vignette of an Oil Field," *Red Heels,* (P.L. Turner Co.) and *New Voices of the Southwest;* "Aunt Gilly" and "Memorabilia," *Red Heels.*

ROGERS, DEL MARIE. "Customs of the Country," *To the Earth,* (The Trilobite Press); "Near the Rio Grande," *New Mexico Magazine* and *To the Earth;* "Some Nights I Love Everybody in Texas," *Images from the High Plains,* (Staked Plains Press); "Great Blue Heron," *Blue Mesa Review.*

Rogers, Pattian. "Moving God," *American Literary Review.*

Ross, Claire Ottenstein. "The Judge," *A Book of the Year 1995,* (Poetry Society of Texas).

Ross, Grace. "Oil Well Fire," *Texas Legacy,* (Poetry Publisher Press).

Ruffin, Paul. "Female Cousins at Thanksgiving," *descant;* "Burying," *Alaska Quarterly Review* and *Southwestern American Literature;* "The Storm Cellar," *The Storm Cellar,* (Cedar Creek Press).

Russell, David. "State Fair," *The Silver Fawn,* (Kaleidograph Press).

Ryman, Sunshine Dickinson. Excerpt from "Street Scenes: Houston," *A Book of the Year 1923,* (Poetry Society of Texas).

Sáenz, Benjamin Alire. "'I Wouldn't Even Bleed,'" "Benjamín," and "Between Worlds," *Dark and Perfect Angels,* (Cinco Puntos Press).

Sale, Richard. "Stilts and Other Vehicles," *Dime Western,* (Chawed Rawzin), *Travois, The Texas Anthology,* and *The Tortilla of Heaven,* (University of North Texas Press); "Farm-to-Market #4," *Concho River Review* and *The Tortilla of Heaven;* "Delayed Love Poem to Odem, Texas," *Dime Western* and *The Tortilla of Heaven.*

Sampley, Arthur M. "South Rim: Big Bend National Park," *A Book of the Year 1948,* (Texas Poetry Society), *Furrow with Blackbirds,* (Kaleidograph Press) and *Selected Poems: 1937-1971,* (North Texas State University Press); "Coronado at Rio Grande Del Norte," *Furrow with Blackbirds.*

Seale, Jan Epton. "Subtropical," *Concho River Review;* "Big Bend: Lion Warning," *New Texas 2000;* "Travel North: The Rules," *¡TEX!,* (The Writer's Garret).

Seibles, Tim. "What It Comes Down To," *Kenyon Review* and *Hurdy-Gurdy,* (Cleveland State University Press),

Shockley, Martin S. "Armadillo," *Southwest Writers Anthology,* (Steck-Vaughn)

Shuford, Gene. "Sam Bass," *Southwest Writers Anthology* and *The Flowering Noose,* (New Mexico Junior College Press); "Celebration," *Gene Shuford: Selected Poems,* (North Texas State University Press); "The Visit," *Selected Poems;* "The Horse in My Yard," *A Book of the Year 1969,* (Poetry Society of Texas) and *Selected Poems.*

Siegel, Marcella. "Waiting Wife," *A Book of the Year 1981,* (Poetry Society of Texas) and *Swift Season,* (Nortex Press).

Simmons, Naomi Stroud. "Black Sunday, April 14, 1935," *A Book of the Year 1996,* (Poetry Society of Texas).

Sjolander, John P. "The Last Longhorn's Farewell," *Salt of the Earth and Sea,* (P. L. Turner, Co.).

Smith, Goldie Capers. "Ballad of a Bombardier from Texas," *A Book of the Year 1944-1945,* (Poetry Society of Texas) and *Deep in this Furrow.*

Smith, James Gregory. "Antonio López and Emily," *Atelier.*

Spears, Rebecca. "Marina's Daughters, 1964," *The Texas Review.*

Spencer, Cherie Foreman. Excerpt from "Desert Symphony: Night," *A Book of the Year 1926,* (Poetry Society of Texas).

Spragins, Anna Word. "Farewell to Texas," *Poets and Poetry of Texas,* (Dixon Press).

Stodghill, Pat. "Rattlesnake Roundup," *A Texas Book of the Year 1970,* (Poetry Society of Texas); "Traitor," *Mirrored Images,* (Nortex Press); "August 1, 1966," *Behold Texas,* (Eakin Press).

Tafolla, Carmen. "This River Here" and "At the Very Last Battle," *Get Your Tortillas Together,* (Rifan Press), *Travois, Five Poets of Aztlán,* (Bilingual Press/Editorial Bilingüe), and *Sonnets to Human Beings and Other Selected Works,* (Lalo Press); "Allí Por La Calle San Luis," *Get Your Tortillas Together, Travois, Five Poets of Aztlán* and *Sonnets to Human Beings;* "Mi Tía Sofía," *Sonnets to Human Beings;* "San Antonio," *Travois;* "Mission San José," *Sonnets to Human Beings* and *Roundup;* "Aquí," *Sonnets to Human Beings.*

Taylor, Chuck. "Poem to Ma Ferguson," *From Hide and Horn;* "our texas economy," *Concho River Review* and *What Do You Want, Blood?,* (Slough Press); "Winterdirge," *Travois;* "renting," *Ordinary Life,* (Cedar Rock Press).

Thomas, Larry D. "The Red Raging Waters," *The Lighthouse Keeper,* (Timberline Press).

THOMAS, LORENZO. "Liquid City," *Liquid City.*

THORN, JAS D. "The Sigh of the Old Cattleman," *Fountain Unsealed,* (Clyde C. Cockrell Co.).

TRAMMELL, ROBERT. "A Nightclub on the Jacksboro Highway," *No Evidence,* (Wowapi Press); "Light Forms," *Southwest Review;* "After Hours," *No Evidence.*

TURNER, FREDERICK. Excerpt from "Texas Eclogues," *Hadean Eclogues,* (Story Line Press); "Early Warning," *Southwest Review.*

ULLMAN, LESLIE. "The Way Animals Are," *Slow Work through Sand,* (University of Iowa Press).

VAIL, ALICE EWING. "Coons in the Corn," *A Book of the Year 1979,* (Poetry Society of Texas).

VANEK, MARY. "Summer Begins Outside Dalhart, Texas," *Concho River Review;* "Homing Instinct," *Texas in Poetry.*

VILLANUEVA, TINO. "Day-Long Day," *Hay Otra Voz: Poems (1968-1971),* (Coleccion Mensaje Press); "The Serving of Water," *Scene from the Movie GIANT,* (Curbstone Press).

VLIET, R.G. "Penny Ballad of Elvious Ricks," *Water and Stone,* (Random House) and *Washing the Cow's Skull;* excerpt from "Clem Maverick," *Events and Celebrations,* (Viking Press) and *Clem Maverick: The Life & Death of a Country Singer,* (Shearer Publishing).

WARD, WILLIAM ALLEN. "Texas," *New Voices of the Southwest.*

WENTHE, WILLIAM. "White Settlement," *Image* and *Not Till We Are Lost,* (Louisiana State University Press).

WIER, ALLEN. Excerpt from *Blanco and Things About to Disappear,* (Louisiana State University Press).

WESTHEIMER, DAVID. "At the Movies," *The Great Wounded Bird and Other Poems,* (Texas Review Press).

WHITBREAD, THOMAS. "Alpine, Texas," *Washing the Cow's Skull;* "Whomp and Moonshiver," *Whomp and Moonshiver,* (BOA Editions); "The Alcohol Question," *From Hide and Horn;* "November 25, 1963," *Whomp and Moonshiver.*

WHITE, BRENDA BLACK. "Tolly Masters" and "Country Boy, City Girl," *Callahan County,* (Plain View Press).

WHITE, C.C. and ADA M. HOLLAND. Excerpt from *No Quittin' Sense,* (University of Texas Press).

WHITTEN, MARTHA E. "Beautiful in Death," *Texas Garlands,* (Triplett & Hutchings).

WILLERTON, CHRIS. "Campsite," *Pawn Review;* "Our Speaker This Morning," *Kansas Quarterly;* "Battle of Adobe Walls," *From Hide and Horn;* "Winter at the Intersection, *Xavier Review.*

WOOD, SUSAN. "Hollow" and "Four Roses," *Campo Santo,* (Louisiana State University Press); "Carnation, Lily, Lily, Rose," *Counting the Losses,* (Jones Alley Press).

WRIGHT, LILLIAN. "West Texas Suicide," *Moon in the Steeple,* (Kaleidograph Press).

YATES, DAVID C. "Century Plant," *Book of the Year 1976,* (Poetry Society of Texas) and *Making Bread,* (Cedar Rock Press); "Sex," *Riding for the Dome,* (Cedar Rock Press); "Washing the Cow's Skull," *Motions,* (Latitudes Press) and *Washing the Cow's Skull;* "Sunset Along U.S. Highway 90 Between Langtry and Sanderson," *Riding for the Dome.*

YAUGER, FAY M. "Planter's Charm," "County Fair," and "I Remember," *Planter's Charm,* (Kaleidograph Press).

Index